To Bob Sullivan,
A "Bob Sell" in
your own right!

# Warning

The Salesperson can no longer "wing it" in a sales interview; they will run out of time reciting boring facts while missing the golden opportunity to get involved with the Prospect. Selling is no longer just products; it is now people and people relationships.

There is a logical mental process the Prospect goes through in buying, so each step of that process must be successfully completed, all while understanding, prompting and controlling their buying emotions.

The planned presentation is a track that allows the Salesperson to move the Prospect through their mental-emotional buying process while allowing:

■ the freedom to develop a mutual liking for each other,
■ the freedom to explore the Prospect's emotions (where the decisions are fast and final),
■ the freedom to get the Prospect involved in your product, and
■ monitoring their emotions for the moment to close.

When you consider the many facets the Salesperson must control, from ferreting out Wanting Prospects through to the successful close, you have to conclude that the subject of selling is overwhelming.

The vastness of selling knowledge across diversified markets has resulted in Salespeople being spoon-fed, often with conflicting ideas. Until now, the various kinds of markets and Prospects introduced so many variables that developing a planned selling presentation was impossible. The problem is due to the incorrect order of emphasis; it has been traditionally the Product, the Market and maybe the Prospect, instead of Prospect first. We don't sell products and markets, we sell people, and fortunately they are uniform and predictable. At least they all go through the same mental-emotional buying process.

The Best Seller simplifies the vastness of this subject by using the overview of an overview of an overview technique. It starts with the Selling Process chart that highlights the necessary steps, the technique to be used, and the logic of that step. The process is detailed further in the Overview chapter wherein the basic steps, Attention, Interest, Conviction, Desire and Close, are related to the emotions of the potential Buyer.

Each chapter begins with a series of one line concept summaries to give the reader an overview of that chapter's content. (Note: Some of these are so self evident that no further reference is made to them in the text, so read them carefully.) Within those chapters, the Selling Process chart is again highlighted for location awareness. Near the end, the Scenario chapter is a sales presentation scripted to show the reader excellent selling skills in action. The book concludes with a quick reference chapter called Selling Summary.

For brevity, the word *product* means both product and service. Similarily, the word Salesperson and its possessive pronominal adjective "their" is used to refer to both genders of Best Sellers.

Just as you can learn to fly an airplane from instructions in a book, you can also learn to sell from a book. But neither are advised. There are better ways. The best way to learn to sell is to take the Dale Carnegie Sales Course, now offered world wide. There you will receive real-life training and a chance to practice in a friendly and professional environment because selling skills must be used by reflex action, rather than by thinking your way through a presentation; there is just too much time-pressure for you to be effective. Nothing in this book conflicts with that course, so we highly endorse it. Let this book be your advanced advisor and friend.

To the reader, may you have the best in selling. Whenever you are in doubt, remember that you are selling people and not products. Whenever you get into an awkward situation keep them talking — about themselves.

# Table of Contents

# Chapter Three: Interest

- ☐ Fan an existing desire rather than create a new one.
- ☐ Questions are the Salesperson's most powerful tool.
- ☐ Describing their Problems convinces them of their need.
- ☐ A question forces the Prospect to think and reply.
- ☐ A two way conversation reduces the tension for each.
- ☐ Questions turn a presentation into an interview.
- ☐ Answering satisfies their ego need to dominate.
- ☐ Questions determine Benefits the Prospect will want.
- ☐ Must find their SIP, MM, and their EBM or Hot Button.
- ☐ They determine both logical and emotional motives.

# Chapter Four:
# Conviction — The Benefits

- ☐ The Prospect's only interest is "What is in it for me?"
- ☐ People buy because they want to and not due to Persuasion.
- ☐ Don't make a presentation unless necessary, they may be sold.
- ☐ The longer the Selling Process the less likely a close.
- ☐ Selling is to convince and not to inform: Sell, not Tell.
- ☐ Present a Fact, Advantage, Benefit, Evidence, Trial Close.
- ☐ Give Advantages and Benefits that satisfy SIP, MM, and EBM.
- ☐ Leave them wanting more so they will be insecure.
- ☐ Emotional decisions: fast, final; Logical: slow, indecisive.
- ☐ Trial Close for interest and concerns after each Benefit.

# Chapter Five:
# Conviction — The Proof

- ☐ Facts and Benefits are claims if they don't believe them.
- ☐ Visualizing is emotional evidence; confirming is logical.
- ☐ A whisper from a happy client is louder than a Salesperson.
- ☐ Testimonials answer a lot of would-be objections.
- ☐ Intangibles are sold primarily on contacts and confidence.
- ☐ Intangibles are difficult to demonstrate and sell.
- ☐ Visual image - "Can't you just see yourself ...?"

- Visualizing is believing because it is an "experience".
- Most brochures preempt the need of the Salesperson.
- Business only goes where it is invited and appreciated.

# Chapter Six: Desire

- You sell people, relationships, Interests and Problems.
- When they stall, Hurt and Rescue them in the Desire step.
- Desire step is romancing the product with a visual image.
- They must be convinced that they have an AWFUL problem.
- Buying is an emotional process justified by logic.
- The Desire step has a magic closing effect that works.
- Visualizing is believing to the subconscious mind.
- Retailers should create the visual image on the Interest.
- In business should create the visual image on the Problem.
- The Desire step is rarely used so it has a freshness.

# Chapter Seven: Close

- The ABC's of selling: Always Be (Trial) Closing.
- Don't make a presentation unless they are UNsold.
- The real secret to good selling is Trial Closing.
- Trial Close often to flush out objections and intentions.
- You must control the weighing of the pros and cons.
- The Alternate Choice is the only true closing question.
- It can be a long way from being sold to buying now.
- If they have no reason to buy now they won't buy now.
- Multiple closes is the only way to get order now.
- Close the sale, close your mouth and close the door.

# Chapter Eight: Trial Close

- The Trial Close is THE most valuable selling tool.
- Selling is questioning, presenting and Trial Closing.
- The Trial Close is the only diagonistic tool you have.
- The Trial Close measures the temperature of their Want.
- Trial Close prevents objections by flushing intentions.
- Close at the earliest wanting moment or oversell them.
- Trial Closer is more successful than a Closer.

- □ There are no surprises with a Trial Close.
- □ A Trial Close can trade off objections with benefits.
- □ A Trial Closer needs one close, the Alternate Choice.

# Chapter Nine: Objections, Understanding and Preventing

- □ Hesitations = Rejections + Objections + Stalls.
- □ Don't suppress objections; flush and conquer them.
- □ An excited Prospect won't raise objections.
- □ Objections appear logical yet are emotional.
- □ Objections are not necessarily permanent.
- □ It doesn't mean that they don't want to buy it.
- □ Clients buy benefits, not answered objections.
- □ Objections are better prevented than answered.
- □ Little doubts create questions; big ones objections.
- □ A closing Stall means indecision due to lack of want.

# Chapter Ten: Objections, Answering Objections

- □ Never again will the Prospect be this interested.
- □ Price is not an objection but lack of perceived value.
- □ Need reflex answers for all expected objections.
- □ Answers to objections need not be brilliant.
- □ Answer must be very brief, concise, - 30 seconds.
- □ Convince them it's a question that needs answering.
- □ Most objections can be reversed or capitalized.
- □ A Stall is a decision not to make a decision.
- □ A Stall means the want or hurt is not strong enough.
- □ Salespeople lose 95% of the successful Stalls.

# Chapter Eleven: Motives

- □ Every Prospect must be sold logically and emotionally.
- □ Wants prompt the desire to buy, logic justifies it.
- □ We buy because we want to and not because we need to.
- □ Several wants can be motivated at the same time.

- A want may not be important until you arouse it.
- Fears speed up and confirms a decision to buy.
- The secret to everyone's surrender is their self-image.
- Everyone needs approval, the stroking of their self-image
- The tougher the Prospect the more image stroking they need.
- The Alternate Choice Close protects their self-image.

# Chapter Twelve: Personalities

- Prospect's personality determines their decision process.
- You must apapt your presentation to their personality.
- Identify their degree of warmth toward you, Responsiveness.
- Degree of people vs task orientation defines their personality.
- Personality behaviors of Prospects are most predictable.
- Interview their Buffer to learn their personality, behavior.
- Expressives are easy to meet and close.
- Drivers are defined as normal to close.
- Analyticals are slow and difficult to close.
- Amiables are almost impossible to close.

# Chapter Thirteen: Appointments: Finding Wanting Prospects.

- Selling is predicated on finding wanting Prospects.
- Referrals are excellent because of the endorsement.
- Phone selling is for closing and not convincing.
- Can't answer an objection so use it as reason to meet.
- Can't compare prices on phone so make concession.
- Be bold, and talk with a feeling of command.
- Promise Prospect an easy exit from the meeting.
- Promise them an early benefit for granting interview.
- Always start at the top to find the decision maker.
- Buffer can assist in pre-approach and follow-up.

# Chapter Fourteen: Appointments: Phone Techniques

- Phone selling is for closing and not convincing.
- People only learn 7% by ear so hard to convice by phone.
- Can't answer an objection so use it as reason to meet.
- Can't compare prices on phone so make a price concession.
- Your attitude on the phone is a supreme success factor.
- Selling an appointment is like selling a product.
- Be bold, and talk with a feeling of command.
- Promise the Prospect an easy exit from the meeting.
- A pre-written script is a great advantage on the phone.
- Never ask a Prospect to return your phone call.

# Chapter Fifteen: Price

- Rarely is price the only deciding consideration.
- A price objection means there is not enough want.
- Every price is too high until they see its benefits.
- People after deals are hard to deal with after deal.
- Features justify purchase; benefits justify price.
- The price must be justified with values and benefits.
- They often will test you to verify the best deal.
- When the price is high, the extra values must be sold.
- Quote Value-Benefit-Value so price is always justified.
- You only cry once when you buy quality.

# Chapter Sixteen: Enthusiasm

- Enthusiasm is the priceless quality in every Salesperson.
- Enthusiasm is the priceless ingredient in every sale.
- Nothing happens until one of you gets excited.
- Act enthusiastic and you will be enthusiastic.
- Enthusiasm is a happy self-confidence in pursuit of a goal.
- Enthusiasm creates endless energy to achieve goals.
- It is not the cause of success, but rather the cause.

- ☐ Your enthusiasm may be your only and best evidence.
- ☐ Suppress the enthusiasm until you have a reason to show it.
- ☐ It may be your only advantage over competition.

# Chapter Seventeen: Attitudes

- ☐ You are exactly what you think you are.
- ☐ Nothing enhances your ability like faith in yourself.
- ☐ Most Salespeople are not sure of their own ability.
- ☐ You are what you do by habit.
- ☐ Improve your self image by forgiving yourself.
- ☐ Compete, but don't compare yourself with others.
- ☐ Winners never quit achieving goals; quitters never win.
- ☐ A lack of self-confidence creates indecision in the Prospect.
- ☐ Most Salespeople's problems seem to stem from their attitude.
- ☐ Most don't know what to change their attitude to.

# Chapter Eighteen: Pep and Faith Talks

- ☐ A Pep talk will give you instant enthusiasm.
- ☐ Faith talks will change your basic personality.
- ☐ Your affirmation becomes a self-fulfilling prophecy.
- ☐ Today's thinking is where and what you'll be tomorrow.
- ☐ You must Tell and Sell yourself that you are successful.
- ☐ 75% of patients are ill because of poor mental attitude.
- ☐ Motivation is a matter of attitude, a habit of your thought.
- ☐ Your subconscious can't distinguish between fact and fantasy.
- ☐ Pep and faith talks are self-motivating.
- ☐ Napoleon: Tell cowards they are brave and they will be brave.

# Chapter Nineteen: Goals

- ☐ "Any port in a storm" leads to career failure.
- ☐ You must measure the cost:benefit of the goal.
- ☐ Goal setting is a life long activity.
- ☐ Ability is not always important to success.
- ☐ First we make the habit, then the habit makes us.
- ☐ Leadership is goal setting and goal getting.

- All great achievers are great planners.
- Visualizing is seeing, is believing.
- The subconscious cannot sort real from imagined.
- A goal without a timetable is a dream.

# Chapter Twenty: Strategy

- Adopt and adapt your selling to the Market and Prospect.
- Consumer sales take fewer calls than Business calls.
- Keep Business interested between calls with Key Events.
- A Stall is a decision not to make a decision.
- Must arrange next visit before Prospect gives Stall.
- The return call must be sold on its own merits.
- Once rejected you have to start over with new curiosity.
- After Stall a Prospect is vulnerable to competition.
- Selling involves protection from predators, in and out.
- Who controls your selling destiny, here and there?

# Chapter Twenty One: Integrated Selling Systems

- Salespeople are sellers and not administrators.
- Automated prospecting will deliver sufficient Prospects.
- Most selling campaigns are destined to failure.
- Few Salespeople have an organized prospecting system.
- A major success factor is organized persistence.
- Computers and non Salespeople can do massive prospecting.
- An Executive computer program is the most sophisticated.
- The Executive program manages other working programs.
- An Executive program is always updated, never obsolete.
- Probability forecasting is the wave of the future.

# Chapter Twenty Two: Scenario

# Chapter Twenty Three: Selling Summary

# Chapter One

# Overview

## Secrets

- ☐ People buy emotionally with logical justification.
- ☐ Behind every logical Need lurks an emotional Want.
- ☐ The hierarchy of Needs differs from the Wants.
- ☐ Selling is motivation and not persuasion.
- ☐ Uncover the Wants and sell to the emotions.
- ☐ Selling is a "Hurt and Rescue" business.
- ☐ Several Wants can be motivated at the same time.
- ☐ People are never satisfied - they are always wanting.
- ☐ If someone really wants something, they need it.
- ☐ If they have no reason to buy *Now*, they won't.
- ☐ A prompted Want can cause disregard for a basic Need.
- ☐ Easier to fan an existing desire than create a new one.
- ☐ People buy because they want to, not because they need to.
- ☐ We all need approval with the stroking of our self-image.
- ☐ The four Prospect personalities require different approaches.
- ☐ Buying must be face-saving since it is succumbing.

- Only present Benefits that aid in solving their *Big* problem.
- A cold Trial Close after a Benefit is an Objection.
- A price Objection means not enough Want so far.
- Every price is too high until they see the Benefits.
- They are interested in owning when they ask the price.
- The price must be justified with Benefits.
- Only problem in closing is overcoming indecision.
- Indecision is due to lack of enough Want.
- People try hard to arrive at a quick decision.
- Objections appear logical but are emotional.
- An excited Prospect won't raise an Objection.
- Objections are better prevented than treated.
- An Objection is a poor selling report-card.
- Little doubts are questions; big ones Objections.
- Prospects buy their Wants, not answered Objections.
- Objections are not necessarily permanent.
- The ABC's of selling: Always Be (Trial) Closing.
- The real secret to good closing is good selling.
- Close emotionally rather than logically.
- You must create a sense of urgency in selling.
- The only way to close is with the Alternate Choice.
- A Trial Close and Alternate Choice differ in firmness.
- A multiple Close is the greatest sales success factor.
- It can be a long way from the Close to the order.

# Motivational Selling
## Sell to the Wants

Behind every logical Need there lurks an emotional Want. If there is no emotional Want, there will be no sale. If there is an emotional Want, but it can't be justified with a logical Need, there will be no sale. Both the emotional Want and the justified Need must exist to consummate a sale. The Salesperson of today must sell both the logical Prospect and the emotional Prospect.

# Sell the Emotions and Close on the Needs

People don't buy because the Salesperson answered the objection effectively, nor do they buy because the Salesperson had a good closing technique. They buy because they want something. Turn on the "Want" emotions and they will buy.

The only way to find out what excites their emotion is to ask them. They will describe their Wants in their own words so you don't need the psychological labels. The technique leading to the answer of the intimate question "What's in it for me?" is quite simple. Just start the Prospect talking about themselves immediately, be clinical, and be an inquisitive listener. People love to talk about themselves and will be most revealing if they feel it is for their benefit.

Motivational selling constitutes the most significant advancement in selling in recent years. The days of "Show and Tell" are gone. The "Needs Satisfier" is assumed! This is now the era of the "Wants Motivator". Uncover the Wants and sell to the emotions!

# Control Their Mental Attitude

When you first approach a Prospect, their attitude overflows with rejection simply because you have invaded their space without any apparent benefit to them. You must immediately get their attention by talking to them about something in which they are interested. You must know why they want the problem solved, their Emotional Buying Motive, EBM.

If you fail to get the Prospect to accept you, there is little point in proceeding to get them disturbed about their problem; they're still disturbed by you. In effect, you cannot move on to the next step until the present step has been "sold". This simultaneous step-by-step Selling Process, wherein you are changing the Prospect's attitude while you are resolving their Interest or Problem with your product, necessitates a preplanned, formula approach as illustrated in the "Selling Process" chart. You just can't "wing" it and still control the direction of the interview.

Resolving their Interests and Problems may be a minor effort in the Selling Process. The probability of the sale is determined more by the Prospect's emotion than by the Advantages of your product. Your competitors may solve the Prospect's physical Needs but can they solve their emotional Needs?

Of special importance in building Rapport and a long term relationship with your Prospect is to recognize, acknowledge and stroke their self-image.

The most important emotion a Prospect has is the defense, maintenance and expansion of their self-image. The defender of that self-image is pride, and it is probably the greatest of buying motivators if you can use your product to nourish or support it. Most personal conflicts in life stem from the bruising of someone's self-image. Rejection by Prospects is largely because you didn't manage their self-image.

# Buying is Emotional

People are wanting beings; they want more of everything. They want more love, more money, more pleasure, more success, more life; just more and more. It is part of the human survival instinct.

A Need is a necessity of life, even a necessary evil in the eyes of the beholder. What amounts to a necessary evil to one person may very well be a Want to another.

A Want is an inner urge which is strictly emotional in nature. It can be turned on instantly when the right emotion is prompted. When a Want is prompted it must be justified to become a necessity or Need and, therefore, a reason to buy.

Selling is motivational and not persuasive. Persuasion is coaxing and it is difficult to coax someone to want something. You may be able to persuade them that it is better than your competitor's; that it is a fair price; even that others will like it, but you can't coax them to *want* it.

A Need is something each person feels is a necessity in their life, even a necessary evil. A Want is an inner urge, strictly emotional in nature. A Want can be turned on instantly if you prompt the right emotions

There is a hierarchy of Needs as well as of Wants. Satisfy one Need and another appears in its place. People work hard to satisfy a Need and once satisfied they move on to fill a higher Need. All higher Needs are Wants until the lower Need is satisfied. The hierarchy of Needs is from survival upward. The hierarchy of Wants is from greatness downward and random.

From a psychological view an orderly progression of attaining Needs is quite logical. People plan to progress in a responsible order: no new car until more basic Needs are fulfilled. Yet, any Want can be easily prompted to priority thereby causing a person to disregard the normal progression of their basic Needs. Here is the hierarchy, along with some of the prompts that can change priorities:

| THE NEED | THE WANT | THE PROMPT |
|---|---|---|
| ACHIEVEMENT | **"I WANT TO BE GREAT"** | "You deserve the very best, don't you?" |
| EGO ENHANCEMENT | **"I WANT TO BE IMPORTANT"** | "That will make you important, won't it?" |
| SOCIAL ACCEPTANCE | **"I WANT TO BE LOVED"** | "This will make you popular, won't it?" |
| SECURITY | **"I WANT TO BE SECURE"** | "You want to maximize your ... don't you?" (Desire for Gain.) |
| SURVIVAL | **"I WANT TO BE ALIVE"** | "You wouldn't want to lose your..., would you?" (Fear of Loss.) |

# The Motivators

From the above basic Wants there are literally hundreds of specific Wants. It is not necessary to label these specific Wants. Rather, you can program the prompts into the discussion of Benefits that will satisfy their Emotional Buying Motive.

| | |
|---|---|
| "I WANT TO BE GREAT" | Stroke self-image with ADMIRATION |
| "I WANT TO BE IMPORTANT" | Stroke self-image with COMPLIMENT |
| "I WANT TO BE LOVED" | Stroke self-image with FRIENDSHIP |
| "I WANT TO BE SECURE" | Appeal to desire for EASY GAIN |
| "I WANT TO BE ALIVE" | Appeal to their FEAR OF LOSS |

If the questioning of the Prospect were to reveal, for example, a strong desire to put their children through college (their EBM), you could prompt it with:

**SP** - "Mr. P, can't you just see yourself at your son's graduation. After the ceremonies your son comes down, looks you in the eye, shakes your hand, and says 'Gee Dad, thanks!' Doesn't that make you feel great?"

# The Prospect's Personality

You will have to adjust the Selling Process for different kinds of Prospects. Personalities, situations and value systems vary widely. Here is a brief summary of the reactions you can expect from these basic personalities:

EXPRESSIVE (Easy to sell) These are the Presidents and Salespeople. They are high on people and aggressive. They are generalists so don't talk details. Instead spend considerable time on Rapport and listen a good deal. They are a mixture of exhibitionist and politician. Stroke the dream in their self-image; after all no one else does and they do deserve it. Use vivid, visual images. Expressives make quick decisions.

DRIVER (Normal to sell) The operating executive is quick, efficient, assertive, though low on people. Definitely job oriented. They refuse to waste their time in the Rapport step. They are more interested in the Benefits, cost justification, and whether the company needs the product.

ANALYTICAL (Difficult to sell) The controllers, engineers, and computer people crave detail, facts, and proof. They do exhaustive comparisons with your competitors. Stay in the Conviction step where they want to see lots of nuts and bolts proof. The decision process is slow.

AMIABLE (Almost impossible to sell) Certain staff coordinators, teachers, and counselors who are very high on people, low on job and assertiveness. They avoid risk. You must build a friendly, personal relationship with them - they need a lot of assurance and proof. Very long time in the decision making process, if there is any. You must emphasize the Rapport step and supply proof, personal assurances, and especially testimonials from happy clients.

Understand and identify these personality types because everyone fits into one of them.

# The ABC's of Selling
## Always be (TRIAL) Closing

Selling can be an almost endless series of pitfalls, most of which are emotional. Competitive services and products have little to distinguish them from one another. If a Prospect has an apparent Need for the Salesperson's product yet does not buy, it is likely due to selling technique rather than product.

The Trial Close should be used often to test the Prospect's Interest. If the response is hot, use the Alternate Choice Close to close regardless of where you are. If it is lukewarm, try another Trial Close to confirm whether hot or cold. If any Trial Close is cold go to the next selling step. Don't do any more selling than necessary for they will lose their emotional involvement.

When a Prospect first meets you (the Attention step) they may be ready to buy. A long dissertation on the product's merits may turn them off. On first meeting a Prospect try for an immediate Close with an Opening Trial Close:

**SP** - "How long have you been thinking about owning a ...?" Then:

**SP** - "Are you serious about owning one now?" Then:

**SP** - "Well, why don't we sign you up for one while they last?"

When a Prospect (as a Consumer) approaches you they may already have an Interest. On the contrary, when you approach a Prospect (as a Business) you try to develop a Problem they may have. Identifying these Probable Interests or Problems (PIP) is critical in that you will want them emotionally involved, really "hurting" over their "awful" situation. You can't sell a satisfied Prospect!

INTEREST: Use a Tradeoff Trial Close, where you trade off the obvious Benefits of your products with their probable hesitations or concerns:

**SP** - "Would it be worth a one time investment of $xxx to be able to speak with ease in public?" Then:

**SP** - "Would it be worth three days of seminars to be able to handle objections successfully?" Then:

**SP** - "Well, why don't we enroll you while space is still available?"

PROBLEM: When developing a business interest you have to assume a problem that you can promise to solve. This gives you the opportunity to search for their real problem, their Specific Interest or Problem, SIP, and what it means to them personally to solve that problem, their EBM. After you present the solution or Benefit test the waters with a Trial Close.

# Questioning

People love to talk about themselves. Usually they won't answer intimate questions until they feel comfortable with you. Put them at ease by starting with simple questions about themselves. As they start to loosen up, develop their problems and then find out "What's in it for them" in solving those problems.

## PURPOSE    KEY QUESTIONS TO PROSPECT

### PERSONAL

| Personal | "What is your title?" |
|---|---|
| Personal | "How long have you been in this position?" |
| Personal | "What is the range of your responsibilities?" |
| Personal | "What part of your position do you like best?" |

## PROBLEM

| | |
|---|---|
| Problem | "What problems does our industry create for you?" |
| Problem | "What help would you normally expect from us?" |
| Problem | "What is preventing you from solving that problem?" |
| Problem | "What are you doing about it?" |

## PAYOFF

| | |
|---|---|
| Payoff | "What would it mean to you to solve the problem?" |
| Payoff | "Why is that important to you?" |
| Payoff | "How will solving this problem make you feel?" |

## PROSPECT

| | |
|---|---|
| Prospect | "Who, besides you, will be making the decision?" |
| Prospect | "Will you introduce me if you are impressed?" |
| Prospect | "What is your step by step decision making process?" |

## PEERS

| | |
|---|---|
| Peers | "What people problems do you perceive in changing?" |
| Peers | "What will you need to win the support of others?" |

## PRIORITY

| | |
|---|---|
| Priority | "When do you plan on making the decision and change?" |
| Priority | "What is the problem costing you now?" |
| Priority | "What sense of urgency do you feel about it?" |

The questioning technique has many advantages:

- The Prospect becomes the center of attention.
- Builds a long-term relationship with the Prospect.
- Answering satisfies the Prospect's need to dominate.
- Lets the Salesperson guide the direction of the meeting.
- Allows time for thinking out the selling strategy.
- By describing their problems they confirm their Need.
- The Salesperson understands the Prospect's Wants.
- Prospect is confident that their problem is understood.
- Easier to fan an existing desire than to create a new one.
- Relieves the pressure that could become an Objection.
- Their answers reveal the secret to closing the sale.

# Create a Sense of Urgency

If the Prospect has no reason to buy NOW they will not buy now but rather postpone it. Time destroys one's desire very quickly.

The way to create the sense of urgency is to sell them on the idea that the problem is really serious. You "Hurt and Rescue" them:

**SP** -"I can appreciate how serious your situation really is. If you don't correct it immediately you will... (Create a Visual Image of the Prospect suffering from their awful problem)... Isn't that correct?"

8

# The Benefits
## The Conviction Step

Now that you have identified their SIP and EBM, but were unable to Trial Close them into a sale in the Interest step, you must start developing the Want, that is, reasons to buy, with the Benefits of your product. But restrict your discussion to solving the problem in a way that personally benefits them. They are only interested in "What's in it for me?"

- Fact/Feature  "We always have agents on duty so…"

- Advantage  "You can call for travel services at any time."

- Benefit  "In an emergency you will never be stranded."

- Evidence  "Here are the National and State 800 numbers for future use. Why not test them tonight?"

- Trial Close  "In your opinion, would you need 4 or 6 agents assigned to your staff?"

  "If you were to start using our travel service, would you want to start with Regional or District offices?"

A Trial Close is an opinion asking question. It doesn't get you in trouble if the Prospect is lukewarm or cold, but if the Prospect is hot you can go directly to the Alternate Choice Close and conclude the sale:

- Alternate Choice: "Would you want the staff introductions to start this week or next?"

Once the solution is apparent the presentation should be restricted to those Facts, Advantages and Benefits which are pertinent to solving the problem. As each is presented it should be tested with Trial Close, progressing toward the Alternate Choice Close:

**SP** - "What do you think of that?" Then:

**SP** - "In your opinion, would you think the small or medium model would be better for you?" Then:

**SP**  "If you were to go ahead with this project, would you want the economy or deluxe model?"

If a Trial Close after a Benefit is cold you have an Objection, probably because you are off on their SIP or EBM. So loop back into the Interest step for more accurate information. If the Objection is a Stall, "Hurt and Rescue" them in the Desire step (emotional persuasion), and then possibly the Weighing Close step for logical justification. Always Trial Cose at the end of each step.

# Indecision - The Stall

As the Salesperson discusses the Benefits of the product with the Prospect, the Prospect becomes emotionally involved because their desire to own the product is being stimulated.

At the same time the Prospect realizes that it is now decision making time. They also know that the emotional Want must be justified by a logical Need for the product. Yet doubts may linger especially when they don't hurt enough from their "awful" problem. Indecision is due to lack of enough Want to buy now. Those doubts could be any or all of the following:

- Will it do the job?          (Product)
- Is the price justified?          (Price)
- What will others think?          (Peers)
- Do I need it now?          (Priority)

The Prospect is looking for justification before buying the product and they need reassurance that it is the right decision. So any doubt that may influence the Prospect's decision must be uncovered and answered.

Questions come from small doubts, but big doubts result in Objections. The Prospect may think there is no solution to a big Problem and they categorically close their mind without even asking. They question by objecting: "You are too far from our plant." instead of asking "How can you serve us from so far away?" With their closed mind the goal is to get the conversation going again. As in any difficult sales situation, "Keep the Prospect talking!"

# Answering an Objection

When you are confronted with an Objection it is imperative that you get it out in the open where you have the opportunity to answer it. An excellent procedure that will uncover the real problem when you suspect a smoke screen is scripted below. Keep in mind that if they don't WANT the product, you don't have an Objection but rather a Rejection - so back to the Interest step to disturb them. Here is the routine:

**P** - "I just don't think it's for us."          The Objection.

**SP** - "I appreciate your sincerity.          Cushions Objection.

Obviously you have a REASON for          Questions Objection.
saying that. Do you mind if I
ask what that reason is?"

**P** - "Well, we have been with our present supplier for ten years and we feel kind of loyal to them."

Prospect explains REASON.

**SP** - "Just suppose you felt that we also deserve that kind of loyalty. Then, in your opinion, wouldn't this product be a real benefit to you?"

Hypothetically resolves the REASON in order to confirm that it is the only hesitation.

**P** - "Yes, I believe so."

If they say "No" then ask them what the real reason is.

**SP** - "Now then, that raises a question. The question is, 'Does our firm have the Benefits and the personalization of service that will warrant long term loyalty?' That is the question, isn't it?"

Converts the REASON to a question.

**P** - "Yes it is."

Salesperson answers objection by:

**SP** - "Your concern for personalized service is the very reason for using our service.

(1) Reversing it and Explaining why.

**P** - "Oh? Why is that?"

OR

**SP** - "Let's look at all the benefits…"

(2) Outweighing or minimizing it, and putting it in perspective.

**SP** - "What do you think about it now?" "In your opinion, do you…?" "If you were to go ahead…?"

A Trial Close.

Follow with an Alternate Choice Close.

People buy because they WANT the product, not because the Salesperson has answered their Objection. With a valid Objection the Salesperson can (1) Reverse it and explain why, or (2) Outweigh it with more Benefits, put it in proper perspective and thereby minimize it. Once they realize that no product is perfect they can see that the Benefits far outweigh other considerations.

The Stall is usually the most difficult hesitation to handle, but it can be effectively overcome with the Desire and the Close steps. By comparison, the other types of hesitations are easier:

| Type | When | Serious? | Handle? | Indicates | How To? |
|------|------|----------|---------|-----------|---------|
| Rejection | early | frivolous | hard | no interest | concede |
| Objection | middle | factual | easy | product doubt | explain |
| Stall | end | emotional | easy | indecision | HURT!!! |

# Price Must Be Justified

The Prospect buys a product for its Benefits, not because the price is right. Even so, it is critically important that they feel the price is justified; that the "price:benefit" relationship is attractive and that it can't be obtained for less elsewhere. They simply don't want to be "taken."

Because speculation about the price can be overwhelming, the Prospect often wants to know the price before hearing what the product will do for them. Nothing kills a sale like revealing the price before they appreciate the product's benefits.

Try to postpone the price until you know exactly what they need. If you must reveal the price before the values have been developed, then do just that because asking shows interest, but give it to them as Value-Price-Value:

**SP** - "This exquisite dress at one ninety five will make you the hit of the reception." (Also leave out the word "dollar".)

You can postpone price questions by making a short, reassuring comment such as:

**SP** - "This product is an exceptionally good value at a price I know you will feel is more than reasonable. I will tell you about it in a moment, but first let me show you how it will benefit you."

Price is rarely the most important criteria in the buying decision. It can even be of minor importance if:

- The Prospect really WANTS it.
- The product is in short supply. or
- They urgently need the product.

Once you have shown how the Advantages of your product will benefit them, price can be discussed and justified. If it is high priced, you must prove that the extra value is worth the extra price and that the Prospect needs the extra values. Most Salespeople feel that price is the biggest objection to overcome but in reality the price problem is in the

Salesperson's mind, and not in the Prospect's mind. It will only be in the Prospect's mind if the higher price cannot be justified. A mispriced product will always be difficult to sell.

Any higher priced product can be made easier to justify by taking the price difference and reducing it to the lowest practical unit, while referring to the Benefits in the largest unit: "This deluxe copier will cost you only $1.00 a day over 5 years of the finest service." Notice that we used the pattern "value-price-value", ("deluxe - $1.00 - finest").

Prospects aren't sure of the value of even a good buy because comparisons are difficult to make, if not impossible. In the end emotion, rather than logic, is the deciding factor. Remember: PRICE IS NOT AN OBJECTION TO THE PROSPECT WHO REALLY WANTS IT!

# PREVENT OBJECTIONS

Objections can be prevented by:

- Selling progressively as per the Selling Process, and
- Preempting Objections that can't be answered.

To avoid Objections the Prospect must be assured that the product:

| | |
|---|---|
| Will solve the problem/do the job | (Product) |
| That it is worth the investment and/or the hassle of changing | (Product) |
| That others will think well of it   and | (Peers) |
| That the Prospect really needs it NOW. | (Priority) |

When the Salesperson has conducted an indepth interview with skillful questioning, and has kept the Prospect involved in discussing the Benefits, there should be no Objections. Questions yes, Objections no.

When the product has a shortcoming that may be raised by the Prospect, or any objection that just cannot be answered logically,then minimize it by boasting about it as a Benefit:

**SP** - "Being one of the largest gives you the benefits of our volume purchasing while you still enjoy personalized service from your assigned agents."

The Salesperson may even be able to capitalize on it and make it a reason for buying:

**SP** - "The high price is the very reason why you should own this product." (Then explain why you say that.) You have exceptionally good taste in ..."

13

# HURT AND RESCUE
## THE DESIRE STEP

Fanning an existing spark into a full flame is quicker than starting a fire from damp wood. From the questioning in the Interest step you learned of their existing problem and their big Hurt. Now you are going to remind them of that awful Hurt, that you can Rescue them from that problem, and then create a Visual Image of them using and enjoying your product.

It doesn't take much to fan the mental embers into flames. It is incredible the imaginations that Visual Images can conjure. A Prospect actually fantasizes themselves hurting from their problem, then enjoying the rescue with your product in their mind's eye. They become emotionally involved in wanting to buy. You can be as descriptive as you want with little risk of overdoing it. Remember, they are keenly aware of their problem, and they do love seeing themselves in a happy situation.

When they have developed real emotional interest in your product, the Prospect will reveal that with Buying Signals or hot responses to your Trial Closes. But when the Prospect is still undecided because of lack of Want you have to remind them of their Hurt and then Rescue them:

**SP** - "We have agreed that the car you have now is in very bad condition, that it is costing you a lot of money in repairs, that you run the risk of it breaking down at a critical business moment, that it is difficult for your family to go on a weekend trip, and that the car you really need has to help you get away from the pressures of city life, isn't that right?" (The Hurt.)

**P** - "Yes, that is true, and it has to be recreational, as well as for business."

**SP** - "Mr. P, can't you just see yourself driving along a country road on the weekend in your beautiful new Porsche, with the top down, and the wind blowing through your hair? Doesn't that feel great?" (The Rescue.)

The only reason for the Desire step is to build up the emotional Want if the Prospect comes out of the Conviction step stalling because of indecision. If they, in turn, come out of the Desire step really wanting your product but still hesitating, it is because they cannot see the logical justification for the purchase. They are desperate for justification both to themselves and maybe to their Peers. They need your help for they are deeply involved emotionally.

14

# The Weighing Close

The only real difficulty in closing is overcoming the Prospect's indecision. Indecision is agony so they need your help in justifying their Want with a Need. You can best do this by helping them clinically weigh the pros and cons:

**SP** - "Mr. P, you are about to make a decision and we want it to be a correct decision. So let's weigh the reasons for hesitating with the reasons for going ahead with us right now."

(Draw a T on a sheet of paper)

| **Reasons for hesitating:**<br>(Let Prospect list) | **Reasons for moving ahead NOW:**<br>(You write in your Benefits) |
| --- | --- |
| Loyalty<br>Price | Cost savings will get you recognition.<br>Nicer packaging will increase sales.<br>24 hr service to serve your clients.<br>Service executive to reduce your work. |

**SP** - "Have I missed any?" Bonuses for your new ideas.
**P** - "No." Free up capital for your expansion.

**SP** - "Now which side weighs heavier - the reasons for hesitating or the reason for going ahead with our product right now?"

**P** - "Your side."

**SP** - "A wise decision."

(Now go to an Alternate Choice Close to Ask for the Order.)

# The Sale And The Order

It is the value of the Benefits to the Prospect that sells them, not the closing techniques. The selling technique facilitates the Close. Closing a sale actually occurs in two steps:

      (1) Overcoming the Prospect's indecision. (the sale)
and (2) Asking for the Order. (the order)

There is no magic in closing. It just takes a little bit of skill in questioning and finesse.

The term Close is used both for overcoming the indecision and Asking for the Order, which is fine since the questions and questioning technique used are virtually identical. They differ only in firmness.

# A Series of Ordering Questions

There may be a time gap between the decision to buy and the actual placing of the order. We started the "buy now" back in the questioning step by evaluating the time-value of delaying the decision. There is no reason to believe that one closing question should actually result in an order. Most often, several closing questions are required.

To be safe always use the Alternate Choice Close. If you find hesitation try a few of the Coaxing Closes by offering more inducements to order now. Failing even those efforts, you should go into the gentle Pressure Closes: "You can't wait too long in deciding since we have another possible buyer."

It really is of paramount importance to try to close and get the order on the first meeting because:

- Ease of a favorable decision.
- Benefits for the Prospect are vivid.
- Their interest is at the highest.
- Hesitations have been minimized.
- Emotional odds are in your favor.

# Closes

| **ASSUMED CLOSES:** | **THE SALE** |
|---|---|
| Alternate-Choice Close | "Would you want 4 or 6 of our staff to be assigned to your ...?" |
| Minor-Point Close | "Would you want to have the ticket packet designed with your logo?" (Half of an Alternate Choice Close.) |
| **COAXING CLOSES:** | **THE ORDER** |
| Instructional Close | "Why don't you try it out and see how nice it is?" |
| Narrative Close | "John Doe had almost the same situation you do. He ..." |
| Service Close | "Here, let me adjust it especially for you ..." |
| Inducement Close | "As an extra feature for you, we can add in the…" |

| | |
|---|---|
| Future-Dating Close | "We have a policy of future dating of 60 days if you order on our first call." |
| Special-Design Close | "You can have this exclusive feature product at a low extra cost of ..." |
| Guarantee Close | "In addition to our regular guarantee, we will also guarantee ..." |
| Return-for-Credit Close | "We will take back for full credit any product that does not sell." |
| Another-Advantage Close | "By the way, we also include free delivery." |

## Pressure Closes

| | |
|---|---|
| Puppy-Dog Close | "Why don't you try it free of charge for a week?" |
| Challenge Close | "Let's put an offer in to see if you can qualify for the loan on the house." |
| Coming-Event Close | "You really should order now since the price will be going up on the first." |
| Last-One Close | "This is the last one we have and the new ones won't be in for quite awhile." |
| Another-Buyer Close | "You can't wait too long since we have another possible buyer." |
| Physical-Action Close | "What I have to do now is call our computer center to set up your file ..." |

**ORDER BLANK:** As our society becomes more service oriented we will see fewer "order blanks". Where personal service is involved the product is only as good as the last performance, so no one wants to be committed in writing for something they may want to get out of quickly. In corporate travel services, for example, there are no order blanks. With this lack of a written agreement, it may take several closing visits before the Prospect actually starts to buy from you. But the longer it takes for them to start doing business with you the less likely they will.

Similarly, where others have to be consulted by the Prospect before ordering, the Salesperson must get as many commitments as possible from the Prospect to perform some activity:

- Set up joint meeting with other decision maker.
- Develop figures for current volume of purchases.
- Do staff survey on value of present service, etc.

You must keep them actively involved between meetings to maintain the sales momentum.

# Conclusion

## *Get them to like you.

If they don't like you they will not buy from you. They won't even be listening to you. When they think of you as a friend they will often buy from you even when it is an inconvenience in price, time, distance or quality.

**You no longer sell products, you sell people and relationships**

...because you no longer have a competitive advantage in product features, advantages, benefits or price in the Prospect's view. Even the Salespeople look and sound alike.

The Prospect will buy from the Salesperson who they believe they can develop a personal relationship with. In essence, YOU, the Salesperson, can be the competitive advantage.

## *Find their real Interest or Problem

It is not your mission to interest them in your product, but rather to find out what they are already interested in that your product will satisfy. It is much easier to fan the spark of an existing desire than it is to create a new one.

The only Prospect-related questions are:
WHAT do they want?    (their Need), and
WHY do they want it?    (their Want).

The selling process is answering those two questions with your product.

## *Sell them their Hurt at every opportunity

First, they must be convinced that they have a serious problem or situation that must be resolved, and then be convinced that your product is the correct solution.

At every opportunity you should stress their problem by making a supporting statement that they have an awful situation. Even a "Tse, tse, tse!" can be most effective.

## *Get them excited about what you can do for them

The Prospect only sees you in terms of "What's in it for me?" Every situation seeks an answer to that question. If there is nothing in it for them, tangible or intangible, they won't get involved.

"What's in it for me?" is the benefits from your product. When they are excited about having their problem solved they will buy NOW. When they are not excited, there is not enough Want or desire and they will reply: "I would like to think it over". They just are not excited enough to want to do something about it now.

# *Offer a solution with a Visual Image

They have to see that they have a serious problem and there is an exciting solution to it right now.

To ensure that they see the seriousness of their problem you "sell" it back to them. You make them Hurt by describing their awful situation with as much visual imagination as you can conjure. Let them see themselves hurting in their awful situation.

Then Rescue them with your exciting solution to their problem. Make it a vivid Visual Image because the scene will make a lasting impression while bland words alone are easily forgotten.

# *Trial Close each selling step

Prospects buy emotionally with logical justification. You can measure their logical justification easily because you can see the reaction of being understood. But the emotional reaction must be tested because it usually doesn't show.

The easiest way is to simply ask the Prospect how they feel about the benefit, i.e., a Trial Close. The Trial Close will never get you in trouble because it is only an opinion-asking question. You can even test their preferences and intentions along with their emotions. The Trial Close is the best diognastic tool the Salesperson has.

# *Close on every hot Trial Close

When the reply to a Trial Close is positive it means they are emotionally excited and will do something about it now if asked. They are ready emotionally and logically. Change the Trial Close opinion-asking question into the decision-asking Alternate Choice Close question simply by dropping the "If":

Trial Close: "If you were to go ahead with this proposal would you want to start this month or next?"

Close: "Would you prefer Green or Blue?"

# *Use the Alternate Choice Close.

The most effective close is the Alternate Choice Close. When the Prospect really wants your product, the close is simply a formality.

The excellence of the Alternate Choice Close is that:
- it bridges easily from a Trial Close
- it avoids the big decision "if" and reduces it to a small decision "which", a choice, not a chance.
- it "saves face" for those who won't succumb with a "Yes"

19

# THE SELLING PROCESS

| PROSPECT'S ATTITUDE | WHAT WE MUST DO | HOW TO DO IT | STEP | WHAT WE MUST SELL | LOGIC OF THE STEP | BUYER ATTITUDE |
|---|---|---|---|---|---|---|
| **REJECTION** | Get them excited about solving a big problem | Prompt their curiosity | **ATTENTION** | It's worth their time to listen | If one of you doesn't get excited there will be no sale | **ACCEPTANCE** |
| | Establish rapport | Justified compliment | | We are a nice person | They won't buy from you if they don't like you | |
| | Disturb Prospect with something better | Ask a question suggesting a need | | They do have a serious problem | There is no hope for a satisfied Prospect | |
| **INDIFFERENCE** | Promise to solve their problem | Relate similar successes | **INTEREST** | We are problem solvers | They must see us as a needs satisfier | **ANXIOUS** |
| | Gather information | Determine •Specific Interest or Problem (SIP) •Mini Motives (MM) •Emotional Buying Motive (EBM) | | They have a very special problem | What does the Prospect need, and why do they want it? | |
| | Be excited about helping them | Fan the spark of existing desire | | There is a way to satisfy their needs and wants | We really are a wants motivator | |
| **SKEPTICAL** | Develop benefits | •Fact/features •Advantage •Benefit •Evidence •Visual Image •Trial Close | **CONVICTION** | Product—will do the job Price/hassle is justified Peers—others will like it Priority—need it now | Tell them what's in it for them | **BELIEF** |
| | Remove any doubts/objections | •Cushion it •Ask what reason •Hypothetically resolve reason •Convert to question •Reverse/minimize (REMEDY) •Trial Close | | Reassurance | Little doubts create questions; big doubts create objections | |
| **DELAY** | Romance the product | Create a visual image | **DESIRE** | That they want the product | Let them see themselves enjoying your product | **ACTION** |
| **FEAR** | Get decision in our favor | Weigh the pros & cons | **CLOSE** | Logical decision based on need | Emotional wants must be rationalized into logical needs | **CONFIDENCE** |
| | Get an order | Assumed closes Coaxed closes Pressure closes | | A sense of urgency | It can be a long way from being sold to buying now | |

# Chapter Two
# Attention

## Secrets

- ☐ If they don't like you, they won't buy from you.
- ☐ The first few seconds determines most of your success.
- ☐ Start with a Close - "Wouldn't you like to own a ...?"
- ☐ You only have one chance to make a good first impression.
- ☐ Their first impression of you is usually correct.
- ☐ You are an intrusion until you get their attention.
- ☐ Make your first impression a big smile.
- ☐ The best channel to their mind is self-interest.
- ☐ Talk to them briefly about one of their interests.
- ☐ Giving the Prospect a sincere compliment feels good.
- ☐ The justified compliment is the best attention getter.
- ☐ MISS GRACE will get their social and business attention.
- ☐ Get them excited about helping solve their big problem.
- ☐ Early attention is focused on YOU and not your product.
- ☐ Don't let Rapport drift into social chatter.
- ☐ Holding attention is more difficult than getting it.
- ☐ If you create enough interest, no Prospect is too busy.

- Curiosity, fear, easy gain, and pride get attention.
- Disturb the Prospect with something better.
- There is no hope to sell an undisturbed Prospect.
- Ask the Prospect a Question Suggesting a Need (QSN).
- Unless one of you gets excited there will be no sale.
- Don't continue until you have their undivided attention.
- Can't successfully close unless you successfully open.
- If you are casual, they will accept you as casual.

# Selling Format

**SP** - "I sure admire someone who will start a business day with a breakfast sales meeting. (COMPLIMENT). The reason I mention this is because the only ones here are people buying for personal reasons. (JUSTIFIED) Why are you so enthusiastic about your job?" (ASKS OPEN QUESTION).

**P** - "I get a great thrill out of my job, it's a great company and your proposal sounds quite interesting."

**SP** - "That kind of INDICATES you have your sights set on really advancing in your company. (ANOTHER COMPLIMENT). That accounts for your enthusiasm and at the same time generates new energy. What is it that you find so exciting?" (ANOTHER OPEN QUESTION).

**P** - (Tells about job, company and future).

**SP** - "Well, reducing your profit leaks is my reason for being here. (BRIDGES TO BUSINESS) Bill, if there were a way to reduce that awful excess of capital tied up in your parts inventory you would probably want to know about it, wouldn't you?" (PROBABLE INTEREST OR PROBLEM (PIP), using the "Ask a Question Suggesting a Need" Attention Getter).

**P** - "Certainly."

**SP** - "We have been very successful in helping several other companies in this area to reduce their capital frozen in parts and just maybe we can help you. To conserve your time and to see if this idea will work here, would it be alright to get the answers to a few questions?" (PERMISSION TO ASK QUESTIONS).

**P** - "Go right ahead." (And off into the Interest step).

| PROSPECT'S ATTITUDE | WHAT WE MUST DO | HOW TO DO IT | STEP | WHAT WE MUST SELL | LOGIC OF THE STEP | BUYER'S ATTITUDE |
|---|---|---|---|---|---|---|
| R E J E C T I O N | Get them excited about solving a big problem | Prompt their curiosity | A T T E N T I O N | It's worth their time to listen | If one of you doesn't get excited there will be no sale | A C C E P T A N C E |
| | Establish rapport | Justified compliment | | We are a nice person | They won't buy from you if they don't like you | |
| | Disturb Prospect with something better | Ask a question suggesting a need | | They do have a serious problem | There is no hope for a satisfied Prospect | |

# Step By Step
## Must Sell Each Step

The five fundamental states of mind as related to the Selling Process are:

| Mind State | Selling Step | Procedural Step |
|---|---|---|
| Curiosity | Attention | Pre-Approach Excitement Favorable Attention Problem Awareness |
| Interest | Interest | Arousing Interest Gathering Information Developing the Hurt Proving the Need or Hurt |
| Conviction | Conviction | Prompting the Wants Selecting the Benefits Proving the Benefits |
| Desire | Desire | Stressing their problem Hurt and Rescue them Romance the product |
| Action | Close | Logical Justification Order the Solution |

The Prospect must go through all of the steps of the selling-buying process before they will buy. Most normal minds follow the same general pattern in shifting from one thought to the next. Once that thinking pattern is understood you have your Selling Process laid out for you. When you act in harmony with the mind's thinking you move in the line of least resistance.

The only way you can be sure that the Prospect takes those critical steps is to walk through them with YOU in command. They may be able to take any of the several steps without your help but you don't want to risk anything, especially in the first few minutes of the sale.

# Rejection

## Prospect's Rejection Attitude

You are an intrusion when you first meet the Prospect. The Prospect has their mind on the pressures of the moment. Their attitude toward you is one of mild to severe rejection.

Even with an appointment they have probably lost the initial excitement that led to the appointment. The specter of pressure from a Salesperson creates a defensive mental barrier, especially about a product that the Prospect may no longer be excited about. We are all conditioned to resist the Salesperson - "Caveat Emptor - Let The Buyer Beware."

There may even be a degree of resistance during subsequent visits though the resistance is lower if they have already bought from you.

This same resistance is true in all fields of selling, from the milkman trying to sell a new line of apple juice, to retail clerks trying to help with the product, to the photocopy Salesperson tugging their heavy demonstrator along on a cart; even the Salesperson collecting money for charity meets it.

To break that invisible resistance you have to seize the Prospect's attention by talking to them about something in which THEY are interested, usually themselves. This will establish the Rapport that starts them liking you.

## Buying Must Be Enjoyable

The logic behind getting them to like you, ie, selling yourself, is that if the Prospect doesn't like you they won't buy from you. Buyers in corporations as well as in private life want to enjoy buying. No one likes to be involved in a buying situation that is distasteful, even when it is the only buy possible. Business flows to where it is invited, appreciated, and serviced. We all love to buy things because it appeals to our possessive instinct, but it has to be an enjoyable activity.

# Getting Their Attention

To move the Prospect mentally away from their preoccupation you have to get their favorable attention. There are nine great opening techniques that will get that favorable attention and when fitted to an easy to remember acronym they become:

**"MISS GRACE" Will Get Their Attention With Her Social Foreplay**

**M**    Mystery
**I**    Information, Items of news
**S**    Startling Statement
**S**    Survey, Service
**G**    Gift
**R**    Referral
**A**    Ask a Question Suggesting a Need
**C**    Compliment
**E**    Exhibit

There are two instances where you must get their Attention:

(1) To get them to talk to you and develop Rapport.
    This is a *Social* Attention Getter.

(2) To prompt an interest in solving their Problem.
    This is a *Business* Attention Getter.

# (M) Mystery Opening

Everyone loves a mystery!

The problem here, as well as all across the profession of selling, is that few Salespeople take the time to develop any new openings. They want to stay with what they have rather than be creative and take the chance of coming up with something new and exciting. All you need is one good mystery and it can open many interesting doors merely by prompting the interest of the "door keeper".

**SP** - "What product you now use could be replaced to reduce your losses by $5,000 a year?"

If your product doesn't save them money, then suggest that yours is faster, easier to maintain, simpler to use, or whatever your special feature is. You fill in your Advantage that will interest them enough to start a dialog.

# (I) Information or Item of News

### Item of News

Interesting things are always happening to your product in the marketplace. You know about it from your trade papers. Such news may never reach TV because of limited interest, but it could have a substantial effect on the Prospect's business with regard to the price, quality and availability. Make the most of it:

SP - "Mr. P, it was reported there was serious damage to the Colombian coffee plantations from the hurricane. Because of that, we can expect that the price of coffee beans will increase by at least 50% in the next six months. To protect yourself, I would suggest that you place a substantial order right now."

### Ideas (And Advice)

Every buyer, whether consumer or business, looks to the Salesperson for advise, and rightly so. The best ideas on the use of the product should come from you. They expect you to be their unbiased consultant.

SP - "Mr. P, if there were a way to double the life of the light bulbs you use in your store, you would probably be interested in knowing how, wouldn't you?"

(The answer is to always leave them burning. The cost of changing bulbs in a commercial building greatly exceeds the costs of the bulbs and the electricity used in burning continuously.)

# (S) Startling Statement

A Startling Statement will literally startle them out of their preoccupation:

SP - "Mr. P, you should hear what I heard about your secretary yesterday."

P - "What did you hear?" (While hoping it won't be too bad).

SP - "I met a man who said that without a doubt your secretary was one of the most professional and business like secretaries he has ever met. That man was Mr. John Jones of the TYU Company. The reason I mention this is because we have a word processing system that can reduce her word processing work load by at least 30%. I'll bet she'd appreciate that, and so would you. It will take less than 15 minutes to show you and your secretary how the system will benefit you. Would Wednesday afternoon or Friday morning be better for you?"

The news will be effective in prompting curiosity, but the news had better be good. They don't expect anything good or exciting, so it is a most welcome surprise.

# (S) Survey or Service

### Survey

Many Prospects don't know if they need your product, or even if it will work in their environment; nor do they know the specifications it would have to meet, or how their people would accept it. In most cases they probably don't have the knowledge, means or even the inclination for conducting such a survey. So YOU offer to do it for them:

The survey is an excellent method of getting serious attention if you *keep the survey honest.*

This method has the potential of misuse by the Salesperson because the Salesperson is within the company and in an influencing position. The Prospect is somewhat at your mercy as far as the recommendation is concerned. This obligates you to remain objective. So be an unbiased consultant. Do not take advantage of them. If you do, it may come back later as a major problem from which there may be no escape.

The same kind of situation exists with a retail store going into the home to measure, recommend, design decor or such other services where the customer lacks information and must trust the Salesperson.

The greatest sale you can make is getting the Prospect to trust you. If you do, they will usually return to you when they need your type of product.

### Service

If you can offer a special service that they cannot buy elsewhere you will have their attention.

The service need not be related to your product. As an example, your VP of Finance may teach Time Management in the evenings at the local University. You could invite the Prospect's staff to sit in on the class free of charge, or even have the VP do a one day seminar for them at their next sales convention.

The service can also be something free accompanying the product. For example, if you are selling copy machines you may include free service calls during the first 3 months.

When you offer the free service, make it a challenging question rather than as a simple statement:

**SP** - "Mr. P, where would you find someone who could teach your people Time Management, free of charge?"

# (G) Gift - Something For Nothing

Desire for unearned or Easy Gain is one of life's most powerful motivators. It enabled Fuller Brush to lead the field for decades. They offered a small, free brush as a "door opener" to set up the interview. Fuller Brush still uses the technique with the same effectiveness as when it began.

The most interesting aspect of offering a free gift is that you gain almost as much interest from a $2.50 item as a $25.00 item. In reality the cheaper gift is much more effective since it does not distract from the interview.

Everyone wants something for nothing even though the value will drop quickly in time, for something for free has little respect. But have it they must.

If you are planning to give a gift as an attention getter, do not put your name on it. If you do, you are opening the sale and not building Rapport. A gift free of commercialism means friendship; a gift with a brand name on it means business.

# (R) Referral

Without a doubt the Referral offers the most effective and efficient way of finding qualified Prospects. A Referral comes from a happy client. Not only is the lead a potential user, but you come to the Prospect with an endorsement, the most convincing of persuasions.

Not every Referral is going to buy. Phone books are filled with names of people that could use your product, yet few want it. To make a lead worthwhile you have to develop it.

DEVELOPING A REFERRER: Before developing methods of getting a Prospect's attention with a Referral, first consider the correct method of cultivating a Referral. To begin with, you need a happy client. Ask the happy client who they know that may need your product by describing your typical Prospect. As you are describing the parameters of your desired Prospect, you trigger their subconscious mind into a memory search.

A typical request by a Salesperson looking for small companies who wish to buy their light-duty copy machine could be:

**SP** - "Mr. Happy Client, we would like to have more clients like you. Would you be so kind as to refer me to one or two people you know that could benefit from this product? Our typical user is a company that has from 10 to 100 employees, is in a growth industry, and is located within 10 miles of here. The person we would probably want to see would be the Executive Secretary or the Controller."

By the time you have finished with the description of your typical Prospect your happy client will have a name or two.

Even when you have made a sales presentation to an impressed Prospect and they cannot buy from you for whatever reason, they can probably give you a qualified lead:

**SP** - "Ms. P, I realize that you can't use our product right now even though you see all of your benefits. Would you be so kind as to refer me to one or two of your associates that could benefit from this product?"

The life insurance industry, one of the largest industries in the world, uses Referral prospecting almost exclusively. They sell an intangible product that most people don't feel a Need for, let alone have a Want for. That is quite an endorsement for the technique. They are trained to get at least 3 qualified leads from every client.

USING REFERRALS: An INeffective way to use the referral is:

**SP** - "I'm John Doe of the ABC Company. Our mutual friend Betty Jones told me I should give you a call."

The prime error is that you waste precious opening words to tell the Prospect about who you are when they are not the least interested. By the time you get to Betty Jones' name, a name they may not even recall, they have already sorted you into the "Oh, another darned Salesperson." At that point you are in a negative position. You have dug yourself a hole, maybe with no way out.

The correct method is:

**SP** - "Mr. Jones?"
**P** - "Yes."
**SP** - "Mr. Paul Jones?"
**P** - "Yes."
**SP** - "Mr. Jones, you don't know me but we have a mutual friend in Carl Randall over at the ABC Company. Carl feels that you would benefit from an exciting new idea/product he is using. By the way, my name is ..."

# (A) Ask A Question Suggesting A Need (QSN)

You have all been conditioned to answer questions. Even when you don't want to answer certain questions you will. Training in our culture is so strong so as to force us to at least listen to questions. When we put our offer in question form we are virtually guaranteed undivided attention while the question is being asked. Compare the same offer as a statement then as a question:

**SP** - "We can show you how to reduce your heating bills."

**Versus**

**SP** - "If there were a way for you to stop losing so much heat from your home, you probably would want to hear about it, wouldn't you?"

The former is much weaker and could lose the Prospect before completing the opening sales approach. At least interest will hover close to zero.

To get favorable attention, ask a question that:
- Prompts their curiosity.
- Makes them feel important.
- Offers and Easy Gain.
- Scares them.

This technique works equally well when:
- Phoning for an appointment.
- Canvassing companies.
- Initiating a sales letter.
- Mass mailing campaign.
- In advertisements.
- In retail selling.

# (C) Compliment - Justified

We all crave recognition for our inherent qualities, and the achievements that demonstrate that ability. So it is most welcome and satisfying for someone to come along and offer sincere praise.

Long ago people found out how powerful compliments were in manipulating people. Because of its immense power it quickly came into misuse, later abuse, and finally disuse. The misuse even became honored with its own name - flattery. In our desire not to be insincere, we stopped making nice comments. The results were harsh. As a result most people have been reluctant to say anything nice to others, even when it was deserved. We now have a nation craving recognition.

Wouldn't it be wonderful if there were an easy way to pay a compliment, yet never have it be considered flattery? Well there is, you simply JUSTIFY the compliment.

Most of the time people are involved in something that deserves recognition or admiration. You merely have to look around for those good things. When you find them, admire them with a compliment, and then each of you win a friend.

## (E) Exhibit

An exhibit can be any kind of device or display whether product related or not. For example, you may mention to the Prospect that you have just received a copy of the latest computer software that was advertised on TV that will interest their children. The exhibit could be a new style golf putter, a sample of your printout of their purchases, etc. Obviously, it must be something in which they will be interested.

When it is not product related it is a Rapport building Social Attention Getter. When it is product related it is a Business Attention Getter, meaning that you are now selling.

# Social vs Business Attention Getters

As noted earlier you have to get their attention for two purposes:

(1) To get them to like you: Social Attention Getter.
(2) To get them to want your solution: Business Attention Getter.

MISS GRACE's techniques can be used for both purposes. In this book we are using those Attention Getters that are the easiest to use and have the widest application, the Compliment and Ask a Question Suggesting a Need.

| SOCIAL | BUSINESS |
|---|---|
| M | M |
| I | I |
| S | S |
| S | S |
| G | G |
| R | R |
| A | ASK A QUESTION SUGGESTING |
| COMPLIMENT | C          A NEED (QSN) |
| E | E |

But that does not mean they are the best in general nor the best for you. The MISS GRACE Attention Getters are so basic that any one of them can be used in combination with any other for either the Social or Business use. As an example, we use the Gift and Mystery openers in this situation where a Salesperson is trying to sell a Prospect a computerized billing system:

**SP** - "Mr. P, I want you to have this fountain pen (GIFT) because it is one of the finest made as you can see. I am also going to show you how NOT to use it (MYSTERY)." (Waits for a reaction).

**P** - "It is beautiful but you sure have got my curiosity going. How are you going to show me how NOT to use it?"

**SP** - "Well, Mr. P, you spend far too much of your personal time doing paperwork that is so easy for a computer to do. This system could free up 20% of your time. I don't want you to ever use this pen during your personal time for billings that a computer can do - you both are too valuable."

It should be a real challenge to your creativity to develop all pairs of Attention Getters for your product. Predictably some will be great. Some may be so great as to increase your sales because of the opener itself. And it is all yours. And it won't cost you anything. Why not make a contest out of creating openers with your Peers?

| PROSPECT'S ATTITUDE | WHAT WE MUST DO | HOW TO DO IT | STEP | WHAT WE MUST SELL | LOGIC OF THE STEP | BUYER ATTITUDE |
|---|---|---|---|---|---|---|
| R E J E C T I O N | Get them excited about solving a big problem | Prompt their curiosity | A T T E N T I O N | It's worth their time to listen | If one of you doesn't get excited there will be no sale | A C C E P T A N C E |
| | Establish rapport | Justified compliment | | We are a nice person | They won't buy from you if they don't like you | |
| | Disturb Prospect with something better | Ask a question suggesting a need | | They do have a serious problem | There is no hope for a satisfied Prospect | |

# Rapport

If the Prospect doesn't like you, they won't buy from you. Conversely, people will go out of their way to do business with you if they do like you.

Your future in selling will be determined in large part by the relationship between you and your client. You sell people and relationships today and not products. You must be a genuine friend.

Personality is the foundation of selling. Sell yourself first and then your product and company. If you don't establish a friendly relationship they won't care, nor will they be listening when you present your product.

You must be liked by the Prospect. You even have to *LIKE* being liked by the Prospect. The easiest way to build Rapport, the first stage of the relationship, is complimenting and showing your admiration for the Prospect.

Of all the techniques MISS GRACE uses in getting attention, the one most likely to win their favorable attention is the compliment. Everyone craves recognition, praise, and admiration so it is always welcome.

Be sincere, compliment them about themselves, their appearance, their goals or ambitions and their actions; What about their accomplishments, their company, their product? Anything that is near to them that is touched by your admiration will make them feel good toward you. Anything they are unsure of is waiting desperately for approval and sincere admiration.

> **SP** - "Mr. P, I really admire your...      (compliment)
> "The reason I say that is because...  (justification)
> "How did you ever ...?"            (open question)

Once you justify the compliment you know you are being sincere and they will believe you as well.

After the justification ask them an open ended question, such as the How and Why type, so they will give you an essay-like answer. This allows them to talk about their greatest interest, themselves.

Listen carefully to their response, for you will discover some other aspects of their lives you can admire. In case they don't warm up enough you can show more admiration by:

**SP** - "Well, that indicates that you ..."

    ...and another admiration is given. It can also be followed by an open question.

The word "indicates" is like the word "therefore" in that anything that follows it doesn't need justification. Its proof is obvious.

When you are selling yourself, you are literally gaining the Prospect's admiration for you by becoming a super listener while they talk about their favorite subject.

The first stage of Rapport building is showing admiration. The second stage (which may come anywhere through out the meeting) is acceptance - getting them to accept you as one of them.

Acceptance is based on a variety of similar experiences, interests, commonality of background, or thinking alike. The more areas of agreement you have, the more acceptance and the more confidence they will have in you. The most important factor in a business relationship, as well as personal relationship, is thinking alike. It transcends all other considerations.

Most people like you because you and they think alike. When you don't think alike, there are several things you can do to minimize the differences:

- Smile, and they will warm up to you.
- Never volunteer your opinions.
- Never criticize, condemn or complain.
- Look for the good in others.
- Never boast about yourself.
- Feelings follow thoughts so control them.

Establishing Rapport at the very beginning should take no more than 3 or 4 minutes. Avoid letting the Rapport step drift into a social exchange. If you allow that to happen you will never be able to bridge back into the business of solving problems for the Prospect.

The development of the second stage will occur during the questioning period. Here the Prospect is asked a good deal of personal and business questions that expose the commonality of interests, background and thinking.

Once friendship is established, maintaining it can be a stressful situation with any account, since you are always on trial. The bigger the account the more servicing you must do. When you close a big account you will have to spend a lot of time servicing the relationship as well as servicing the account.

# Trial Close

Depending on how you came to be in contact with the Prospect determines your next step.

CONSUMER: If the Prospect is a consumer and has come to you, it is possible that your new Prospect knows all about your product and their need for it. They may already be sold.

In keeping with the strategy of the ABC's of Selling: Always Be Closing -you should immediately try to close the Prospect. The most effective way is with a Trial Close:

**SP** - "How long have you been considering owning such a product?"

**P** - "About one month."

**SP** - "Are you seriously considering owning one today?"

**P** - "Yes I am."

**SP** - "Why don't we go ahead with it right now. Would you prefer the green or the blue?" (A Close).

BUSINESS: If you called on the Prospect, as in the business world, then go to the Interest step with it's PROBABLE PROBLEM statement. Your chances of closing off a Trial Close in the Attention step is unlikely for business protocols demand study and consideration before a purchase, even if they are ripe to buy in the opening.

| PROSPECT'S ATTITUDE | WHAT WE MUST DO | HOW TO DO IT | STEP | WHAT WE MUST SELL | LOGIC OF THE STEP | BUYER'S ATTITUDE |
|---|---|---|---|---|---|---|
| R E J E C T I O N | Get them excited about solving a big problem | Prompt their curiosity | A T T E N T I O N | It's worth their time to listen | If one of you doesn't get excited there will be no sale | A C C E P T A N C E |
| | Establish rapport | Justified compliment | | We are a nice person | They won't buy from you if they don't like you | |
| | Disturb Prospect with something better | Ask a question suggesting a need | | They do have a serious problem | There is no hope for a satisfied Prospect | |

# Disturbing The Prospect
## Probable Interest or Problem (PIP)

When you approach the Prospect offering to solve one of their problems with your product, start with the PROBABLE PROBLEM's Question Suggesting a Need (QSN). To do this find a transition word in their comments to use as a bridge and build the QSN around that. Suppose that you pick up on the word "golf" in the Prospect's social conversation:

**SP** - "Mr. Prospect, golf is the very reason why I am here. If you were able to reduce your time in ... so you could spend more time on the golf course, you'd want to hear about it, wouldn't you?"

    **P** - "Why certainly."

  **SP** - "In order to save you time and see just how well this idea might work for you, would it be alright to get the answers to a few questions?"

    **P** - "Sure."

Now go into the questioning procedure detailed in the Interest chapter. Here you will find their Specific Interest or Problem (SIP), Mini Motives (MM), and their Emotional Buying Motive (EBM). With that data you select the Fact/Feature-Advantage-Benefits to convince them that your product will solve their problem as you bridge into the Benefits presented in the Conviction step.

# THE SELLING PROCESS

| PROSPECT'S ATTITUDE | WHAT WE MUST DO | HOW TO DO IT | STEP | WHAT WE MUST SELL | LOGIC OF THE STEP | BUYER'S ATTITUDE |
|---|---|---|---|---|---|---|
| **R E J E C T I O N** | Get them excited about solving a big problem | Prompt their curiosity | **A T T E N T I O N** | It's worth their time to listen | If one of you doesn't get excited there will be no sale | **A C C E P T A N C E** |
| | Establish rapport | Justified compliment | | We are a nice person | They won't buy from you if they don't like you | |
| | Disturb Prospect with something better | Ask a question suggesting a need | | They do have a serious problem | There is no hope for a satisfied Prospect | |
| **I N D I F F E R E N C E** | Promise to solve their problem | Relate similar successes | **I N T E R E S T** | We are problem solvers | They must see us as a needs satisfier | **A N X I O U S** |
| | Gather information | Determine<br>•Specific Interest or Problem (SIP)<br>•Mini Motives (MM)<br>•Emotional Buying Motive (EBM) | | They have a very special problem | What does the Prospect need, and why do they want it? | |
| | Be excited about helping them | Fan the spark of existing desire | | There is a way to satisfy their needs and wants | We really are a wants motivator | |
| **S K E P T I C A L** | Develop benefits | •Fact/features<br>•Advantage<br>•Benefit<br>•Evidence<br>•Visual Image<br>•Trial Close | **C O N V I C T I O N** | Product—will do the job<br>Price/hassle is justified<br>Peers—others will like it<br>Priority—need it now | Tell them what's in it for them | **B E L I E F** |
| | Remove any doubts/objections | •Cushion it<br>•Ask what reason<br>•Hypothetically resolve reason<br>•Convert to question<br>•Reverse/minimize (REMEDY)<br>•Trial Close | | Reassurance | Little doubts create questions;<br>big doubts create objections | |
| **D E L A Y** | Romance the product | Create a visual image | **D E S I R E** | That they want the product | Let them see themselves enjoying your product | **A C T I O N** |
| **F E A R** | Get decision in our favor | Weigh the pros & cons | **C L O S E** | Logical decision based on need | Emotional wants must be rationalized into logical needs | **C O N F I D E N C E** |
| | Get an order | Assumed closes<br>Coaxed closes<br>Pressure closes | | A sense of urgency | It can be a long way from being sold to buying now | |

# Chapter Three

# Interest

## Secrets

- ☐ Fan an existing desire rather than create a new one.
- ☐ Selling the "Hurt" deepens an existing Interest.
- ☐ Questions are the Salesperson's most powerful tool.
- ☐ No thoughts of a problem, no need to think of a solution.
- ☐ The problem and dissatisfaction must be in clear focus.
- ☐ Describing their problems convinces them of their Need.
- ☐ A question forces the Prospect to think and reply.
- ☐ A two way conversation reduces the tension and pressure.
- ☐ If they aren't talking they may not be listening either.
- ☐ Questions turn a presentation into an interview.
- ☐ The Prospect satisfies their need to dominate by answering.
- ☐ The Salesperson guides the interview with questions.
- ☐ The one who asks the question controls the interview.
- ☐ You must find their SIP, MM and their EBM, or Hot Button.
- ☐ Forget labels for the EBM, just ask them what they want.
- ☐ If they have no reason for buying NOW, they won't.
- ☐ Questions get the Prospect emotionally involved.
- ☐ They determine both the logical and emotional motives.
- ☐ Questions determine which Benefits the Prospect will want.
- ☐ "How would you use...?" and they own it emotionally.

- Questioning personalizes the sales presentation.
- Today's great Salespeople question their way to success.
- Ask them a question and shut up; the silence pressures them.
- Their answers contain the secret to closing the sale.
- Questioning enables you to select a selling strategy.
- They also give the Salesperson time to think.
- Questions should reveal any prejudices they may have.
- Questions relieve Objections created by the pressure.
- They also preempt many would-be Objections.
- Whenever their interest wanes ask them a question.

# Selling Format

### (A) CONSUMER PROSPECT:

**SP** - "How long have you been thinking about owning one?" (Trial/Close)

**SP** - "Are you seriously thinking about owning one today?" (Trial/Close)

**SP** - "The major benefits of this product are: (1) ...... (2) ...... (3) ...... (4) ...... (5) ...... Which one are you most interested in?" (Determining Specific Interest - SIP)

**SP** - "What would that do for you?" (MM or EBM)

**SP** - "What would that mean to you?" (MM or EBM)

**SP** - "What would you do with that?" (MM or EBM)

**SP** - "If you were able to achieve ... would it be worth a one time investment of ...?" (Trade off price using a Trial Close)

**SP** - "In order to eliminate your problem in ... you would probably want to go ahead with this now, wouldn't you?" (Close)

### (B) BUSINESS PROSPECT:

**SP** - "If there were a way for you to reduce those awful losses in your ... you would probably want to know about it, wouldn't you?" (PIP)

**SP** - "Well, we have helped other companies such as yours with this and maybe we can help you also. In order to save your time and maximize your benefits, would it be alright to get the answers to a few questions?"

(Ask the questions to define their SIP, MM and EBM)

**SP** - "Based on what you have told me there is a way to resolve your awful ...(SIP)... and at the same time help you achieve your ...(EBM)... Let's look at how we would do that."... And off into the Fact/Feature-Advantage-Benefits.

| PROSPECT'S ATTITUDE | WHAT WE MUST DO | HOW TO DO IT | STEP | WHAT WE MUST SELL | LOGIC OF THE STEP | BUYER'S ATTITUDE |
|---|---|---|---|---|---|---|
| **INDIFFERENCE** | Promise to solve their problem | Relate similar successes | **INTEREST** | We are problem solvers | They must see us as a needs satisfier | **ANXIOUS** |
| | Gather information | Determine<br>•Specific Interest or Problem (SIP)<br>•Mini Motives (MM)<br>•Emotional Buying Motive (EBM) | | They have a very special problem | What does the Prospect need, and why do they want it? | |
| | Be excited about helping them | Fan the spark of existing desire | | There is a way to satisfy their needs and wants | We really are a wants motivator | |

# Probable Interests or Problems (PIP)

The secret in selling is not so much a process of creating interest as it is *discovering* the Prospect's present interest. It is by far easier to fan the glowing embers of an existing desire, than to create a new one. Determine their Interest or Problem and sell it back to them with a lot of Hurt!

In the Attention step you focused the Prospect's attention on getting them to like you, and then prompted their curiosity about some problems they have. Now with their undivided attention you want to find out what their most pressing problems are, and why it is important to them to have those problems solved.

Once the Prospect is excited about what your product can do for them they will want to hear more. You want them to say: "Yes, I have some serious interest in this product!" From the Salesperson's view, the questions that must be answered are "What problem are they interested in solving and why do they want it solved?" You must know:

- What Benefits you should emphasize so you will hold them in rapture, and

- What emotion to excite so you can take them out of the logical thinking pattern and put them into the emotional-visual mind where the decisions are made fast and forever.

We must discover what their most pressing Interests or Problems are. Then we must find out their personal reasons for for wanting those Problems solved. These become the Specific Interest or Problem (SIP) and Emotional Buying Motive (EBM).

There are only two reasons why a Prospect won't buy:

(1) They don't realize they have a problem - No Hurt.

(2) They are not concerned with the problem - Not enough Hurt.

Asking questions is the only way to develop that information. The more questions asked the more clearly you define their Interests or Problems. This in turn leads to a greater opportunity to understand the motives and emotions of their Want.

THE INTEREST STEP consists of:

PROBABLE INTEREST or PROBLEM (PIP)    "If there were a way to ... you would want to know about it, wouldn't you?"

ASK QUESTIONS (defines SIP, MM, EBM) "What, How, Why...?"

SPECIFIC INTEREST or PROBLEM (SIP) "Based on what you have told me there is a way..."

# What Does a Prospect Buy?

What we think we sell versus what our Prospect buys can be shockingly different. What the Prospect wants is not in the Salesperson's eyes but in the Prospect's eyes. Generally, though, most Prospects buy for the same major reasons.

The most probable reasons a Prospect is likely to have for buying (Probable Interests) from several industries are:

| REAL ESTATE | INSURANCE | SALES COURSE |
|---|---|---|
| Location | Investment | Closing skills |
| Investment | Protection | Answering Objections |
| Convenience | Future income | Self-motivation |

Knowing their most probable reasons is valuable when:

- ■ Searching for their Probable Interests or Problems.
- ■ Trial Closing in the Interest step.
- ■ Designing an Ad campaign.

Let's examine an industrial situation where the Prospect is not the user, and where several Prospects can be involved in the buying decision. Typically that could be a widely used product like business travel from a Travel Agency where the:

Secretary    - sets up the travel plans with the agency.
Traveler    - makes many changes and demands excellence.
Controller   - controls expenses and invoicing confusion.

The Probable Interests for each person involved will be quite different. Each is only concerned with "What's in it for me?"

**PROBABLE INTERESTS:**

| SECRETARY | CONTROLLER | TRAVELER |
|---|---|---|
| Fast response | Savings | Stress relief |
| Pleasant agent | Control | Fine hotels |
| Advice | Reporting | VIP services |

**EMOTIONAL BUYING MOTIVES:**

| | | |
|---|---|---|
| To be liked | Profit | Security |
| Recognition | Recognition | Recognition |

Obviously the only way to approach these Prospects is with a presentation tailored to each person's specific Needs and Wants. Otherwise, we are simply rolling dice.

# Consumer vs Business

In most selling situations, the Prospect has an Interest in your product, or they have a Problem you feel you can solve. Generally the situation depends on who approaches whom.

When a Consumer Prospect approaches you, use the Interest approach. It is much shorter and it assumes that they are already seeking one of the major Benefits of your product. When they have a special problem just swing into the detailed questions to define their SIP and EBM.

When you are approaching the Business Prospect you take the Problem approach. The Problem method should be used because it is more detailed and lends itself to a tailored solution to a very specific problem.

It is critical in completing the sale *today* that the Prospect Hurt enough to want to do something about their Interest or Problem *today*. To assure a *today* sale you literally have to SELL them into wanting to do something about it - *today*.

In retail sales, where the selling time is short; where decision making is fast because the Prospect is usually pre-sold; and where the product price is relatively low, you should prompt and fan their glowing *INTEREST* with a:

**SP** - "Can't you just see the flames from the fireplace flickering across the top of this beautiful coffee table?" type of Visual Image.

In business sales, where the Prospect must be SOLD on the seriousness of their PROBLEM, the emotions can be prompted with:

**SP** - "Well, I can certainly see how having too many dollars tied up in inventory could create real problems for you; the nasty phone calls from suppliers for payment; the bounced payroll checks; the COD shipments that hold up production; the collection agencies; the threatening lawyers. That does make for an awful scene, doesn't it?"

Doesn't that create the Visual Image of a distressful situation? Doesn't that make them Hurt a lot? Will they do something about it *now*? You bet they will! Remember you do not sell products; you sell people, relationships, *interests* and *problems*. You sell them *their* Interests and Problems!

We will study the Consumer Prospect first since you can try this type of Close on any kind of Prospect, Consumer or Business.

# Consumer Prospects
## Closing On Interest

A Salesperson should not do a full sales presentation unless it is necessary. It is more than possible that the Prospect has already compared the product with your competition and the Need-Desire has been well established. The Prospect may even be somewhat desperate for your product. Before you go into the presentation try to close as soon as you have established Rapport with the Prospect:

**SP** - "How long have you been thinking about owning this product?"

**P** - "For several weeks."

**SP** - "Are you seriously thinking about owning one today?"

**P** - "I am somewhat interested."

**SP** - "Mr. P, the major benefits of a Sales Training Course are:

    Selling Skills
    Answering objections
    Enthusiasm
    Self-motivation
    Self-confidence

    … Which one would you select?"

**P** - "To learn how to *answer objections* better." (SIP)

**SP** - "What would that do for you?"

**P** - "I could close *larger accounts*." (MM)

**SP** - "If you had more of them, what would that mean to you?"

**P** - "A lot *more income*." (MM)

**SP** - "What would you do with that extra income?"

**P** - "I could raise the *standard of living* for my family." (MM)

**SP** - "Why is that important to you?"

**P** - "Well, it is my basic responsibility to my family." (EBM)

**SP** - "If you were able to achieve that ability to answer objections with ease, would it be worth a one time investment of $xxx?"

**P** - "It certainly would."

**SP** - "In order to eliminate that problem in answering objections and move yourself closer to that higher standard of living for your family, you would probably want to start with our new class next month, wouldn't you?"

**P** - "Yes I would."

**SP** - "Well, let's enroll you now while the space is still available. Just approve this agreement here and a check for $xxx will start you on your way to your new life."

The Prospect's Interests and Motives are:

| Specific Interest | Mini Motives | Emotional Buying Motive |
|---|---|---|
| | | Responsible to family |
| | Higher living | |
| | More income | |
| | Larger accounts | |
| Handling Objectives | | |
| | | Emotional content! |
| | Tangible or | |
| | Intangible | |
| | Benefits. | |
| Emotional DIScontent! | | |

# MM vs EBM

What is the difference between a MM and an EBM? The EBM is the highest level of emotion the Prospect has for wanting the product or problem solved. A Mini Motive is what the Prospect will have when satisfied. A Mini Motive can be either tangible (more income) or intangible (better job, or higher standard of living), while the EBM is always emotional (the feeling of having fulfilled their family responsibilities, etc).

You may never find their EBM for it may be too personal. But any one of the MM's in the chain that leads to the EBM may be strong enough to close the Prospect. So try to develop as many MM's as possible with such questions as:

**SP** - "What would that do for you?"

**SP** - "What would you do with that?"

**SP** - "How would you benefit from that?"

How far you delve into their buying motives is a matter of appro-priateness. A low priced, standard item is less an emotional buy than a high priced, non-essential product which can be motivated by pride.

Remember that they rarely buy on logic alone, that emotion will be the deciding factor. Whether they were emotionally involved because of problem awareness or were prompted to action by the Salesperson's motivation matters little. It is all the same emotion. The important fact is that you have them upset about their current situation and they are in an emotional state where you want them.

Once you hit their *EMOTIONAL* reason for wanting something, that reason is the EBM. It may not be the only one but it is strong enough for a close.

While questioning the Prospect for their SIP, MM and EBM, you can respond with Hurt:

**SP** - "I can see how answering objections would be important to you. I guess there is nothing that shocks us with fear the way a major objection does just when we think we have wrapped up a major sale. What would an improved skill in answering objections do for you?"

"Hurt" and support any comment they make which will take you closer to the sale. When they disagree with anything you say, withdraw that support either with silence, or by confirming their comment:

**P** - "This sure costs a lot of money!"

**SP** - "Yes it does, doesn't it?"

When the Prospect has some hesitations about the course then trade those hesitations off against the major Benefits. Remember that their hesitation may be just a self justification that they took reasonable precaution before buying. They simply need some logic to rationalize their desire. Let's continue with the sales course example:

| | Hesitation | | Benefit To Prospect |
|---|---|---|---|
| **SP** - "Is it worth | $xxx | to be able to | handle objections?" |
| **P** - "Yes, indeed." | | | |
| **SP** - "Is it worth | 12 nights | to be able to | close more sales?" |
| **P** - "Yes it is." | | | |
| **SP** - "Is it worth | homework | to be able to | speak in public?" |

**P** - "It sure is."

**SP** - "Well, let's get you enrolled now while there is still space available. Just approve this agreement and a check for $xxx will open a whole new career for you."

**P** - "It sure sounds good, but I would really like to know more about it?"

**SP** - "Great. I'm really happy to hear of your interest."

… you tried to close but they want to learn a little more about the product so and move into the Information Getting questions.

# Business Prospects
## Problem Solving

In order to capture the Prospect's immediate interest, you prompt them with one or all of the following:

- Arouse their curiosity.
- Promise a benefit.
- Offer a service.

A great way to use all of the above is to ask a question that suggests a solution to a problem they PROBABLY have:

**SP** - "If there were a way you could *REDUCE YOUR LOSSES* by *$X,XXX A MONTH*, you would probably want to know about it, wouldn't you?"

This is virtually guaranteed to get their interest. The question arouses their curiosity, offers to solve a major problem, and promises a Benefit.

Notice that the problem addressed is rather general. It is a shot-in-the-dark at a problem that everyone in that business experiences. It is general enough to apply to the Prospect even without knowing much about their affairs. If it is too specific the Prospect may reject you because some specific doesn't apply. As an example, suppose you are selling the services of an Employment agency and you want the ABC Company as a client:

**SP** - "As Controller of the ABC Company, it would make sense for you to know how to *REDUCE THE TURNOVER IN YOUR ACCOUNTING STAFF*, wouldn't it?"

Maybe it would and maybe it wouldn't. They would be interested if they were indeed experiencing a large turnover in their staff. If they don't, you will be rejected. You have to make the curiosity promise general enough to be assured of interest but not so specific as to cause rejection. For now, you only want to meet with them to start the Selling Process. You can work on their specific problems in the meeting.

Of course, if you have advance information about a specific problem so much the better. That is not usually the case since the size of the sale may not warrant too much advance study other than interviewing one of the Prospect's associates over the phone.

# Typical Probable Problems

**Some Probable Problems in the business world are:**

**SP** - "If there were a way to ...

  ... improve your quality ...

  ... increase inventory turnover ...

  ... make your customers happier ...

  ... increase your profit ...

  ... increase your cash flow ...

... you would probably want to know about it, wouldn't you?"

**P** - "I certainly would."

Business Interests focus on the main areas:

| | |
|---|---|
| Financial: | how to reduce costs or improve profits. |
| Performance: | how they can do their work better. |
| Image: | how they can look better to their public. |

Those areas will be the Prospect's problem. The reason why the Prospect wants to resolve the problem will be for their personal benefit.

The Prospect may also have a concern about their present vendor. Some of their concerns, and your opportunities could be:

- Dislikes the Salesperson.
- Unhappy with the service.
- Not important to them.
- Price was never justified.
- Fears their future ability.

**Be neither too general, nor too specific**

The *Probable* Problem should be broad enough to capture their interest but not specific enough to cause rejection (when the specific does not apply).

When it is too general there will be limited interest:

**SP** - "If there were a new idea to save money for your company you would probably want to talk about it, wouldn't you?"

Maybe they would, but probably not because the benefit is too general. It would be better to give them an estimate of the savings involved and in which area:

**SP** - "If there were a new idea on how you could save over $1,000 a year in photocopy paper, you would probably want to talk about it, wouldn't you?"

The $1,000 per year could be interesting and most companies do use photocopy paper. On the other hand, you may be rejected by mentioning a particular type of paper may because they don't use it.

It can be a fine line between being too general and being too specific about the problem, but you are most interesting when you indicate the amount of the benefit.

# Make Them Hurt!

The above is a question suggesting a benefit that works well. Better if you ask a question suggesting a need or problem. Not only remind them that they have a problem but make the problem HURT! If they do not have a reason to buy NOW they won't buy now! You have to sell them on the severity of the problem. The more they hurt the more reason they have to buy NOW: NO PAIN, NO GAIN. Selling is a "Hurt and Rescue" business. Let's make the problem HURT them more:

**SP** - "If there were a way to ...
  ... reduce your customer complaints ...
  ... reduce your losses in labor costs ...
  ... reduce your losses in production overruns ...
  ... take the stagnation out of your inventory turnover ...
  ... reduce your rejects and quality complaints ...
  ... cut down your late deliveries ...
... you would probably want to know how to correct it, wouldn't you?"

**CONTINUE:**

**SP** - "The reason I mention this is because we just solved a similar problem for several other companies in your area and maybe we can help you."

It is simply a statement reassuring them that you can solve a major problem in their business. If you have that capability then you can probably solve any related problem they may have. You aren't sure of the specific problem, but you can arrive at it by asking questions.

At this point, ask if it would be alright to get the answers to a few questions. If you don't, you will be rejected for being too forward:

**SP** - "In order to save you time and see just how well this idea might work for you, would it be alright to get the answers to a few questions?"

# VALUE OF QUESTIONS

Few Salespeople understand the value from questioning the Prospect. If they did there wouldn't be such a great preponderance of "Show and Tell" selling. With an understanding of the value of questions you are ready for questions that lead to the sale. Here are the major benefits:

- Enables the Salesperson to select a strategy.
- The answers contain the secret to the sale.
- Creates equality between Prospect and Salesperson.
- Gives the Saleperson time to think and gain composure.
- Prospect can give their opinion of the solution.
- Their need to dominate is satisfied through answering.
- Answering questions builds and strengthens rapport.
- Questioning shifts pressure from Salesperson to Prospect.
- Two way conversation reduces the tension and pressure
- Get the Prospect into an agreeable YES mood.
- Requires a reluctant Prospect to talk and get involved.
- Turns a presentation into a sales interview.
- Compliments the Prospect by asking for their viewpoint.
- If they aren't talking they may not be listening either.
- Questioning identifies the spokesman of a buying group.
- Narrows a talkative Prospect down to your subject.
- Keeps the Salesperson off the defensive.
- Adds tempo and interest to the sales interview.
- Helps keep the Salesperson's courage up.
- Keeps the Salesperson from talking too much.
- Keeps the Salesperson from making a mistake.
- Qualifies the Prospect, qualifies the Salesperson.
- Forces the Prospect to substitute reason for prejudgement.
- It appeals to Prospect's pride, a most powerful motivator.
- Enables the Salesperson to understand their point of view.
- Can pinpoint the area where you may be able to help them.
- Find an existing desire rather than create a new one.
- Determines both rational and emotional buying motives.
- Will determine what benefits the Prospect will want.
- Arouses and directs the Prospect's emotions toward the sale.
- Talking about their needs convinces them of those Needs.
- Prospects will tell the Salesperson what is important.

- Can uncover Peer pressures: likes, dislikes, prejudices.
- They reveal to the Prospect themselves why they want to buy.
- Gives Prospect the pleasure of an attentive listener.
- Relieves the pressure that may have become an objection.
- Questioning should reveal any prejudices they may have.
- Enables the Salesperson to isolate and answer objections.
- Can force a Prospect to answer their own objections.

| PROSPECT'S ATTITUDE | WHAT WE MUST DO | HOW TO DO IT | STEP | WHAT WE MUST SELL | LOGIC OF THE STEP | BUYER'S ATTITUDE |
|---|---|---|---|---|---|---|
| I N D I F F E R E N C E | Promise to solve their problem | Relate similar successes | | We are problem solvers | They must see us as a needs satisfier | A N X I O U S |
| | Gather information | Determine<br>•Specific Interest or Problem (SIP)<br>•Mini Motives (MM)<br>•Emotional Buying Motive (EBM) | I N T E R E S T | They have a very special problem | What does the Prospect need, and why do they want it? | |
| | Be excited about helping them | Fan the spark of existing desire | | There is a way to satisfy their needs and wants | We really are a wants motivator | |

# THE QUESTIONS

## BASIC QUESTIONS

To detect their compelling interest and problems, and why they want them resolved, ask them most if not all of these questions. The questions cover other areas of influence that may have a direct effect on their decision, that is, their Peers, Priorities and whether they are a real Prospect. Add any questions which are pertinent to your business. Remember this is an interview so be thorough.

Questions have the innate ability to involve the Prospect in convincing themselves that they need to solve their problem, whether great or small. Keep in mind that you want to move the questions toward the Close.

| Purpose | Question To Prospect |
|---|---|
| Personal | "What is your title?"<br>(Verifying their position with a simple question) |
| Personal | "How long have you been here in this position?"<br>(Qualifying their ability in knowing the situation) |
| Personal | "What is the range of your responsibilities?"<br>(Encourages them to talk about themselves) |

| Personal | "What part of your position do you like best?"<br>(Easier to get them to talk about the good first.) |
|---|---|
| Problem | "What problem does our industry create for you?"<br>(Their problems, our opportunities.) |
| Problem | "What kind of help would you normally expect from us?"<br>(Are we capable of keeping them satisfied?) |
| Problem | "What is keeping you from solving that problem?"<br>(Flushes out any internal conflicts or politics.) |
| Problem | "What are you doing about it?"<br>(A status update. If nothing, "Why not?") |
| Payoff | "What effect would it have on you and your business?"<br>(To measure impact on the business and the people.) |
| Payoff | "How would the solution make it easier for you?"<br>(To find out what they see in "What's in it for me?") |
| Payoff | **"WHY IS THAT IMPORTANT TO YOU?"**<br>(What emotion will be satisfied with a success?) |
| Prospect | "Who besides you will be making the decision?"<br>(By assuming there are others it saves them face.) |
| Prospect | "Will you introduce me if you are impressed?"<br>(Commits them to a meeting with the decision maker.) |
| Prospect | "What is your step-by-step decision process?"<br>(Gives you the Key Events that must happen.) |
| Peers | "What people problems would you perceive in changing?"<br>(Will it be easy or are there political problems?) |
| Peers | "What will you need to win the support of others?"<br>(Others may not agree with the decision.) |
| Priority | "When do you plan on making the decision/change?"<br>(Tells you about priorities and alternatives.) |
| Priority | "What is the problem costing you now?"<br>(Starts to create a sense of urgency to buy now.) |
| Priority | "What sense of urgency do you feel about solving it?"<br>(To preclude the "We'd like to think it over.") |

You don't have to ask all of these questions, but you should have most of the answers. Before meeting with the Prospect, outline just which answers you do need. These are the KEY questions and can be marked on your questioning form. As the discussion develops you may want to explore an area with CLARIFYING questions:

...Oh? ...Why is that? ... What does that mean? ... Why? etc.

Detailed answers come from:  How,  What,  Why      questions
Brief answers come from:         Who,   When,  Where   questions

| PROSPECT'S ATTITUDE | WHAT WE MUST DO | HOW TO DO IT | STEP | WHAT WE MUST SELL | LOGIC OF THE STEP | BUYER'S ATTITUDE |
|---|---|---|---|---|---|---|
| I N D I F F E R E N C E | Promise to solve their problem | Relate similar successes | I N T E R E S T | We are problem solvers | They must see us as a needs satisfier | A N X I O U S |
| | Gather information | Determine <br>•Specific Interest or Problem (SIP)<br>•Mini Motives (MM)<br>•Emotional Buying Motive (EBM) | | They have a very special problem | What does the Prospect need, and why do they want it? | |
| | Be excited about helping them | Fan the spark of existing desire | | There is a way to satisfy their needs and wants | We really are a wants motivator | |

# Specific Interest Or Problem

From these answers we know their Specific Interest or Problem (SIP), their emotional reasons (EBM) for resolving that Interest or Problem and some of the lesser buying motives (MM). With that we can zero in on the Features of our product that will give them the Benefits they need to satisfy their EBM and maybe a MM or two.

SP - "Well, based on what you have told me there is a way that we can solve your awful problem with the ...

... (Describe their Hurt from their SIP) ...

and at the same time give you the ...

... (Benefits that satisfy their EBM) ...

... you deserve. You may be wondering how we can do this, so let us look at the facts. Mr. P, we have ...

Facts/Features          Advantages          Benefits

...and then into the Conviction step.

# THE SELLING PROCESS

| PROSPECT'S ATTITUDE | WHAT WE MUST DO | HOW TO DO IT | STEP | WHAT WE MUST SELL | LOGIC OF THE STEP | BUYER'S ATTITUDE |
|---|---|---|---|---|---|---|
| **REJECTION** | Get them excited about solving a big problem | Prompt their curiosity | **ATTENTION** | It's worth their time to listen | If one of you doesn't get excited there will be no sale | **ACCEPTANCE** |
| | Establish rapport | Justified compliment | | We are a nice person | They won't buy from you if they don't like you | |
| | Disturb Prospect with something better | Ask a question suggesting a need | | They do have a serious problem | There is no hope for a satisfied Prospect | |
| **INDIFFERENCE** | Promise to solve their problem | Relate similar successes | **INTEREST** | We are problem solvers | They must see us as a needs satisfier | **ANXIOUS** |
| | Gather information | Determine<br>•Specific Interest or Problem (SIP)<br>•Mini Motives (MM)<br>•Emotional Buying Motive (EBM) | | They have a very special problem | What does the Prospect need, and why do they want it? | |
| | Be excited about helping them | Fan the spark of existing desire | | There is a way to satisfy their needs and wants | We really are a wants motivator | |
| **SKEPTICAL** | Develop benefits | •Fact/features<br>•Advantage<br>•Benefit<br>•Evidence<br>•Visual Image<br>•Trial Close | **CONVICTION** | Product—will do the job<br>Price/hassle is justified<br>Peers—others will like it<br>Priority—need it now | Tell them what's in it for them | **BELIEF** |
| | Remove any doubts/objections | •Cushion it<br>•Ask what reason<br>•Hypothetically resolve reason<br>•Convert to question<br>•Reverse/minimize (REMEDY)<br>•Trial Close | | Reassurance | Little doubts create questions;<br>big doubts create objections | |
| **DELAY** | Romance the product | Create a visual image | **DESIRE** | That they want the product | Let them see themselves enjoying your product | **ACTION** |
| **FEAR** | Get decision in our favor | Weigh the pros & cons | **CLOSE** | Logical decision based on need | Emotional wants must be rationalized into logical needs | **CONFIDENCE** |
| | Get an order | Assumed closes<br>Coaxed closes<br>Pressure closes | | A sense of urgency | It can be a long way from being sold to buying now | |

## Chapter Four

# Conviction
## The Benefits

# Secrets

- ☐ The Prospect's only interest is "What's in it for me?"
- ☐ People buy because they want to, not because of conviction.
- ☐ Don't sell to them unless necessary, they may be already sold.
- ☐ The longer the Selling Process, the less likely a close.
- ☐ Half of all completed sales occur in the Conviction step.
- ☐ No one wants to be sold, only helped in solving problems.
- ☐ Selling is to convince and not to inform: Sell, not Tell.
- ☐ "Show and Tell" and "Bring and Brag" should be gone forever.
- ☐ Be concerned with Product, Price, Peers, and Priority.
- ☐ They want to know what it will *do*, not what it *is*.
- ☐ State the Benefit so the Prospect won't see it negatively.
- ☐ Give a Fact, Advantage, Benefit, Evidence, and Trial Close.
- ☐ Only give Advantages and Benefits that satisfy the SIP, EBM.
- ☐ Every Fact you give the Prospect is a chance to back out.
- ☐ A Benefit means nothing unless there is a Hurt to heal.
- ☐ The confused won't buy; Keep it Simple and Specific (KISS).
- ☐ Benefits should be 5 second emotion stroking messages.
- ☐ Always leave them wanting more so they will be insecure.
- ☐ You can minimize Objections with a clear presentation.
- ☐ Sell you and your company's Benefits with the product

- ☐ Most Salespeople don't know enough beneficial facts.
- ☐ Should have 25 Fact/Feature - Benefits for each product.
- ☐ Difference between all products and Salespeople is Benefits.
- ☐ You only need to know what the Prospect needs to be told.
- ☐ Every decision is made by weighing the costs and benefits.
- ☐ Emotional decisions are fast, final; Logical slow, indecisive.
- ☐ Benefits have to be more personalized for big sales.
- ☐ They won't comment on the Benefits unless they have a chance.
- ☐ Trial Close for interest and concerns after each Benefit.
- ☐ You must be dominantly persuasive while stroking their ego.
- ☐ Never argue to defend a shortcoming in your product.
- ☐ Don't leave Conviction until they are logically satisfied.
- ☐ Facts and Benefits are claims if they are not convincing.
- ☐ Make it easy for them to buy, hard for them to get.

# Selling Format

**SP** - "Based on what you have told me, there is a way we can help you reduce your losses of capital and cash from that awful parts inventory situation, that will keep you free of COD shipments, bounced payroll checks and help you move closer to your goal of promotion to General Manager. You may be wondering how this can be done so let's look at some of the Facts."

"We have a warehouse in this area (FACT) so we can inventory over 90% of your parts (ADVANTAGE) and thereby free and up your critical cash." (BENEFIT)

**P** - "That is excellent but how much does that cost extra?"

**SP** - "The extra cost is really quite small in comparison to the great relief on cash you will get. We will include one free delivery each day but we will surcharge you $50 for any order less than $500 to insure efficient ordering. To make sure we can control our investment, and yet insure that your parts will always be available, we will need your complete cooperation. We will assume the control as though it were a partnership, which it is. The benefits to each of us are substantial."

**P** - "That is great but I have a few concerns."

**SP** - "What are they?"

**P** - "What assurances do we have that ...?"

　　(Prospect wants some assurances.)

| PROSPECT'S ATTITUDE | WHAT WE MUST DO | HOW TO DO IT | STEP | WHAT WE MUST SELL | LOGIC OF THE STEP | BUYER'S ATTITUDE |
|---|---|---|---|---|---|---|
| S K E P T I C A L | Develop benefits | •Fact/features<br>•Advantage<br>•Benefit<br>•Evidence<br>•Visual Image<br>•Trial Close | C O N V I C T I O N | Product—will do the job<br>Price/hassle is justified<br>Peers—others will like it<br>Priority—need it now | Tell them what's in it for them | B E L I E F |
| | Remove any doubts/objections | •Cushion it<br>•Ask what reason<br>•Hypothetically resolve reason<br>•Convert to question<br>•Reverse/minimize (REMEDY)<br>•Trial Close | | Reassurance | Little doubts create questions; big doubts create objections | |

# They Don't Buy Facts

## Show & Tell is Terrible

　　Traditionally, the Conviction step has been the longest part of the Selling Process. In most cases it has been the only step.

　　Early selling was basically one of "Show and Tell" and "Bring and Brag". It was the idea that "If you throw enough 'mud' against the barn door some of it is bound to stick". The Salesperson force-fed the Prospect with all the information about their product. It didn't matter what the Prospect wanted, they got the full treatment anyway. The sales that were made were usually because the Prospect needed the product even before meeting the Salesperson.

Unfortunately much selling today is conducted this way. Companies therefore have to rely on advertising to create the Attention, Interest and Desire steps for the Salesperson. The Salesperson performs the Conviction step to an excess. The Close step is often left out presumably because of the fear of rejection.

The Prospect tends to see little difference between products and Salespeople. Products features are almost identical as well as prices. It is now becoming very difficult to be different and to offer Benefits that are significantly better than competitors. Often the only difference is you, the Salesperson.

Selling must put the emphasis on the Prospect rather than on the product. Little time should be spent telling the Prospect about what the product *IS*. Maximum effort must be spent on what the product can *DO* for them.

# To Be or Not To Be?

Of the five fundamental states of mind, Curiosity, Interest, Conviction, Desire, and Action, Conviction is a major turning point. It is where the Prospect decides if the product is a valid consideration.

We assume the Salesperson has aroused the Prospect's curiosity, and they have learned enough to display a definite interest in the product's potential. Now they need to know the details.

# Facts to Benefits

A fact by itself tells the Prospect very little. It is only a bit of information about the product. Unless the Prospect is very familiar with the product, they won't see the real personal gain for themselves. As such, there is a great chance that they will either not think about the Benefits or even see the Features as a negative.

There are many Features which have obvious Benefits, but there are many that can be negative when viewed from the Prospect's viewpoint. The Salesperson tends to see the Features in terms of the Salesperson's values, rather than from the Prospect's view. For example, a home with a large back yard is:

Positive  - For a family with children.

Negative - For a person who hates yard work.

Even though all of the actions and decisions in our lives revolve around the question of "What's in it for me?" people don't listen too well when someone tries to explain the Benefits to them. For example, of the 11,000,000 US military personnel who were eligible for the Benefits under the GI bill only 5% used it. Was someone not listening or was someone not explaining the Benefits clearly, or both?

The Prospect's only interest is "What's in it for me?" They want to know what it will mean to them in Benefits. If it doesn't benefit them, then there is no logic in having it.

**FACT/FEATURE:** "This lawnmower is made of aluminum."

To different Prospects this fact may mean different things. Some may not attach any significance to that bit of information. Others may see the advantage immediately, while still others, who have heard about the bad experience with aluminum house wiring and car engines, will be reminded of those unhappy times. To avoid problems, the Salesperson should carefully translate the facts into Benefits so the message comes across accurately:

**ADVANTAGE:** "The advantage is that it is lighter in weight and easy to use.

So aluminum lawnmowers are lighter in weight. "What does that mean to me?" "What's in it for me?" Translate that advantage of the product into a Benefit for the Prospect:

**BENEFIT:** "... which means that mowing the lawn will be a pleasure instead of a back-breaking effort. Can't you just smell the wonderful aroma of the new mown grass?"

Now we have the chain:

Fact/Feature ➤ Advantage ➤ Benefit

| | |
|---|---|
| **Fact/Feature:** | "This lawnmower is made of aluminum so ..." |
| **Advantage:** | "... it is lighter in weight and easy to use ..." |
| **Bridge:** | "... which means that ..." |
| **Benefit:** | "... you may even enjoy mowing the lawn." |

Not every Benefit has to be presented in the Fact/Feature, Advantage, Benefit order. For variation you can state the Benefit first:

**SP** - "You will save $xxx dollars with the high speed capabilities of this machine."

Be careful not to confuse Fact/Features, Advantages, and Benefits with one another:

| | |
|---|---|
| **FACT/FEATURE:** | Physical, tangible product information. |
| **ADVANTAGE:** | What it *DOES* for the Prospect. This satisfies the Need. It solves the problem. |

| **BENEFIT:** | Emotional. What it means to the Prospect in a personal way. The Benefit satisfies the EBM, the Want. |
|---|---|

Don't worry about the fine difference between Advantages and Benefits. As long as the Prospect sees something "in it for me" in the Feature you are on the right track.

# Bridge

We have added a few connecting words, "which means that", to the chain. These words are a bridge. It puts the "you" into the statement as it converts the Advantage to a Benefit. Several examples of such bridges are:

so ... which means ... which will allow you to ... therefore ... that's important to you because ... thus ...

# Whose Benefits?

When you are in a sales interview with a Decision *INFLUENCER* instead of the Decision *MAKER* you must arrange it in such a manner that the Influencer will not end up making your presentation to the Decision Maker. The Influencer will only present the Fact/Feature-Benefits that interest the Influencer.

During the Information Gathering in the Interest step you should obtain this commitment:

**SP** - "Who besides you will be involved in the decision?"

**P** - "Mr. (Decision Maker)."

**SP** - "If you are favorably impressed, will you accompany me while I present these Benefits to Mr. (Decision Maker)?"

# Examples of Fact/Features with Benefits:

"We have an 800 number so you will save on your telephone costs."
"This hotel is on the beach so you will be able to go sailing."
"Your name will be engraved on it free so it will be forever."
"This office is open 24 hours so you will never be stranded."

To be professionally prepared the Salesperson should have at least 25 Fact/Feature-Benefits for each product. Even 50 for an intangible product is realistic and desirable. Remember that *BENEFICIAL FACTS* are the Prospect's only interest, and in a way they are your real "product".

# Trial Close

The first Benefit presentation should solve their major Problem (SIP/EBM), so automatically Trial Close them to test the waters. The Trial Close keeps the Prospect involved and guides the rest of your sales interview. The more they are involved, the closer you are to closing.

The dialog also gives you total feedback on where you are and how to proceed. It will enable you to find out:

- How the Benefit is received?
- How interested is the Prospect?
- Are we on the right track?
- Any hesitations or Objections?
- Do they need more Benefits?
- Do they want to buy now?

**EXAMPLES:**

**SP** - "What do you think of that?"

**SP** - "Do you think you would prefer the economy or the deluxe?"

**SP** - "If you were to go ahead with this program do you think you would want the green or blue?"

**SP** - If you could overcome this problem you would probably want to go ahead with the program now, wouldn't you?"

The answer to a Trial Close's opinion asking question shows you how to proceed:

**Cold:** Handle as an Objection. Cushion - "May I ask why you say that?" and on into the Objection answering procedure, the Desire step, Weighing Close and the Alternate Choice Close.

**Warm:** Try another Trial Close.

If the Trial Close is *COLD* go to Objection answering for there is a problem with either the identification of the SIP/EBM or there is a hidden problem.

If it too is *WARM* go back into the Conviction step and give the Prospect another Benefit followed by a Trial Close.

If *HOT* try another Trial Close, the Alternate Choice Close, and a few Order asking questions.

**Hot:** Use the Alternate Choice Close, followed by one or more order asking questions.

# Prospect's Mental Concerns

There are questions or concerns in the Prospect's mind:

**Product:** ■ "Will it do the job?"
**Price:** ■ "Is it worth the investment, or hassle-of-change?"
**Peers:** ■ "What will my associates think of it?"
**Priority:** ■ "Do I need it now?"

The prospect won't ask you these questions. Perhaps they won't even consciously think about them, but these concerns must be resolved if they are going to buy the product.

The Conviction step MUST answer the first three questions, the Problem-Product questions. If indecision still exists, (Do I need it now?), by virtue of the Prospect wanting to think it over, the Salesperson must go into the Desire and Weighing Close steps. The indecision exists because the Prospect doesn't Hurt enough from the problem to want the solution *now*. The Desire step will remind them of how much it does Hurt and then creates a happy Visual Image of them enjoying the solution. The Weighing Close will clinically weigh their hesitations against their Benefits and give them the *logical justification* of their Want. Then give them an Alternate Choice to close the sale.

## *Will it do the job?

It is basic that the Prospect believe your product will solve the problem under consideration.

Normally this is where most Salespeople spend their time unnecessarily. They are in their "comfort zone" with product knowledge. The usual method is to talk the product's Features to death at the expense of the other critical steps in the Selling Process.

What usually develops is an overkill situation. The Salesperson presents the facts about their product, then presents more facts, and then even more facts. Most of those facts are boring to the Prospect. The few that are of interest are buried amongst the no-interest facts. The whole thing becomes so muddy with no-interest facts that they can no longer see the interesting aspects. The Prospect loses their emotional want; they have slipped back into the logical state of mind.

Present only those Facts/Features that are of interest to the Prospect. You found out those Interests during the questioning in the Interest step.

Give them only the Facts/Features that interest them, then show the Prospect how they will benefit from them. The Facts/Features and Advantages will cover the logical part of their interest. The Benefit will motivate them emotionally.

Give the Prospect only enough Facts/Features, Advantages, and Benefits to demonstrate that your product will do the job, ie, solve their PROBLEM. If they want to know more, let them ask. In the words of show business, "always leave them wanting more!"

# * Is is worth the investment or hassle-of-change?

### Worth the Investment?

Every Prospect weighs the costs against Benefits. Business people call it the "cost:benefit ratio". The "cost:benefit ratio" is the *LOGICAL* evaluation of the product.

The cost or price can consist of "now" dollars (purchase price), "future" dollars (maintenance costs), and "people" dollars (the hassle-of-change). Make the Prospect aware of these costs in the evaluation of the cost:benefit ratio. Such costs are often not considered but they are real and maybe substantial.

### Hassle-of-change?

INTANGIBLE PRODUCTS

When buying an intangible product such as insurance, where very few people are involved in its use, the hassle-of-change may not exist. But where many people are involved, the potential for people problems and politics can be great.

An example would be corporate travel services where a number of secretaries are frequently involved with the travel agents. Each secretary has their own concept of personal service and may be dealing with a different travel agent for each reservation. Positive or negative feelings may develop with any travel agent. Those feelings can become a serious problem when the company wants to evaluate, compare or change vendor. The secretary may resent the change and subtly try to upset the new arrangements. Contrarily, the secretary may become an instrument of change and try to force a change if they can't establish a phone-friend relationship with the agents. Where people are involved on a continuous basis there will be people problems and politics. That is the hassle-of-change.

The smart Salesperson ferrets out any potential people problems during the questioning phase. If any exist maybe an independent survey of current services should be conducted to prove that the service is inadequate and a need to change exists. The Salesperson can arrange for the survey forms but let the Prospect run the survey to keep it unbiased. To complete the transition and build Rapport, arrange for introductions of your personnel to the client's staff by setting up joint training sessions, etc.

TANGIBLE PRODUCTS

When acquiring a tangible product there may be a change of technique; a reduction in people who no longer are qualified to operate the machine; perhaps there could be a change in the environmental atmosphere (noise, scene, dust, odor); perhaps there could be problems with startup; or emotional upsets because the operators weren't consulted first. The Salesperson and the Prospect should evaluate such problems if experience indicates concern in a certain area, for any unresolved problems may very well fall back on the Salesperson.

# * What will my peers think?

Peer reaction is the hidden question or Objection that will rarely surface. No one wants to buy something that creates an argument, questions their taste or indicates poor decision making ability. Pressure may come from family, friends, coworkers, and bosses.

The Prospect won't mention their concern for the approval of others, yet it is there. The best way to handle such a potential Objection is to preempt it by assuring that the Prospect's Peers will enjoy it as well:

**SP** - "Mr. P, your family will be proud that you have bought the finest quality."

**SP** - "Mr. P, your friends will really envy you when they see this beautiful new ..."

**SP** - "Mr. P, your boss will probably congratulate you on the selection of this really cost-effective unit."

Occasionally you will find a person who deliberately buys an item they hope will raise eyebrows. This may be simply to attract attention. If it happens, they will usually boast about it. That is their Want and they may be very easy to close.

People are only interested in what it will do for them. If the Benefit appeals to them they will be interested. They have desire tempered with resistance. If there were no resistance Salespeople would not be needed.

It is in the Conviction step (the Benefits and the Proof) where the Salesperson overcomes the logical resistance. They don't always believe the Salesperson so evidence is necessary to support your statements.

## *Do I need it now?

When there is no sense of urgency about the Prospect solving their problem *now*, they will postpone action.

Each Prospect has many Wants all competing for their limited resources, especially money. Prospects rarely have a list of their Wants and action plans for satisfying those Wants. Rather, the Wants are a mixture of vague emotions each varying in intensity according to their current environment.

Any Want may be prompted into a passion to own or possess at any time with the right prompt. Since most Prospects do not have a priority list of their Wants, or even a list at all, any Want may be satisfied at any time by the Salesperson who can prompt the Want to purchase their product.

Since most Prospects will spend their money down to their quilt or comfort level of savings, it really doesn't matter much what the Prospect buys as long as it makes them feel good.

To that end, the Salesperson should not feel quilty about urging the Prospect to make the purchase *now* as long as the Prospect has a legimate Need and Want for the product.

When the Prospect does not act on the Want now, it is because they do not feel that their problem is serious enough. They may be concerned and have some Want or Desire, but not enough to do something about it now. If they don't, they will postpone it until a later date. But with time this Want cools and other Wants become important. As a result, your sale is dead.

You must therefore create the impression that they now have a serious situation, that it is urgent and that it must be resolved NOW.

All through the selling process you should be taking every opportunity to "sell their problem back to them", that is, convince them that it is a serious situation that must be resolved now.

The Prospect must be convinced of three ideas:

(1) They have a problem
(2) The problem is serious and needs a solution NOW
(3) Your product will solve their problem

Your solution without a serious product-problem has nowhere to go. Their response will be: "I'd like to think it over".

Hurt and Rescue is detailed in the Chapter: Desire.

# THE SELLING PROCESS

| PROSPECT'S ATTITUDE | WHAT WE MUST DO | HOW TO DO IT | STEP | WHAT WE MUST SELL | LOGIC OF THE STEP | BUYER'S ATTITUDE |
|---|---|---|---|---|---|---|
| R E J E C T I O N | Get them excited about solving a big problem | Prompt their curiosity | A T T E N T I O N | It's worth their time to listen | If one of you doesn't get excited there will be no sale | A C C E P T A N C E |
| | Establish rapport | Justified compliment | | We are a nice person | They won't buy from you if they don't like you | |
| | Disturb Prospect with something better | Ask a question suggesting a need | | They do have a serious problem | There is no hope for a satisfied Prospect | |
| I N D I F F E R E N C E | Promise to solve their problem | Relate similar successes | I N T E R E S T | We are problem solvers | They must see us as a needs satisfier | A N X I O U S |
| | Gather information | Determine <br>•Specific Interest or Problem (SIP) <br>•Mini Motives (MM) <br>•Emotional Buying Motive (EBM) | | They have a very special problem | What does the Prospect need, and why do they want it? | |
| | Be excited about helping them | Fan the spark of existing desire | | There is a way to satisfy their needs and wants | We really are a wants motivator | |
| S K E P T I C A L | Develop benefits | •Fact/features <br>•Advantage <br>•Benefit <br>•Evidence <br>•Visual Image <br>•Trial Close | C O N V I C T I O N | Product—will do the job <br>Price/hassle is justified <br>Peers—others will like it <br>Priority—need it now | Tell them what's in it for them | B E L I E F |
| | Remove any doubts/objections | •Cushion it <br>•Ask what reason <br>•Hypothetically resolve reason <br>•Convert to question <br>•Reverse/minimize (REMEDY) <br>•Trial Close | | Reassurance | Little doubts create questions; big doubts create objections | |
| D E L A Y | Romance the product | Create a visual image | D E S I R E | That they want the product | Let them see themselves enjoying your product | A C T I O N |
| F E A R | Get decision in our favor | Weigh the pros & cons | C L O S E | Logical decision based on need | Emotional wants must be rationalized into logical needs | C O N F I D E N C E |
| | Get an order | Assumed closes <br>Coaxed closes <br>Pressure closes | | A sense of urgency | It can be a long way from being sold to buying now | |

# Chapter Five

# Conviction
## The Proof

## Secrets

- ☐ Facts and Benefits are claims if they don't believe them.
- ☐ If the truth won't sell your product, don't lie to sell it.
- ☐ They don't like to buy on unsupported facts or claims.
- ☐ Never prove anything the Prospect already believes.
- ☐ If they don't believe you, guarantee the product claim.
- ☐ You need both emotional and logical evidence.
- ☐ Confirming is logical evidence, visualizing is emotional.
- ☐ Exhibits, Demonstrations and Statistics are logical.
- ☐ Stories, Testimonials and Understatements are emotional.
- ☐ When they push for logical details, tell them a story.
- ☐ Nothing builds confidence like successful experiences.
- ☐ A whisper from a happy client is louder than a Salesperson.
- ☐ Testimonials answer a lot of would-be Objections.
- ☐ They will never ask you to prove an Understatement.
- ☐ Intangibles are sold primarily with contacts and confidence.
- ☐ Intangibles are hard to sell because difficult to demonstrate.
- ☐ Can dramatize the Fact, Advantage, or Benefit of any product.
- ☐ Dramatizing your product will REAP CASH for you. (Acronym)

- ☐ Your presentation is boring if they saw your competitor's.
- ☐ Learning is 87% by sight and only 7% by listening.
- ☐ They will spend more time with you if you use visuals.
- ☐ Visual Image: "Can't you just see yourself...?"
- ☐ Buying is not a spectator sport so get them involved.
- ☐ Emotional involvement: "How will you use this product?"
- ☐ Get them to "try" your product with a Visual Image.
- ☐ If you can't demonstrate it do another Visual Image.
- ☐ Visualizing is believing because it is an "experience".
- ☐ Visualize the Prospect using and enjoying the Benefit.
- ☐ Brochures cannot sell; only tell, create curiosity and image.
- ☐ Most Brochures preempt the need of the Salesperson.
- ☐ Never refer to competition; let Prospect do the comparing.
- ☐ Loyalty to competition is usually because of one person.
- ☐ Your appearance tells them what you think about yourself.
- ☐ Dressing in good taste builds your belief in you.
- ☐ Confidence in you is a great substitute for product proof.
- ☐ They want to know you care, as well as know the product.
- ☐ Familarity breeds confidence and scatters fear.
- ☐ Never express any opinion except on what you sell.
- ☐ The more you need the sale the less obvious it should be.
- ☐ Service and showmanship sell more than all other factors.
- ☐ Business only goes where it is invited and appreciated.
- ☐ Never forget a client; never let a client forget you.

# Selling Format

**P** - "Those are great benefits but I have a few concerns."
**SP** - "What are they?"
**P** - "Well, how do I know just what parts you have in stock?"
**SP** - "We run a computer printout every hour of the entire inventory. Here is the startup copy from this morning."
(STATISTICAL: LOGICAL EVIDENCE)
**P** - "Impressive."
**SP** - "Bill, do you know John Smith over at TMG Company?"
**P** - "I don't."

**SP** - "If you did you'd appreciate this even more. John has been using this same system for six months now and he says he really likes it. His business is a little different from yours but they have the same problems with parts."
(STORY: EMOTIONAL EVIDENCE)

**P** - "That's good."

**SP** - "If you were to go ahead with this program when would you want to start?" (TRIAL CLOSE)

**P** - "Almost immediately. First, I would like to talk to Smith."

**SP** - "That's great. He's a great guy. I'll tell you what, why don't we get started on your program tomorrow? In about two weeks we can meet with Smith and exchange ideas. Maybe we can help each other even more."

**SP** - "Great idea. I'll set up the program for tomorrow right now."
(BUILDING RELATIONSHIP)

| PROSPECT'S ATTITUDE | WHAT WE MUST DO | HOW TO DO IT | STEP | WHAT WE MUST SELL | LOGIC OF THE STEP | BUYER'S ATTITUDE |
|---|---|---|---|---|---|---|
| S K E P T I C A L | Develop benefits | •Fact/features<br>•Advantage<br>•Benefit<br>•Evidence<br>•Visual Image<br>•Trial Close | C O N V I C T I O N | Product—will do the job<br>Price/hassle is justified<br>Peers—others will like it<br>Priority—need it now | Tell them what's in it for them | B E L I E F |
| | Remove any doubts/objections | •Cushion it<br>•Ask what reason<br>•Hypothetically resolve reason<br>•Convert to question<br>•Reverse/minimize (REMEDY)<br>•Trial Close | | Reassurance | Little doubts create questions;<br>big doubts create objections | |

# Facts vs Claims

Wouldn't it be wonderful if the Prospect believed everything the Salesperson told them? Some do, some don't. Proof is very personal. If they believe it, it is called a FACT, if not it is a CLAIM.

The difference between a fact and a claim is merely academic because most often the Prospect won't tell you what they don't believe. When you say your product is the best, they probably are not going to challenge your statement, but they probably don't believe it either. To be safe, you must prove ALL your Facts and Claims with appropriate evidence.

At this point you may be frightened about the spectre of needing overwhelming proof. After all there are numerous Fact/Features-Advantages-Benefit statements you could make about your product line.

Well, don't worry. Recall that in the questioning phase you were only looking for Needs and Wants, the SIP and EBM. The whole effort was to find the problems they were concerned about, to spark an interest in those problems they were not aware of.

If the Prospect is only concerned with one or two problems, they will be bored to death while you are presenting them with all the superfluous Facts and Benefits about your product. It will kill your chances of the sale. So zero in on the Key Benefits, that is, the Benefits that will satisfy their Specific Interest and Emotional Buying Motive. If they will not close on that then appeal to one or two of their Mini Motives. If they are still reluctant, sell them confidence in you and your company. But don't do any more selling than necessary.

At the MOST you should have five Fact/Feature - Advantage - Benefit presentations to make:

- Major problem - SIP and EBM.
- Minor problem - Mini Motive.
- Minor problem - Mini Motive.
- Your personal service - their personal benefit.
- Company's prestige - assures satisfaction.

The evidence you need is now more manageable and will, in fact, become a dynamic part of your conviction and persuasion.

# Evidence
## Logical Persuasion vs Emotional Motivation
### Conviction can be logical and emotional.

The conviction of the *logical* mind is one of confirming. You claim that your product has the lowest rate of wear in the industry, so you confirm it by showing evidence. On the other hand, the conviction of the *emotional* mind endorses as it sells. Emotional decisions are fast and final as long as the emotion can be properly supported by justification. Logical decisions are slow and loaded with indecision because they are a continual weighing of costs and Benefits. They are not as final as emotional decisions unless they are supported by an emotional emphasis.

### ■ LOGICAL PERSUASION IS MERELY CONFIRMING

The logical persuasion is by CONFIRMING rather than by CONVINCING. It usually consists of Exhibits, Demonstrations and Statistics:

■ EXHIBIT: An exhibit can be any type of chart, photo, map, brochure, diagram on a marker board or flip chart. An exhibit is to confirm a fact, feature, advantage or benefit. If you can do something with the exhibit then it would also be classed as a demonstration.

■ DEMONSTRATION: A demonstration confirms by performing. The basic idea is to show your product in actual use, doing what you claim it does. The power of the demonstration is that it gets the Prospect involved, and it is memorable.

■ STATISTICS: Statistics have been the long time standing method of convincing. They can read all about the merits of your product, at least in terms of numbers. But this can be boring if the statistics are not humanized, that is, converted into people examples. Statistics would seem to be at their best when generated by an independent source, but in reality it seems that even your company's own brochure will be accepted as a final authority. The assumption is that the company wouldn't dare print it unless it were true.

## ■ EMOTIONAL MOTIVATION IS A "LIVING" EXPERIENCE

The Emotional Motivation consists of Stories about similar situations, Understatements, and various forms of Testimonials:

■ STORIES: A story about others in a similar predicament that turns out well with your product is an excellent method of conviction.

The believability is so phenomenal that most Salespeople don't even reference them with names. The Prospect accepts the "endorsement" as is. They rarely question the story. Life insurance Salespeople are great story tellers, and they have a story for almost every conceivable situation.

Stories must be selected with certain purposes in mind. They should:

- Have a basic theme, moral, or idea to sell.
- Try to reverse a Prospect's negative thought.
- Prompt an emotion, eg, fear, fun, confidence.
- Contain some self-humor, if possible.
- Allow Prospect to see themselves as - an individual.
  - all alone.
  - an underdog.
  - injustice.

The Stories have several distinct advantages:

- They give you self confidence.
- They can be powerfully persuasive.
- They love to hear about similar situations.
- They can overcome Objections.

Stories work magic unto themselves. They are so powerful in persuasion that they almost preempt the Desire Step and the judicial Weighing Close. They allow the Close to happen easily, pleasantly, naturally and definitely.

Magic happens to the Prospect when they see themselves in the story using, enjoying and benefiting from your product. It is a visual proof, a "trial run", because visualizing is believing.

Whether the stories are created for the occasion is not the issue. If we equate the "created" stories to the Desire step's Visual Image, we can conclude that the important issue is that once the Prospect sees themselves painted into a happy situation with your product the effect is the same: what the mind's eye can see, it accepts! It's a successful "experience".

Given that the mind's eye believes what it sees, it is important to build in as much "visual" benefit as possible.

| Logical | ■ Proof - "Look at it work!" |
| | ■ Testimonials - "See what they said." |
| Emotional | ■ Similar story - "Can't you just see yourself in that wonderful situation?" |
| | ■ Desire step: "Let's suppose you were using our product for six months and this is what happens. You are sitting in your office with your ..." |

Logical conviction runs a distant second to emotional conviction in real life. It must be considered on a "analyze-accept/reject" basis for proof. On the contrary, the emotional visualization merely has to include the Prospect in the Image. They accept the happy conclusion along with whatever caused it.

■ UNDERSTATEMENT: An Understatement can be the most powerful force in the Conviction step. In an understatement you "admit" a limitation in one area to gain credibility for a more important area. Like a gambit in chess, you give up something you probably couldn't get anyway for something that you really want.

Example: A Volvo Ad - "This car won't go 150. It just looks like it will. But it will do an honest 110 mph!" ... honest and believable!

Many Salespeople use superlative words to describe their product: best, most, finest, cheapest, fastest, their product is perfect. But if we admit the limitations of what it will do, or what it won't do, then we build credibility in areas where we excel. In other words, they won't believe us until we demontrate that we are believable. Example:

SP - "Well, when it comes to general insurance we are merely adequate. We will do a respectable job and that is all. But when it comes to casualty insurance there are none that can touch us."

The understatement is like magic in that it tells the story in a way that self-justifies itself to believability.

**No One Ever Asks A Salesperson To Prove An Understatement!**

Exaggerating, on the other hand, sounds like desperation, as though the Salesperson is in a hurry to tell the truth. The desperation feeling creates a lower value and the Prospect ends up with less interest for the product.

If the truth won't sell, don't sell it! Tell the truth and be emphatic but try not to exaggerate. Exaggerating is like using profanity to make your story stronger. Not only does the profanity not help, but it actually degrades it. The same thing happens when you exaggerate a truth - it becomes less believable. People want to believe things that are in their best interests. But when exaggerated they fear being "conned".

Your product can't be everything to everyone. It has it's limitations. You can create very serious problems if you promise that it will do something for which it was never designed.

When you sell a service, you are probably more inclined to exaggerate. That is the nature of selling services. Yet, the more you exaggerate the less they believe you. The only resolve is to use Testimonials.

■ TESTIMONIALS: The Testimonial is likely the most effective form of conviction. It says that others are using your product and are happy with it.

There are several forms of testimonials:

- Letters from happy clients.
- Client list as references.
- Phone call to happy clients.

LETTERS FROM HAPPY CLIENTS: Even though most clients are happy with their current product very few will write a letter. Testimonials are rare, and that makes them valuable.

There are few Testimonials because Salespeople wait until the happy client initiates the letter. Since clients are busy they will only write such a letter when your product is really outstanding, if then.

Work with your happy clients to generate a steady flow of letters. A simple and effective method is to call them and ask why they like your product. Make a note of those reasons:

SP - "Mr. P, in summary, you said that the reasons you like our product is because ...
... the price is quite reasonable
... orders are delivered promptly and complete
... and service is excellent
... is that right? Mr. P, we would like to have more clients like you and certainly a letter from you would go a long way to helping others. May I do this? I'll write a brief memo of your comments and send it

along to you. Would you look it over and correct where necessary, have your secretary type it on your letterhead and then return it to me? Would you do that to help me?"

This method produces Testimonials and builds a great team spirit between you and your client.

In real life there is a strong tendency for your happy client to improve on the letter. If you merely give a client's name as a reference without their permission, they will tend to tell the truth, the good and the bad. On the other hand, if you ask the client's permission to list them as a reference they will tend to "sell" you because they are on your "team".

When you have the Testimonial letters reprinted for future Prospects, leave off the date. Even a great Testimonial with an old date will immediately raises a question in the Prospect's mind, "Are they still that good?" That could turn a positive situation into a negative question that must be resolved before the Prospect will buy. The problem is that they may never ask you that question.

When reprinting Testimonials, make sure they are top quality. If you can afford it have them printed in the original letterhead colors to look more authentic. Do not give the originals to your Prospect, you may not get them back.

CLIENT LIST: An impressive, though less efficient method, is to show the Prospect your entire client list of Decision Makers and phone numbers. Ask the Prospect to randomly select names to call. That is impressive!

There are disadvantages though:

- You may lose the client list and it could fall into the hands of your competitors,
- The Prospect may not call any clients because they are certain of the response. That is unfortunate for they will not hear great things about your product. It is a dynamic endorsement in a general way, but it has no real sell because the happy client doesn't get the chance to convince them.

PHONE CALL TO A HAPPY CLIENT: An on-the-spot phone call by your Prospect to your happy client is most effective if:

- You have asked your happy client's permission to do so, and
- Your client is available. If not it can be an anti-climax.

Ask for such phone call permission from all of your testimonials, its worth it.

## Proof Book

As soon as you can, create a presentation book that can be used to prove any feature of your product or company. This would consist of test-imonials, brochures, reprints, special reports, media articles, charts, statistics, etc. Highlight the areas of greatest interest to the Prospect.

Like a brochure, it should be shown and not given to the Prospect to hold. Like answering an Objection, you use the KISS formula, Keep It Simple and Specific. Don't get into your or their comfort zone by talking logical facts. Simply flash and refer to the proof, then get back into the emotional mind.

# Sales Brochures

## Sales Brochures Do Not Sell

Brochures do not sell. If they did, you could mail them by the thousands and have all of the business you could use. So would your competitors.

A sales brochure has a built in disadvantage in that it explains too much. It tells the Prospect everything they want to know, thereby eliminating the need for you. There is no more selling from that point on. The Prospect picks up the brochure, starts to read it, hears absolutely nothing more, and begs off with:

**P** - "Let me take a few days to study this."

The Salesperson leaves, falsely elated, and that is the end of the sales attempt.

The correct use of sales literature is:

- To create an image.
- To arouse their curiosity as in a mail campaign.
- As evidence to prove some Fact/Feature, Advantage or Benefit.

When the proof is in your brochure, highlight the area of interest and show it briefly, but don't let them hold it. If they take the brochure, be silent until until they return it. The pressure will maintain your control and keep them from reading it for long.

If they want to keep the brochure, tell them that your company doesn't want it made public, but once they become a client you will see that they get a "personal copy".

When they insist that you leave it with them make an appointment to come back the NEXT day to pick it up (and close the sale while they are still hot).

Once the Salesperson is replaced by a brochure the Prospect no longer needs you. Curiosity and novelty have been completely satisfied without any risk of them buying. You are now out of the picture. They have everything they need to know and you will only sell when they are desperate!

You have to build subtle suspense into the Conviction step. You originally got their attention with curiosity and now you need a little suspense to carry you over to the Visual Images. You must keep the emotion up!

Maintain suspense, always keep them wanting MORE! That's the theme of show business. And it works. This should be the whole theme of the Conviction Step: Benefits enough to do the job, but always leave them wanting more information. That which you can't have has value. That which is scarce has value. That which is plentiful has little value or interest.

This impacts on the type of sales literature you should have:

CREATE AN IMAGE: The appearance of the brochure creates an image in the Prospect's mind. That image will be their impression of the company. If the brochure looks outstanding the company is outstanding. If the brochure is cheap, it's a cheap company. This is a logical conclusion because a company or person will only accept that which is in their own likeness, or what they feel comfortable with.

GENERATES CURIOSITY OR NOVELTY: This is the kind you leave behind. It suggests many questions, tickles them with Benefits, but never tells them about it.

OPERATIONAL DETAIL: This you never leave behind for it tells it all. This should either be a detailed operational manual, or the ring binder presentation book that many Salespeople use. Make it obvious that it can't be left behind.

## Sales Brochures Are Necessary

It is most difficult to sell without a brochure just as it is difficult for a Prospect to remember you without a business card.

The ideal sales brochure is one that creates a positive image while highlighting benefits rather than details. During the selling process there is usually no need to educate the Prospect in detail; that detail only confuses them and attracts their attention away from their emotional benefits. Once the Prospect is in the logical state of mind the decisions are slow and indecisive; in the emotional mind they are fast and final. The brochure should be simple, only detailed enough to cover the major benefits, usually less than four (4) pages.

# Rules of Evidence

To be effective, evidence should meet certain criteria. In order to make the rules easy to remember use this acronym:

## Evidence Will Convict The "Rascal"

**R**  Relevant to the problem and situation.
**A**  Accuracy is a must.
**S**  Specifics make it more believable.
**C**  Clarity for easy understanding.
**A**  Acceptable to the Salesperson.
**L**  Long enough to convince,
       short enough to hold interest.

# Dramatize

Dramatizing is also referred to as Showmanship. The word Showmanship is somewhat of an overkill in that it suggests that one has to be spectacular. It's nice if you can do it, but certainly dramatizing does not have to qualify for prime time TV, nor anything close to it. The desired effect is that it play to the emotions.

You can dramatize a Fact/Feature, Advantage, or a Benefit. For some products you may want to dramatize all or do only the Benefit. For example, an annuity that will put your daughter through college may be dramatized with a photograph of the local University, the Benefit.

The rules of Dramatizing can be remembered as the acronym:

## Dramatizing "Reaps Cash"

**R**  Relevant to the product and its use.
**E**  Emotions should be excited.
**A**  Appropriate to the situation.
**P**  Personally acceptable to the Salesperson.
**S**  Something different to make it interesting.

**C**  Contest: see if the Prospect can do it.
**A**  Action should make it more exciting.
**S**  Striking in conception to make it memorable.
**H**  Hands of the Prospect should be on it.

An example of Dramatizing that illustrates many of the above guidelines would be to send a letter with a blank telegram to a Prospect. The telegram is to be returned collect:

TELEGRAM

Dear Mr. Salesperson,

"Will be pleased to meet with you on ... at ... in my office."
Signed: (Mr. Prospect)

Selling does have a strong parallel with show business:

- You must be entertaining.
- You have script lines to memorize.
- Your attitude controls your performance.
- You always play to a new audience.
- You must get the audience involved.
- You must make a favorable impression.
- You must control your facial expressions .
- You must leave them wanting more.

# Confidence

Critical to closing the sale is that the Prospect have confidence in the Salesperson, the company and the Product.

The Prospect is vitally concerned about:

- The relationship with the Salesperson.
- The quality of the product.
- The price they will pay.
- The future service.

That all spells integrity and confidence. Most Prospects don't have much belief in their own judgement, so it's logical that part of the Selling Process is building confidence all along the way.

Prospect's like a strong Salesperson, one who:

- Can understand the Prospect's point of view.
- Can advise on how to implement the solution.
- Knows what they are doing in selling.
- Knows their product.
- Knows their industry.
- Makes the Prospect confident of their decision.

Because the Salesperson is under constant exposure to rejection by Prospects, the fear of failure looms high in the Salesperson's emotion. A human error is that most people fail because they are afraid of failure.

The fear of failure may overcome the Salesperson and that attitude may show. That attitude destroys self-confidence. For details on how to exude a positive attitude, see the chapter on Pep and Faith talks.

The Salesperson must have a good deal of confidence in their own product and what it can do for the Prospect. This is necessary if the Salesperson is to get excited and enthusiastic about it. Often a Salesperson's enthusiasm about the product and what it will do for the Prospect is their best evidence. Those emotions are most contagious and you want them to be. The essence of selling is transferring that enthusiasm to the Prospect. That means that if one of you doesn't become excited there will be no sale. The burden of enthusiasm is therefore on the Salesperson.

The Prospect's confidence in the Salesperson can be destroyed by:

- Poor or inappropriate appearance.
- Anti-social habits, such as chewing gum, smoking, talking too much, nervous habits.
- Not looking the Prospect in the eye; letting the gaze wander.
- Completing the Prospect's sentences for them; interrupting them; and taking the conversation away from them.
- Answering questions and objections nonchalantly rather than waiting a few judicial seconds to show serious thinking.
- Comparing their problems to others rather than showing them how unique their problem really is, and that it requires a unique solution. (It is embarrassing to the Prospect to have a major problem that is quickly solved because others have already done it.)
- Treating their comments as minor, easy to solve, or a ridiculous situation, rather than being very concerned about it.

Prospect's like to hear success stories about the product and the company. They have a problem and they want the problem solved. They want to be assured that the product is the best possible. So tell the Prospect of your product's successes, the company's awards for excellence and your personal service.

The advantages you may have over competition are:

- Your product.
- Your company.
- Your personal service.
- Your personality.
- Your dramatic presentation.

If your product or company don't have some outstanding Benefits for the Prospect, then it falls back on your selling skills and service! Buyers of intangible products are seldom aware of being serviced well so your personal service will probably be your only competitive advantage.

# Competition

When you are in a bidding contest for an account you have to use a little strategy.

■ A most effective strategy is to let competition have their sales interview before you: They may not know you are scheduled to be there as well, so they may conduct an ineffective "off the cuff" interview which gives you the advantage. They do develop the Prospect's Need-Desire, so when you meet with the Prospect, they should be quite knowledgeable about the product. You can then "Sell instead of Tell." But make sure you have a commitment from the Prospect not to buy before you revisit them; to assure the return meeting create a special program, gift or incentive for them.

■ Ask many questions in your interview. Most Salespeople don't ask enough questions so they never zero in on the Prospect's problem (SIP) or their reason for wanting it solved (EBM). Their sales presentation misses the target.

■ Include a Miscellaneous list off Fact/Features, Advantages and Benefits as one liners and without further explanation. The reason for this is that you might run into a skilled competitor who is limiting themselves to the SIP, MM and EBM in their presentation and thereby presenting limited benefits. Similarly, some unskilled Salespeople do win out with their "throw enough mud against the barn door and some is bound to stick" type of selling: the Prospect may pick up on something minor that tickles their fancy and turns the sale.

■ Convince your Prospect that all of your competitors have virtually identical products so the Prospect can limit their survey. Then emphasize your exclusive Benefits that can solve their unique problem.

■ Prompting the Prospect that they have outgrown their present situation grabs their interest. Point out the weakness in it and suggest that their current happiness is contentment at a lower level. There is nothing wrong with their present product but they are missing a lot:

**SP** - "Mr. P, you really have outgrown your present situation."
**SP** - "Mr. P, you should have a better product. You deserve it."
**SP** - "Mr. P, a company like yours deserves more sophistication from this product."

Don't criticize what they currently have. That reflects on their judgment and they will have to defend it. Rather, create a Visual Image of their awful situation. Make it really Hurt.

■ From time to time it becomes quite popular to do "competitive advertising", fancy words for bad-mouthing your competition in an ad. Here again it is like using profanity; instead of adding impact to the message it actually distracts from it due to a lack of dignity. The result is bad publicity.

The best way to knock competition is simply to cast doubt. One good unanswered question has more impact than a blistering sermon from the mountain:

**SP** - "Yes, we have heard that their price is lower. I wonder what they are leaving out?"

■ It is a normal part of our memory process to remember only favorable experiences and suppress the unfavorable. So the competitor has an advantage in that the loyal Prospect will discount the problems of the past, unless the problems impacted on the Prospect personally. Fortunately, loyalty to a competitor is usually based on only one person in either company. Your approach is to discretely remind the Prospect of the problems of the past with their current supplier and that "the past is the key to the future".

Ask if their present level of personal service would be adequate if problems occur. Most clients do not feel the personal service from their representative is ever adequate, even without problems.

■ When the Prospect is happy with your competition and you really want the account, your strategy should be:

- Become a real friend.
- Make frequent service calls - more than competition.
- Offer an incentive: price, terms, service, prestige.
- Offer to become second (10%) supplier, not a backup.
- Wait for the competition to stumble.

■ Keeping the competition away from your current clients is also an excellent strategy. Your client's memory is always the strongest about the most recent past. Their unasked question to you is "What have you done for me lately?"

### Never Forget a Client; Never Let a Client Forget You

Always assume that competition is calling on your best Clients and your best Prospects. They probably are or will be. Historically a well run company will lose 15 to 20% of its clients each year due to a wide variety of reasons, many beyond control. When it is your company's fault, then 68% of the problem is due to indifference of your staff toward the client. These statistic mean that your company must be on its toes in serving your present Clients.

# THE SELLING PROCESS

| PROSPECT'S ATTITUDE | WHAT WE MUST DO | HOW TO DO IT | STEP | WHAT WE MUST SELL | LOGIC OF THE STEP | BUYER'S ATTITUDE |
|---|---|---|---|---|---|---|
| REJECTION | Get them excited about solving a big problem | Prompt their curiosity | ATTENTION | It's worth their time to listen | If one of you doesn't get excited there will be no sale | ACCEPTANCE |
| | Establish rapport | Justified compliment | | We are a nice person | They won't buy from you if they don't like you | |
| | Disturb Prospect with something better | Ask a question suggesting a need | | They do have a serious problem | There is no hope for a satisfied Prospect | |
| INDIFFERENCE | Promise to solve their problem | Relate similar successes | INTEREST | We are problem solvers | They must see us as a needs satisfier | ANXIOUS |
| | Gather information | Determine<br>•Specific Interest or Problem (SIP)<br>•Mini Motives (MM)<br>•Emotional Buying Motive (EBM) | | They have a very special problem | What does the Prospect need, and why do they want it? | |
| | Be excited about helping them | Fan the spark of existing desire | | There is a way to satisfy their needs and wants | We really are a wants motivator | |
| SKEPTICAL | Develop benefits | •Fact/features<br>•Advantage<br>•Benefit<br>•Evidence<br>•Visual Image<br>•Trial Close | CONVICTION | Product—will do the job<br>Price/hassle is justified<br>Peers—others will like it<br>Priority—need it now | Tell them what's in it for them | BELIEF |
| | Remove any doubts/objections | •Cushion it<br>•Ask what reason<br>•Hypothetically resolve reason<br>•Convert to question<br>•Reverse/minimize (REMEDY)<br>•Trial Close | | Reassurance | Little doubts create questions;<br>big doubts create objections | |
| DELAY | Romance the product | Create a visual image | DESIRE | That they want the product | Let them see themselves enjoying your product | ACTION |
| FEAR | Get decision in our favor | Weigh the pros & cons | CLOSE | Logical decision based on need | Emotional wants must be rationalized into logical needs | CONFIDENCE |
| | Get an order | Assumed closes<br>Coaxed closes<br>Pressure closes | | A sense of urgency | It can be a long way from being sold to buying now | |

82

## Chapter Six

# Desire

# Secrets

- [ ] You sell people, relationships, interests and problems.
- [ ] The desire to own is a fundamental state of mind.
- [ ] When they stall, "Hurt and Rescue" them in the Desire step.
- [ ] The Desire step romances the product with a Visual Image.
- [ ] The Desire step is rarely used so it has freshness.
- [ ] They must be convinced that they have an *AWFUL* problem
- [ ] Buying is an emotional process justified by logic.
- [ ] Help the Prospect logically justify their purchase.
- [ ] If they can't justify it, help them rationalize it.
- [ ] Subconscious can't distinguish between real or imagined.
- [ ] A Visual Image to the mind is like a real experience.
- [ ] Visualizing to the subconscious mind is believing.
- [ ] Fears vanish when they see it in the mind's eye.
- [ ] The Desire step has a magic closing effect that works!
- [ ] Retailers should create the Visual Image on their *Interest*.
- [ ] Business should create the Visual Image on their *Problem*.
- [ ] The Visual Image can and should be used in all steps.
- [ ] It should appeal to all the senses that make sense.
- [ ] Creating a Visual Image is like method acting.
- [ ] Go for the juglar: greed, fear, importance and pride.

# Selling Format

**P** - "I want to think it over." (STALL from the Conviction step)

**SP** - "I can understand how you feel. I can also understand the awful problems you can have with too many dollars tied up in your inventory, the nasty phone calls from your suppliers; the COD shipments, and the collection agencies, not to mention the bounced payroll checks. (REMIND THEM OF THEIR HURT) Isn't that right?" (GET THEIR AGREEMENT)

**P** - "Yes it is."

**SP** - "We can resolve that problem with our nearby warehouse and the 24 hour delivery service..." (REMIND THEM THAT YOU CAN HELP THEM)

"... Let's assume that you have been using our service and it is six months from now. Your President is examining your inventory control report at the quarterly management meeting. With a smile on his face he says: 'You have done an excellent job in selecting your new parts vendor, and have the inventory under fine control. Congradulations!' Now that is the kind of scene you want to be in, isn't it?"(VISUAL IMAGE OF THEM ENJOYING YOUR PRODUCT)

**P** - "Yes it is. It looks great."

**SP** - "Mr. P, do you have a plan of action or would you want me to suggest one?" (Alternate Choice close)

**P** - "Let's both work on it." (And they are closed)

OR THEY ARE STILL UNDECIDED:

**P** - "Well, it looks good but I'm still undecided."

**SP** - "Well, I'm not sure you are going to be in that scene or not. It all depends on the decision you are about to make."

... and into the Weighing Close step to help them resolve their indecision with logical justification.

| PROSPECT'S ATTITUDE | WHAT WE MUST DO | HOW TO DO IT | STEP | WHAT WE MUST SELL | LOGIC OF THE STEP | BUY ATTI |
|---|---|---|---|---|---|---|
| D E L A Y | Romance the product | Create a visual image | D E S I R E | That they want the product | Let them see themselves enjoying your product | |

# To Visualize Is To Desire

The desire to own is one of the five fundamental states of mind. It occurs naturally in the mental process of Curiosity (Attention), Interest, Conviction, Desire and Action (Close).

The Desire step is to be used *only* when the Prospect is *Stalling*, that is, not buying now: "I want to think it over". They want to think it over because they don't want it enough to buy it now. They are in a state of indecision.

The Desire step reminds them of their big Hurt from the Problem and then shows them how happy they are with the solution to that Problem. In short, you HURT and RESCUE them - emotionally.

The Desire step is the shortest step in the Selling process yet it works like magic. It is also the least used technique so it has a great freshness.

You are never sure of their emotional involvement when they come out of the Conviction step unsold. It is risky to assume that the persuasion (logical) and motivation (emotional) of the Conviction step will be sufficient. The Conviction step is a *logical* process blending into an *emotional* process: Fact/Feature (Logical), Advantage (Logical), Benefit (Emotional). We are unsure of the degree of emotional excitment and desire but we know it was not enough because they are stalling on the Trial Close with indecision or lack of want.

To increase their desire you remind them of the awful problem they have.  Make them Hurt all over, then get their agreement. Then immediately create relief with a happy Visual Image of them using your product and benefiting from it. In short, you Rescue them.

**EXAMPLE:**

SP - "Mr. P, I can understand how you feel. I can also understand the awful problems you can have with too many dollars tied up in your inventory, the nasty phone calls from your suppliers, the COD shipments, and the collection agencies, not to mention the bounced payroll checks. Isn't that right?" ..." ("Yes.")

"... As discussed, our nearby warehouse and 24 hour delivery service will solve your problem and the new cash flow will give you the recognition you so rightly deserve ...

"... Mr. P, Let's assume you have started receiving your spare parts from us. It is now six months later, and you are in a management meeting with your President. He is studying your inventory report. It is down 65%. He scans the report, looks up, smiles and says, 'John, you have done an excellent job in selecting your new parts vendor. Congratulations!'

"... Now that's the kind of picture you want to be in, isn't it?"

(In a retail situation you can use a shortened version:

**SP** - "Mrs. P, can't you just imagine the flames from the fireplace flicking over the top of this beautiful coffee table? It's gorgeous, isn't it?")

Procedurally, we must do these three things for the full Desire step:

(1) Remind the Prospect of their AWFUL problem. Get their emotional agreement: "Isn't that right?" ("Awful" is much more effective than the word "terrible".)

(2) Tell the Prospect that you can solve that awful problem, with a very brief reminder of what that solution is: "... Our nearby warehouse and 24 hour delivery service will solve that awful problem and help you get the recognition you so rightly deserve ..."

(3) Create a Visual Image of the Prospect using and enjoying your product.

## Logical Justification Of a Want

When the purchase is small the buying action usually follows the buying desire in a spontaneous way. When the buy is big it must be justified, or rationalized.

JUSTIFICATION is necessary when the Prospect really wants the product but does not feel there is an obvious need in the eyes of others. RATIONALIZING is scraping the bottom of the barrel for even the Prospect can't justify the purchase to themselves; they have to dream up a need. To help with this the Salesperson should always be on the lookout for LOGICAL reasons for them buying it, just in case.

# Visual Image

Strange as it may seem, most fears, if not all, are vaporized once the Prospect sees themselves in their mind's eye using and enjoying the product. They see it because you visualize it for them.

Once you can visualize the scene in your mind's eye you experience it. If you like the scene, you accept it. The mind's eye, the subconscious, cannot distinguish between the real and the imagined. Therefore, creating a scene of them using and enjoying your product is like a successful experience.

Buying is an emotional process justified or rationalized by a Need. Once the Prospect wants the product they can adjust their Needs to assure that

Want. First, though, they need to have some logical reason for justifying that Need.

The Desire step has been affectionately called "Romancing the Product", an apt description of the step. You are getting them to fall in love with what your product will do for them.

Whether you are in retail or business sales you can easily find an opportunity to use a simple Visual Image like:

**SP** - "CAN'T YOU JUST SEE YOURSELF sitting by the fireplace, with the flames flickering off the top of this beautiful coffee table?"

**SP** - "Can't you just see yourself in the warehouse with your President as he admires all of that neat inventory that your new forklift just stacked?"

You see them in a happy scene with your product and you simply tell them what you see. If you can't see it you cannot describe it. So turn on your imagination. It is whatever you see in the scene and your imagination can create any scene that you feel is appropriate and comfortable to *you*.

Creating the Visual Image in the Desire step is rarely used even by trained Salespeople. It does depart from the normal conversation. To go from a bland sales talk into a full blown description of an excursion into their happy future takes a little courage, but it is worth it.

To become proficient with it, you start out with a simple image and build on it. Take it step-by-step instead of ignoring the technique altogether and missing the most dynamic and persuasive tool in selling.

A simple Visual Image can and should be used anywhere in the Selling process. When you feel good about a brief Visual Image then try setting up a more elaborate scene of them seeing themselves enjoying your product:

**SP** - "Just imagine you and your sweetheart on a cool winter's evening sitting by the fireplace. Can't you just see the flames flickering off this beautiful coffee table?"

As you increase in experience you will add more dialogue:

**SP** - "Just imagine you and your sweetheart on a cold winter's evening sitting on the rug in front of the fireplace; you can smell the wonderful aroma of the burning wood, while light from the flames flickers all around the room. Your sweetheart looks over at you and says, 'Isn't it gorgeous the way the flames are reflecting off the coffee table?'"

Just how elaborate a scene you create depends on the Prospect, the product, the situation and you.

If this begins to feel like method acting then you are getting the idea. A lot of selling is acting. You have a script to follow. You must be nice when you don't particularly feel like being nice, smile when you must, and say things that are vital even if those things aren't a part of your normal day-to-day conversation. The more acting you can conjure the easier it is to sell.

The Visual Image can become even more effective by sprinkling it in other parts of the Selling Process. The prime areas of use are in the selling the Problem back to the Prospect in the Interest step, the Benefit in the Conviction step and the Hurt and Rescue of the Desire step. For example after you have given the Prospect a Fact/Feature, Advantage, Benefit you can romance the Benefit with:

**SP** - "Can't you just see yourself walking into the ballroom and everyone stops to look at you in your beautiful new gown?"

**SP** - "Can't you just see yourself being congratulated for your fine taste in office furnishings?"

**SP** - "Just imagine your happy family in the living room enjoying the beautiful sounds from your new stereo system. Wonderful, isn't it?"

**SP** - "Just imagine yourself lying on the deck of a Spanish clipper, soaking in the sun, the light breeze blowing through your hair, as the Clipper cuts through the blue water of the Caribbean? Isn't that beautiful?"

**SP** - "Can't you just see your Secretary thanking you for getting her a new photocopier?"

# The Five Senses

We appreciate the world around us with five human detecting devices all of which are intimately connected to the mind's eye. Those five senses are sight, hearing, smell, taste, and touch. We should prompt as many senses as is practical, in short, appeal to as many senses as make sense:

**SP** - "Just listen to the quiet purr of the engine; smell the new leather of the seats; see the long, sleek lines of the body; feel the softness of the upholstery; it's gorgeous, isn't it?"

In retail sales, where selling time is short, where decision making is fast because the Prospect is generally pre-sold, and where product price is relatively low, you should SELL their INTEREST by prompting their senses routinely with:

**SP** - "Can't you just see the flames from the fireplace flickering across the top of this beautiful coffee table?"

In business sales, where the Prospect must be SOLD on their PROBLEM, the senses can be prompted with:

SP - "Well, I can certainly see how having too many dollars tied up in inventory could create real problems for you, the nasty phone calls from suppliers for payment, the bounced payroll checks, the COD shipments that hold up production, the collection agencies, the threatening attorney calls. That does make for an awful scene, doesn't it?"

Convincing? You bet that is. It promises a lot of Hurt if that problem isn't corrected. Does it hurt enough to make them want to correct it NOW? It depends on how vivid you make it.

Remember you do not sell products; you sell people, relationships, interests, and problems!

# Buying And Selling Is a Visualizing Process

Most people are instinctively cautious about becoming involved with something that is unfamiliar to them. They have fears that fuel caution:

- Will it work?
- Will I waste money?
- Will I be ridiculed or admired?

Yet they have the desire for the product and that desire is based on a feeling of:

- Greed.
- Fear of loss.
- Wanting to feel important.
- Pride has been prompted to support or defend their self-image.

We are visual people. We want to see nice scenes. Once it looks good to our mind's eye it is acceptable.

Let's try a little test. A Salesperson is selling space in two beautiful Cemeteries and has photos of both. One photo shows the Cemetery landscape from a visitor's view. The other photo is the landscape the other Cemetery over looks.

Which one would you choose? Which one do you think others will choose? Virtually every one chooses the Cemetery that overlooks the beautiful landscape. Doesn't that tell you a powerful story about the mind's eye? What is that strange power?

The Visual Image basically is a scene where the Prospect is using the Product NOW and happy about it; even with their peers showing their admiration if that is necessary for them to see. Then you tell them what you see. It'll do it every time.

Visual Images always succeed when words fail. Fears are vanished when they can visualize a happy experience with your product. People don't like to buy from words. They like to buy with their mind's approval. A well written novel will capture and hold the reader with more tenacity than will the movie of that same book simply because the reader must create their own Visual Images.

Although the full Desire step should be used only when the Prospect stalls, you should use the magic of the Desire step - the Visual Images -everywhere you can in the Selling Process. It is vitally necessary in selling the Interest or Problem to the Prospect in the Interest step, and again at the end of each Benefit in the Conviction step. The more often you use it the more effective your closing will be because ...

## Visualizing is Believing!!!

# Selling is a Hurt and Rescue business!

When their problem doesn't Hurt them enough you cannot Rescue them with your product solution.

The Conviction Step is to convince them that your product is the solution to their problem. If they do not see that they have a serious problem to solve, then the solution doesn't have much impact. To ensure that they will be excited about the solution, not only do they have to see the Problem/Interest as being serious, but they must also do something about it NOW, that there is a sense of urgency.

You do this by selling their problem back to them by making their problem HURT them. Describe their problem to them vividly so they can appreciate what an awful situation they have:

**SP** - "Mr. P, I noticed your car when you drove in. It is about five years old, probably served you well in it's day, but the repair bills are getting quite high and you know they will go higher. It is also just a matter of time until it lets you down when you are due for an important meeting. Besides, you are probably getting bored with it and you do deserve something better, don't you?" (The Hurt)

**P** - "I suppose you are right."

**SP** - "Now this elegant sports convertible, at twenty-nine-nine, is an engineering delight. It has power and at the same time economy; it has speed and at the same time safety. Above all it has the look of a successful person, wouldn't you agree?" (The rescue with a Trial Close)

**P** - "It certainly does."

**SP** - "You can be driving this motor car today. Would you perfer to have the 2 door or the 4 door?" (The Alternate Choice Close)

**P** - "Oh, the 4 door for certain."

**SP** - "Well, let's write it up before some other person takes it!" (The Physical Action Close)

**P** - "Great." (The Sale is complete)

Yes, selling is a Hurt and Rescue business. They have the Hurt; you expose it then remind them of it vividly. You have the Rescue with a product that will emotionally and logically satisfy them. People buy emotionally with logically justification. The Hurt and Rescue is most effective in that effort.

# Epilogue

When the bruising and healing of the Desire step cannot move the Prospect out of indecision you will have to help them by laying out the pros and cons, that is, you will have to move from emotional motivation to logical persuasion. They want it and now they must justify it to themselves and/or others. This is done with the Weighing Close technique and it is the only effective method for clarifying one's thinking about dissimilar factors. This is the the subject of the Close Chapter next.

# THE SELLING PROCESS

| PROSPECT'S ATTITUDE | WHAT WE MUST DO | HOW TO DO IT | STEP | WHAT WE MUST SELL | LOGIC OF THE STEP | BUYER ATTITUDE |
|---|---|---|---|---|---|---|
| **REJECTION** | Get them excited about solving a big problem | Prompt their curiosity | **ATTENTION** | It's worth their time to listen | If one of you doesn't get excited there will be no sale | **ACCEPTANCE** |
| | Establish rapport | Justified compliment | | We are a nice person | They won't buy from you if they don't like you | |
| | Disturb Prospect with something better | Ask a question suggesting a need | | They do have a serious problem | There is no hope for a satisfied Prospect | |
| **INDIFFERENCE** | Promise to solve their problem | Relate similar successes | **INTEREST** | We are problem solvers | They must see us as a needs satisfier | **ANXIOUS** |
| | Gather information | Determine <br>• Specific Interest or Problem (SIP) <br>• Mini Motives (MM) <br>• Emotional Buying Motive (EBM) | | They have a very special problem | What does the Prospect need, and why do they want it? | |
| | Be excited about helping them | Fan the spark of existing desire | | There is a way to satisfy their needs and wants | We really are a wants motivator | |
| **SKEPTICAL** | Develop benefits | • Fact/features <br>• Advantage <br>• Benefit <br>• Evidence <br>• Visual Image <br>• Trial Close | **CONVICTION** | Product—will do the job <br>Price/hassle is justified <br>Peers—others will like it <br>Priority—need it now | Tell them what's in it for them | **BELIEF** |
| | Remove any doubts/objections | • Cushion it <br>• Ask what reason <br>• Hypothetically resolve reason <br>• Convert to question <br>• Reverse/minimize (REMEDY) <br>• Trial Close | | Reassurance | Little doubts create questions; big doubts create objections | |
| **DELAY** | Romance the product | Create a visual image | **DESIRE** | That they want the product | Let them see themselves enjoying your product | **ACTION** |
| **FEAR** | Get decision in our favor | Weigh the pros & cons | **CLOSE** | Logical decision based on need | Emotional wants must be rationalized into logical needs | **CONVINCE** |
| | Get an order | Assumed closes <br>Coaxed closes <br>Pressure closes | | A sense of urgency | It can be a long way from being sold to buying now | |

# Chapter Seven
# Close

## Secrets

- ☐ The ABC's of selling: Always Be (Trial) Closing.
- ☐ The Close is the natural and logical end to the sale.
- ☐ The presentation sells, the Close consummates.
- ☐ There is no magic in closing, just simple choices.
- ☐ Most completed sales are closed on implied consent.
- ☐ Your first words to the Prospect should be to close.
- ☐ You can start with: "Would you like to own a ... now?"
- ☐ Don't make a presentation unless they are UNsold.
- ☐ The Close is the beginning and the end of the sale.
- ☐ Prospects often are ready to buy before the formal Close.
- ☐ Most decisions are made on the first call, even if not stated.
- ☐ The real secret to good closing is Trial Closing.
- ☐ Trial Close often to flush out intentions and Objections.
- ☐ Close early and often; not too little, nor too late.
- ☐ The Close can be tried any time after a hot Trial Close.
- ☐ You shouldn't try to close in a social situation.
- ☐ If an Objection appears in the Close, go back to Conviction.
- ☐ Sell the emotions, justify logically, close emotionally.
- ☐ People don't like to buy emotionally or sentimentally.
- ☐ Let the Prospect think they are buying logically.

- ☐ The Visual Image can be extremely powerful in closing.
- ☐ The only problem in closing is simply overcoming indecision.
- ☐ Indecision is agony, so the Prospect needs your help.
- ☐ Every decision is a weighing process of the pros vs cons.
- ☐ You make the decision and get them to agree with it.
- ☐ You must control the weighing of the pros and cons.
- ☐ Alternate Choice Close decides which and not if.
- ☐ Silence after a closing question gives time to think.
- ☐ Silence can be a greater pressure than words.
- ☐ No sale is closed until you have the order in hand.
- ☐ Omit the invitation to buy and they will procrastinate.
- ☐ Many a Prospect is "sold" but no order taken so no Close.
- ☐ It can be a long way from the Close to getting the order.
- ☐ You must create a sense of urgency in the presentation.
- ☐ You should have several reasons for them to buy now.
- ☐ If they have no reason to buy *now* they won't buy *now*.
- ☐ Easier to close *now* if there is a Benefit or gift *now*.
- ☐ Multiple Order Asking is the greatest closing success factor.
- ☐ Make the product hard to get, easy to buy.
- ☐ Make it financially easy for them to own it.
- ☐ Don't be obvious about how elated you are for the order.
- ☐ The tension relief may make your emotions uncontrollable.
- ☐ Assure them their decision was wise as well as desirable.
- ☐ Congratulate them on their wise decision then leave quickly.
- ☐ Close the sale, close your mouth and close the door.

# Selling Format

**P** - "Mr. P, I don't know if you are going to be in that scene or not. That depends on the decision you are about to make. We want that to be a correct decision so let's weigh the reasons that may cause you to hesitate against the reasons for going ahead with this program right now.

(Draw a T on a sheet of paper)

(Draw a T on a sheet of paper)

| **Reasons for hesitating:** (Let Prospect list) | **Reasons for moving ahead NOW:** (You write in your Benefits) |
|---|---|
| Loyalty | Cost savings will get you recognition. |
| Price | Nicer packaging will increase sales. |
| | 24 hr service to serve your clients. |
| | Service executive to reduce your work. |
| **SP** - "Have I missed any?" | Bonuses for your new ideas. |
| **P** - "No." | Free up capital for your expansion. |

**SP** - "Now, which side weighs heavier, the reasons to hesitate or the reasons for going ahead right now?" (WEIGHING CLOSE)

**P** - "Why, your side."

**SP** - "A fine decision. Would you prefer the red or the blue line?" (ALTERNATE CHOICE CLOSE)

**P** - "The red is good."

**SP** - "Would you want weekly or monthly billings?" (ALTERNATE CHOICE CLOSE)

**P** - "Weekly."

**SP** - "Shall I ask them to send along an introductory order next week?" (MINOR POINT CLOSE)

**P** - "Sounds great."

**SP** - "Let me use your phone please to call the Computer center to open your file." (PHYSICAL ACTION CLOSE)

**P** - "Sure, go right ahead."

| PROSPECT'S ATTITUDE | WHAT WE MUST DO | HOW TO DO IT | STEP | WHAT WE MUST SELL | LOGIC OF THE STEP | BUYER'S ATTITUDE |
|---|---|---|---|---|---|---|
| F E A R | Get decision in our favor | Weigh the pros & cons | C L O S E | Logical decision based on need | Emotional wants must be rationalized into logical needs | C O N F I D E N C E |
| | Get an order | Assumed closes Coaxed closes Pressure closes | | A sense of urgency | It can be a long way from being sold to buying now | |

# Sold vs Close

## The Confusion In Terminology

Never has so much been written about any one subject in business, and to such little avail, as there has been on the subject of closing. Part of it is due to confusing terminology, because closing is seen as the Selling Process itself rather than just the natural conclusion.

The term "close" has been a catch-all for everything to do with finalizing a sale. The lack of specific terminology indicates the state of confusion because conflict surrounds the words Sold, Close and Ask For The Order.

**SOLD:** The Prospect wants to own your product, perhaps very much, yet does not necessarily want to buy it. At times they will admit it, other times they will not. It is an emotional commitment.

**CLOSE:** The Close is the act of getting the Prospect motivated to want to buy your product *now*. It is a verbal commitment.

**ASK FOR ORDER:** Often they may want to "own" your product but not buy it now for they may be concerned about peer pressure, or money, etc. The Selling Process consists of getting the Prospect to (1) *want* your product and (2) buy your product *now*. Asking For the Order forces them to realize that they are going to make a *decision* now. Otherwise they will decide *not* to decide now and time will erase their desire.

If they don't have a reason or pressure to buy now they won't. All through the presentation you must create a sense of urgency, thereby relieving the need for selling pressure at this delicate "go-no go" decision making time.

## The Apparent Problem In Closing

The Close is not the Selling Process itself, but rather the natural and logical end to the interview. The Selling Process must be accomplished step by step, and each step must be sold. You just can't "wing" it anymore!

If the Prospect does not like you, if you did not get the Prospect Hurting, and then excited with a solution to their problem (SIP), if you failed to locate the Prospect's Hot Button (EBM), if the Prospect could not see what was in it for them, if you did not carefully explain the solution and benefits; if you did not help clarify the pros and cons in the Prospect's mind, there will be no sale. That is a guarantee! Remember that it is the Process that sells; the Close merely consummates the sale.

There is a widely accepted belief that the more Closes you know the better closer you are. That attests to the fact that Salespeople consider closing to be an objective unto itself rather than the natural conclusion to a diaglog about mutual benefits.

If the Salesperson knows that the Prospect really wants to buy their product, then a simple Alternate Choice would suffice. Since they often don't know the Prospect's Problems nor their intentions, they probably haven't done a very good job of convincing. They end up resorting to closes that are little better than trick closes.

Many of the books on selling lay out a countless number of closes. Few are generic closes that can be used in a variety of situations. They are so specific that the Salesperson must maintain total recall under rather stressful conditions to know which one is applicable. Because of the prevalent use of these trick closes, the Prospects end up with Buyer's Remorse instead of long lasting satisfaction.

When you find the Prospect's Emotional Buying Motive and they are excited about wanting your product, they will show it even though they have some minor hesitations or tradeoffs. If you didn't get them excited, then your work has just begun, for now come the hesitations that loom large because real indecision is present.

In real life there are two closing situations:
    (1) When the Prospect wants to buy now, and
    (2) When the Prospect is in a state of indecision.

# (1) Wants to Buy Now

A Prospect may want to buy your product *now*, at any point in the sales presentation. They may even want to buy it before you meet them. If you try to sell them after they have developed their own want, you may talk yourself out of the sale since any new comment may turn them off emotionally. It is therefore imperative that you Trial Close them every chance you get:

## Attention Step

The Prospect may already want to buy at time of meeting:

**SP** - "How long have you been looking for this type of product?"

**SP** - "Are you seriously considering owning this product today?"

If "Yes", close immediately with the Alternate Choice Close:

**SP** - "Would you like it in green or blue?"

**SP** - "Cash or credit card?"

## Interest Step

In the Interest step you have two ways to go:

■ If the Prospect is a CONSUMER then start off with the "major reasons for buying" question.

■ If the Prospect is a BUSINESS buyer then start off with the Probable Problem - QSN question ("If there were a way ...?"), then the Personal, Problem, Prospect, Payoff, Peer and Priority questions to get their SIP, MM and EBM. Once you have their SIP and EBM you can then try the "Major reasons for buying" question:

**SP** - "Which of the following major reasons for buying our product would be the most interesting to you? ...

- Selling skills.
- Answering Objections
- Self-Motivation.
- Self-Confidence.
- Enthusiasm.

**P** - "It would be answering objections." (Their SIP)

**SP** - "What would that do for you?"

**P** - "More sales and I would be able to try bigger accounts."

**SP** - "What would that mean to you?"

**P** - "I would be able to make more money for less effort."

**SP** - "What would you do with all of that money?"

**P** - "Early retirement." (Their EBM)

**SP** - "If you were able to overcome the inability to answer objections, you would probably want to go ahead with this program, wouldn't you?"

**P** - "Yes I would."

**SP** - "In order for you to achieve this higher standard of living and move you closer to an early retirement, would it be worth a one time investment of $xxx?" (Price introduction.)

**P** - "Oh, definitely."

**SP** - "We have classes beginning next month. Would you prefer Monday or Wednesday nights?"

**P** - "Wednesday."

## Conviction Step

If the Prospect wants to know more about your product, by virtue of them not closing in the Interest step, then you give them the:

Fact/Features ⟶ Advantages ⟶ Benefits

...appropriate to solving their problem.

As each Benefit is given, Trial Close them:

**SP** - "What do you think of that?"

**SP** - "In your opinion, do you think this will help reduce the losses you are now experiencing in your business travel?"

**SP** - "If you were to go ahead with this program, do you think you would want to start with the Economy model or the Executive model?"

**SP** - "Do you want the Executive model in mahogany or walnut?"

# (2) Indecision

There is no magic in closing, merely finesse; finesse in helping the Prospect overcome indecision. When the sale fails to close naturally during the Benefit presentation, the Prospect is in a state of indecision. You must set up a decision-making ritual to help them overcome that indecision.

Spinning about in the Prospect's mind are a series of questions:

"Will it do the job?"
"Is the price justified?"
"Will it be a hassle in change?"
"What will others think of it?"
"Do I need it now?"
"Am I acting logically or rashly?"

Indecision dominates because either the appeal to the emotional Want isn't strong enough and/or the justification with Benefits has not been made. The Prospects are in a value-judgement syndrome. They want the product BUT ... Their Want is simply not strong enough to outweigh the perceived tradeoffs.

At this point they need help! If they have been actively involved in the discussion during the presentation of Benefits then there is substantial interest, maybe not enough to swing the decision, but nevertheless some.

Confusion prevails and there is no agony like indecision. If you let them take the easy way out by postponing the decision, "I want to think it over", you will lose 95% of the time. Rarely do they think it over. Of those who want to shop around only about 50% do so. After that, time has a way of waning desire and thereby generating more indecision. Obviously then it is important to close immediately. Why? Because:

■ The best time for a favorable decision.

■ The Benefits are vivid in their mind.

■ The Objections have been minimized.

■ The desire to own is at a peak.

■ The emotional odds are in your favor.

The Conviction step is to convince them that your product will:

　　　■ Do the job intended,
　　　■ That it is worth the investment, or hassle-of-change,
　and　■ That your peers will like it,

... but it doesn't do much in convincing the Prospect that they need it NOW. That can only come from the Prospect seeing the big Hurt in their mind's eye. If they Hurt enough they will buy now. If they have no reason to buy NOW, they won't buy NOW! Indecision is simply not having a big enough reason to buy now, that is, they don't Hurt enough.

The way to keep the Hurt vivid enough is to go into the Desire step. Here you remind them of the awful "mess" they are in, get their agreement, and then rescue them via a Visual Image "mental experience" that shows them enjoying your product and its Benefits.

SP - "Mr. P, let's summarize your situation so far. At the moment you are suffering from serious losses in your business travel, and that is causing you real grief, isn't that right?" (SIP - and make it Hurt!)

P - "Yes it is."

SP - "We can reduce those losses substantially and get your budget back in line where your president wants it. (EBM)...

...Can't you just see yourself in the next Board meeting as your President looks over your travel budget. It is in excellent shape. He looks up and says 'John, congratulations. This is great.' Now that is the kind of scene you want to be in, isn't it?'

P - "Yes, indeed, but I would like to think about it." (Stall)

SP - Mr. P, I don't know if you are going to be in that picture or not. It all depends on a decision you are about to make ..."
... and into the Weighing Close.

# The Weighing Close

Clarity comes while putting ones thoughts down on paper. One of the best ways of weighing dissimilar thoughts is the Weighing Close. It goes like this:

SP - "Mr. P, you are about to make a decision and we want it to be a correct decision. So let's weigh the reasons for hesitating against the reasons for moving ahead with us right now:

(Draw a T on a sheet of paper).

(Ask the Prospect for their hesitations or concerns. Write them on the left side as logical one word reasons if possible. Don't volunteer any help. If it is important to them, they will list it. On the "reasons for" side, you stay emotional with them by enlarging on their personal BENEFITS in the decision. (Which do you think has more impact?) Let them keep the sheet; it becomes a silent seller.)

(Draw a T on a sheet of paper)

| **Reasons for hesitating:** (Let Prospect list) | **Reasons for moving ahead NOW:** (You write in your Benefits) |
|---|---|
| Loyalty<br>Price | Cost savings will get you recognition.<br>Nicer packaging will increase sales.<br>24 hr service to serve your clients.<br>Service executive to reduce your work. |
| **SP** - "Have I missed any?"<br>  **P** - "No." | Bonuses for your new ideas.<br>Free up capital for your expansion. |

**P** - "No."

**SP** - "Now, which side weighs the heavier, the reasons to hesitate or the reasons for going ahead right now?" (Point to the paper as you ask the question.)

**P** - "Your reasons."

**SP** - "A very wise decision."

The excellence of the Weighting Close is that it is the only way of getting the Prospect to make a true, unbiased decision that will stand the test of after-thoughts. It sets you in the role of an independent consultant who the Prospect can trust. Also, it gives the Prospect the opportunity to express all of their hesitations discussed during the presentation. It is better to have all hesitations revealed so they can be evaluated, minimized, and buried forever through the weighing process.

# Progressive Order Asking

| PROSPECT'S ATTITUDE | WHAT WE MUST DO | HOW TO DO IT | STEP | WHAT WE MUST SELL | LOGIC OF THE STEP | BUYER'S ATTITUDE |
|---|---|---|---|---|---|---|
| F E A R | Get decision in our favor | Weigh the pros & cons | C L O S E | Logical decision based on need | Emotional wants must be rationalized into logical needs | C O N F I D E N C E |
| | Get an order | Assumed closes<br>Coaxed closes<br>Pressure closes | | A sense of urgency | It can be a long way from being sold to buying now | |

Being "sold" doesn't always mean being closed. Nor is there reason to believe that one closing question actually results in a signed order blank. Most often several are required. In reality there are two sales you must make:

(1) That they WANT the product.
(2) That they want it NOW.

It is best to separate these two decisions. While the Prospect is trying to make the decision that they really want it, they are being pressured to order NOW. It is best to get them to clinically agree, first, that it is something they need and want without pressure. Once the Want decision has been made, you can then assume, coax or even pressure them into giving you the order now.

The Weighing Close is the only known WANT Close, but there are many NOW Closes. Here are some NOW closes:

Inducement.
Future dating.
Special design.
Guarantee.
Return for credit.
Another advantage.

It is quite professional to have these printed as a paper form checklist in the priority that is best for your product. That could be in the order of increasing cost, and/or benefit to the Prospect. The checklist is also a good way to record any special arrangements agreed to.

You should assume that the Prospect will place an order. Always use the Alternate Choice Close to get the emotional commitment. The Alternate Choice substitutes a small, easy decision for the larger, fear creating buying decision. Most people would rather avoid such decision:

**SP** - "Would you want it in blue or green?"

**SP** - "Would you want four or six agents assigned to your account?"

Or try a Minor Point Close (half an Alternate Choice):

**SP** - "Would you like to have your logo embossed on the product?"

# Selling The Order

If they are cool to these Assumed Choice questions, you may sweeten the offer with a new inducement. Examples are listed under the Coaxing Closes.

If the Prospect is still reluctant to buy now, then move gradually into pressure Closes, ending up with the Physical Action Close, where you are setting the stage for a denial if they do not want to buy now:

**SP** - "Mr. Prospect, may I use your phone to call the computer center to reserve/ship/design, etc., a product for you?"

If they want to order now they won't say anything. If they don't/can't order they will stop you. If they stop you, you have an Objection to take care of:

**SP** - "May I ask what is causing you to hesitate?" And off you go into the Objection answering procedure.

## Assumed Closes:

| | |
|---|---|
| Alternate-Choice Close | "Would you want 4 or 6 of our staff to be assigned to your ...?" |
| Minor-Point Close | "Would you want to have the jacket decorated with your logo?" |

## Coaxing Closes:

| | |
|---|---|
| Instructional Close | "Why don't you try it out and see how nice it is." |
| Narrative Close | "John Doe had almost the same situation you do. He ..." |
| Service Close | "Here, let me adjust it especially for you ..." |
| Inducement Close | "As an extra feature for you, we can add on the ..." |
| Future-Dating Close | "We have a policy of future dating of 60 days if you order on our first call." |
| Special-Design Close | "You can have this exclusive feature at a very low extra cost of ..." |
| Guarantee Close | "In addition to our regular guarantee, we will also guarantee ..." |
| Return-for-Credit Close | "We will take back for full credit any product that does not sell." |
| Another-Advantage Close | "By the way, we also include free delivery." |

## Pressure Closes:

| | |
|---|---|
| Puppy-Dog Close | "Why don't you try it free of charge for a week?" |
| Challenge Close | "Let's submit an offer to see if you can qualify for the loan on the house." |
| Coming-Event Close | "You really should order now since the price will be going up on the first." |
| Last-One Close | "This is the last one we have and the new ones won't be in for quite awhile." |
| Another-Buyer Close | "You can't wait too long since we have another possible buyer." |
| Physical-Action Close | "What I have to do now is call our computer center to set up your file ..." |

# Get The Order And Leave

Once you have the order do not let the Prospect see that you are elated. Often the Salesperson is so excited about getting the order that their emotions become somewhat uncontrolled and they emote in an unbusiness-like way.

Best to congratulate the Prospect on their wise decision, since they need that assurance, and then leave quickly. To further discuss the product or socialize will degrade your excellent selling. Do not buy it back:

**SP** - "Mr. P, you have made a wise and desirable decision. You and your associates will be very pleased with the results."

It is a great feeling of accomplishment to close. Be proud of yourself, treat yourself to some special reward, you've earned it. Remember, however, that you still must service the CLIENT:

### Never Forget a Client, Never Let a Client Forget You

Business goes where it is invited, serviced and appreciated. The Invitation is your offer to help them. The Service is for the product and also for the Prospect, who is now your Client. They want to be appreciated and serviced even when they don't need it.

## Chapter Eight

# Trial Close

# Secrets

- ☐ The Trial Close is THE most valuable selling tool.
- ☐ A Trial Close is safe, it only asks for an opinion.
- ☐ The Trial Close measures the temperature of their Want.
- ☐ It gives you reserve power to control the interview.
- ☐ Asking how they FEEL vs THINK changes their emotions.
- ☐ Selling is questioning, presenting and Trial Closing.
- ☐ The Trial Close is the only diagnostic tool you have.
- ☐ Trial Closes should be used everywhere in selling.
- ☐ Trial Closes prevent Objections by flushing intentions.
- ☐ A Trial Close will trade off Objections with Benefits.
- ☐ The Trial Close catches them at their peak of interest.
- ☐ Always leave them wanting more, as in show business.
- ☐ Closing too early can create a barrier resulting from a "NO".
- ☐ Closing too late will bore the Prospect.
- ☐ A Trial Close is infinitely more valuable than a Close.
- ☐ A Trial Closer is more successful that a good Closer.
- ☐ You can't sell well even with the best closing technique.
- ☐ There are no surprises with a Trial Close.
- ☐ A Buying Signal shows they see themselves owning it.
- ☐ At times an Objection is often a Buying Signal in disguise.

- ☐ Always Trial Close on a Prospect's Buying Signal.
- ☐ Prospects don't always give Buying Signals.
- ☐ Salespeople don't always recognize Buying Signals.
- ☐ Closing on a Buying Signal can get you in trouble.
- ☐ With a Trial Close you don't need a Buying Signal.
- ☐ A Trial Closer only needs one Close, the Alternate Choice.

# Selling Format

**SP** - "What do you think of that?"

**COLD:**
   **P** - "Well, not too much."  (CONSIDER THIS AN OBJECTION)

**LUKEWARM:**
   **P** - "It sounds quite good."  (DO ANOTHER TRIAL CLOSE)
   **SP** - "In your opinion, do you think you would prefer the Regional or the National version?"
   **P** - "Probably the Regional one." (Do ANOTHER TRIAL CLOSE)
   **SP** - "If you were to go ahead with this program would you want the Economy model or the Executive model?"
   **P** - "The Executive model."  (DO AN ALTERNATE CHOICE CLOSE)

**HOT:**
   **P** - "That sounds super!"  (DO AN ALTERNATE CHOICE CLOSE)
   **SP** - "Would you want the red or the blue?"

# Trial Closes

A Trial Close is any attempt to start closing the sale before the completion of the Selling Process. It is exactly what the name implies. It is a test to see how near the Prospect is to buying. The Trial Close is the only way of fulfilling the ABC code of selling, Always be (TRIAL) Closing.

Just as talking too much is a characteristic of American Salesmanship so is the aversion to asking the Prospect what they think about the product. Yet, the most important success factor in selling is knowing just what the Prospect thinks as you resolve their Interest or Problem with the Benefits of your product.

The Trial Close is a "thermometer" on how much the Prospect wants the product at any given point. You must know what the Prospect is thinking in order to know how and where to proceed with the presentation. You must know when and how much they emotionally want the product. If they have only a little desire you simply add more Benefits until they want it so much that they see themselves owning it. Once they want it, you can start the close.

When the Prospect sees themselves wanting to own your product their desire is at its highest point. If you don't track their reactions you will talk them out of the sale. Any further selling effort will satisfy their curiosity and erode their desire. Rather, "always leave them wanting more" as in show business.

# Perpetual Use

The Trial Close can be used anywhere, at any time, and as often as you wish. The wonderful part of it is that you can ask the Prospect how much they want your product without causing a problem. There is no penalty for getting a cold response, it is only an opinion.

The Trial Close MUST be used in the:

| | |
|---|---|
| Attention step | - The Prospect may be ready to buy now. |
| Interest step | - May be able to close on an Interest or Problem. |
| Conviction step | - Any Benefit may be enough to sell the Prospect. |
| Objection | - Your answer may have relieved their concern. |
| Desire step | - When you have revisited and soothed their Hurt. |
| Close step | - When you have logically justified their Need. |

# Trial Close vs The Close

A Trial Close is an OPINION asking question, whereas the Close is a DECISION asking question. A Trial Close is like a:

| | |
|---|---|
| Report card | - it tells you how you are doing. |
| Thermometer | - it gives you the degree of Want. |
| Guide | - it moves you into the ordering stage. |

## The Question

A TRIAL CLOSE is an OPINION asking question:

**SP** - "What do you think of that?"

**SP** - "If you were to acquire this unit would you want the Regional or National version?"

**SP** - "In your opinion, would you want the Economy or Executive model?"

A CLOSE is a Decision asking question:

**SP** - "Would you prefer the green or blue?"

# The Response:

The Trial Close can result in a cold, lukewarm, or hot, ready-to-close response:

**Cold:**

> **P** - "Well, I really can't see how it would fit our operations." (You have an Objection to handle. Flushing out their concern may take you back to the Attention, Interest, Conviction or even the Desire step.)

**Lukewarm:**

> **P** - "It does sound interesting. How does it ...?" (Try another Trial Close. If it is hot try for a close. If it is lukewarm add more Benefits. If it is cold you have a real concern or Objection.)

**Hot:**

> **P** - "That sounds great! What is delivery like?" (Go to a closing question.)

A Trial Close is more valuable than a Close, because it flushes out valuable information that allows you to plan your way through to a successful conclusion. The Close is easy when the Prospect is ready to buy but impossible if they aren't.

Because of the difficulty in closing, Salespeople think that a better closing technique will improve their sales. Not so. You can't close someone who does not want your product unless you trick them. You can't sell with only a *CLOSING* technique. Neither can a good closing technique bail you out of bad selling.

When you ask a Prospect a *closing* question that results in a *NO*, you have dug yourself a hole. You have a serious problem to overcome for the Prospect must defend that decision and the reason given, valid or not. If you were to use a series of Trial Closes all through the interview you would have learned long before the Close just what the Prospect wants, thinks, and expects of you. The Close then becomes a formality rather than a major decision.

A Trial Close is the only "diagnostic" tool the Salesperson has. The questions in the Interest step determine what the Prospect's Interest or Problem is (SIP) and what it would mean to them to have it resolved (EBM). The Trial Close is the testing device you use to see how the Prospect is accepting your solution. If the Prospect is not accepting the solution then you have the necessary feedback to come up with a better solution. You can't do that with a Close that gives you a NO, for that's a dead end. Better is this simple Trial Close:

**SP** - "On a scale of 1 to 10, 10 being tops, where are you?"

  **P** - "About a 3 or 4."

**SP** - "Oh! I guess that means I don't really understand your problem. Let's talk about it in more detail. When you said ..." (and back into the Information Getting of the Interest step to reevaluate their SIP and EBM).

    OR

  **P** - "About an 8."

**SP** - "Great, what does it take to move you to a 10?"

**THERE ARE NO SURPRISES WITH TRIAL CLOSES!**

## Emotional vs Logical

Bearing in mind that the Prospect has two states of mind to satisfy, the emotional and the logical, you should be aware that you can move the Prospect from one to the other by the choice of question:

**SP** - "What do you THINK of that?" (LogicaL)
**SP** - "How do you FEEL about that?" (Emotional)

THINKING is logical, FEELING is emotional. The Trial Close can be used everywhere throughout the Selling Process, at any time at the Salesperson's discretion. If the Prospect starts to get too logical then Trial Close them with emotional questions back into the emotional state of mind:

**SP** - "If you were to go ahead with this, would you FEEL better with the red or the blue?"

# Psychological Moment

It is controversial as to whether or not there is one definitive psychological moment for closing a Prospect. Most sales trainers do not believe there is such a moment. They believe the Prospect can be closed at any time after they are ready to buy. So Trial Close early and often, rather than too little, too late in order not to miss the Want.

## Too Early

The problem with trying to close the Prospect before they are ready to buy is that their response will be negative. Once they give a negative decision they may feel they have to defend it. The Salesperson ends up with a barrier to penetrate, and maybe a premature Objection to answer.

## Too Late

The problem with waiting too long is that the Salesperson may talk too much about the product, bore the Prospect past curiosity and excitement and into the no-interest stage. Their Want emotion will turn cold.

So there is a special time to close - when the Prospect WANTS to buy. It may last longer than a moment but don't wait too long. Whether it is a psychological moment or not is a moot point. It doesn't really matter as long as you Trial Close often to monitor their desire. If they telegraph their interests with a Buying Signal, immediately Trial Close them, and if lukewarm or hot try for a Close.

# Buying Signals

There are moments when the Prospect is showing a lot of interest. These moments are called Buying Signals. They don't mean the Prospect wants to buy, rather the Prospect can see themselves owning it.

Buying Signals are good clues to the Prospect's thinking IF the Prospect gives a Buying Signal and IF the Salesperson can spot it.

Most Buying Signals are triggered by the Prospect as they see themselves enjoying the benefits in their mind's eye. Emotionally they want it even though they may not yet be ready to commit to buying it.

Once the emotional commitment has been made it will be evident. Their physical and emotional responses to you will change. It is much like the polygraph lie detection test. When they are emotionally involved a lot of things change, and some will show. A change is obvious by their questions, actions, expressions or comments. Changes likely to take place are:

> Change in attitude, warms up.
> Pulls ear, rubs chin.
> Leans forward, scratches head.
> Tone of voice changes, up or down.
> Facial expression changes, eyes come alive.
> Prospect studies the product judiciously.
> Questions about the product.

The Salesperson can't always rely on the Prospect giving a Buying Signal nor being able to spot one if given. So the Salesperson must Trial Close with a continuous series of questions on how the Prospect feels now. Always, the big question is: Do they emotionally own it? Are they thinking past the sale?

In Real Estate sales they have no interest as long as the Prospect is commenting favorably about the house; they just respond with "it is very nice". But the minute they start criticizing the house about needed repairs, they are seriously thinking about owning it. They are thinking past the sale.

# Objections or Buying Signals?

Buying Signals may take different forms. Don't mistake a Buying Signal for a NO decision and try to handle it as an Objection:

**P** - "I don't know if I can afford it." A Buying Signal?

**P** - "I don't think I can afford it." A Buying Signal?
    ... they may want it but are concerned about payment.

**P** - "I can't afford it." A No Decision!

**P** - "Do you have it in green?" A Buying Signal?
    ... real interest to the point of asking availability.

At times you may want to close on a Buying Signal but that can be dangerous:

**P** - "Can you get it in green?"

**SP** - "Would you want it if I can get it in green?"

**P** - "No, I don't. I was just curious." (A NO decision)

You are answering an apparent Buying Signal with a decision asking Close. That is dangerous. It may get you a NO decision that the Prospect may have to defend.

Rather than trying to close on a Buying Signal and end up with premature objections, it is best to test their Want with a Trial Close. If it shows the Prospect is not ready to close then no damage is done since the Trial Close only asked for an opinion.

**SP** - "Yes, you can have it in green. Why would you want it in green?" (An opinion asking question.)

#### When Really a Buying Signal:

**P** - "I don't *think* I can afford it."
**SP** - "If you could afford it, would you prefer green or blue?"
**P** - "Definitely the blue."

**When Really an Objection:**

**P** - "I can't afford it."

**SP** - "If you could afford it, would you prefer green or blue."

**P** - "Definitely the blue, but I can't afford it."

**SP** - "I can understand your concern. The question then is "How can we arrange a payment program for you that fits your budget." That is the question, isn't it?"

**P** - "Yes it is."

**SP** - "Well, we have a program designed ..."

The moral is don't try to handle it as an Objection until you have confirmed that it is a real concern and not a Buying Signal.

## Advantages of Buying Signals

Given that a Prospect may not always give a Buying Signal, that a Salesperson may not always spot the Buying Signal, and that a Trial Close will tell you everything that you need to know, what then is the advantage of a Buying Signal? TIME! Whenever you do spot a Buying Signal stop what you are doing, even in the middle of a Story, Testimonial, Demonstration, etc, and Trial Close. A Buying Signal does indicate high interest and that is where you want to Trial Close and Close:

**SP** - "This is how ABC company ..." (Interrupted)

**P** - (Gives Buying Signal)

**SP** - "How do you feel about ...?" (A Trial Close)

# Tradeoff Trial Close

There is a natural progression of Trial Closes from the opening remarks all the way through to the Close:

OPENING TRIAL CLOSE
TRADEOFF TRIAL CLOSE
PROGRESSIVE TRIAL CLOSE
ALTERNATE CHOICE CLOSE
CLOSE

... The Tradeoff Trial Close requires more explanation.

If they know a lot about your product then they are probably aware of the major Benefits and disadvantages. To attempt a Close you simply trade them off.

The trading off of major Benefits against major concerns logically is quite sound to the Prospect. Again, if they say NO, or just MAYBE, you have new information to redirect your selling efforts.

The Prospect may be ready to buy at any time, even in the first few minutes of the sales meeting because of prior knowledge and interest. You will never know unless you test the waters. To miss that opportunity and go into a full selling presentation may bring up more questions or doubts in their mind. Ask the Prospect if they are ready to buy. The idea is to test them early to see if they are presold; if so, close them quickly:

Selling a Sales course as an example:

> The major benefits are:
> (1) At ease in front of people.
> (2) Able to answer Objections easily.
> (3) Opportunity for more income.
>
> Their major concerns:
> (1) The high cost.
> (2) Weekly night classes.
> (3) The homework.

**SP** - "Would you like to take a sales training course now?"

**SP** - "How long have you been thinking about taking one?"

**SP** - "Mr. P, what do you know about our course?"

**P** - "Well, I've heard a lot about it. It has a very good reputation and I may be able to benefit from it."

**SP** - "I'm pleased that you are so impressed. Mr. P, would it be worth one night a week for 10 weeks to be able to stand in front of a group of people, feel at ease, and be in full control?"

**P** - "It probably would."

**SP** - "Would it be worth $xxx to be able to answer objections with ease?"

**P** - "That I could use."

**SP** - "Would it be worth 2 hours of homework a week to be your able to earn substantially more income for the rest of your life?"

**P** - "Definitely!"

**SP** - "Well, let's do it! All you have to do is print your name here as you would want it on your certificate. Then approve it down here. As soon as I have your check you are on your way to a more successful career in selling."

All we did here was trade off the pros with the cons. Don't worry about them bringing up Objections that you never mentioned. Once the major concerns have been minimized, others will vaporize. If they do have other concerns, trade them off with other Benefits.

When you trade off concerns with Benefits you are preempting those major Objections or concerns from being raised by the Prospect. By trading them off you expose them, minimize them and bury them forever.

Once you get used to the idea of trading pros for cons you can try trading the Specific Interest or Problem and EBM off with the concerns:

**SP** - "Would it be worth the change in loyalty from your present supplier for a cost reduction of $xx,xxx a year?" (SIP)

**SP** - "Would it be worth the hassle of changing to a new system to be able to get the recognition (EBM) for being at the state of the art in your product?"

# The Alternate Choice Close

Most things are bought without the Prospect ever having to say "I'll take it". Some just don't like the idea of giving in. So you have to make it easy for them to say YES without them getting the feeling that they've been sold. You have to let them "save face" because they are succumbing to your selling effort; the Alternate Choice Close does that nicely.

**The Alternate Choice Close is The Ideal Close!**

**SP** - "If you were to want one, would you prefer red or blue?"

**P** - "Definitely blue."

**SP** - "Well why don't we write you up for one right now before they are all gone. Will this be cash or credit card?"

**P** - "Cash."

... They've bought it! If you Trial Close often, the Alternate Choice Close is the only close you will ever need.

The progression from the Trial Close to the Alternate Choice Close has allowed them to transition them from passive listener, to interested Prospect, through to an active buying stage.

# Where To Use

## Use The Trial Close:

Attention step - after Rapport.
Interest step - after SIP and EBM.
Conviction step - after each new Benefit.
When Prospect shows interest.
When Prospect asks a question.
When Prospect picks up product.
When Prospect objects to the price.
When Prospect becomes friendly.
When Prospect's tone changes.
When Prospect relaxes.
When Prospect leans forward.
When Prospect rubs their chin.
When you discuss an Objection.
After every Buying Signal.
Anytime you feel like you should.

# How To Use

Although the Trial Close should be used everywhere along the Selling Process to test the waters, it's form should be adapted somewhat to the particular situation. We end up with 3 different versions:

## Opening Trial Close:

OPENING Trial Close: they may want to buy as soon as you meet them.

**SP** - "How long have you been considering owning a ...?"

**SP** - "Are you seriously considering owning a ... today?"

## Tradeoff Trial Close:

TRADEOFF Trial Close: as soon as you determine their major Problem in the Interest step test to see if they are ready to buy:

**SP** - "In order to achieve ... would it be worth a one time investment of $xxx?"

**SP** - "Would it be worth ten night classes to be able to answer questions easily?"

**SP** - "Would it be worth two hours homework each week to have a smooth sales presentation?"

## Progressive Trial Close:

PROGRESSIVE Trial Close: to see if the Benefit is what they want. It starts out rather general and becomes more specific.

**SP** - "What do you think of this plan?"

**SP** - "If you were to go ahead with this when would you want it to go into effect?"

**SP** - "If you were able to overcome ... you would probably want to go ahead with this, wouldn't you?"

OR

**SP** - "Does this sound like something you would like to go ahead with?"

**SP** - "If you were pretty sure you could ... you would want to get involved, wouldn't you?"

**SP** - "In order to eliminate ... you would probably want to start with us on ... wouldn't you?"

## Alternate Choice Trial Close:

The Trial Close blends into the Alternate Choice Close simply by removing the "If ... " or "In your opinion ... ":

**SP** - "Would you want it in green or blue?"

**SP** - "Cash or credit card?"

# Selling by Questions

Questions are the most useful tool the Salesperson has. In the Attention step you get their attention with one of the MISS GRACE methods; you get them personally involved with a few personal questions.

In the Interest step you question them intensly about their interests and problems and even intimately about their personal Wants that are to be satisifed.

In the Conviction step you ask them how they think and feel your benefits will help them.

In answering an Objection you question them about why their concern is important to them, and again for their reaction after you assure them there is no concern.

Whenever you detect a Buying Signal you are ready to go into a Trial Close about how they feel (emotional) and think (logical) your product will help them.

When the Trail Close is hot you bridge into the Alternate Choice Close and conclude the sale.

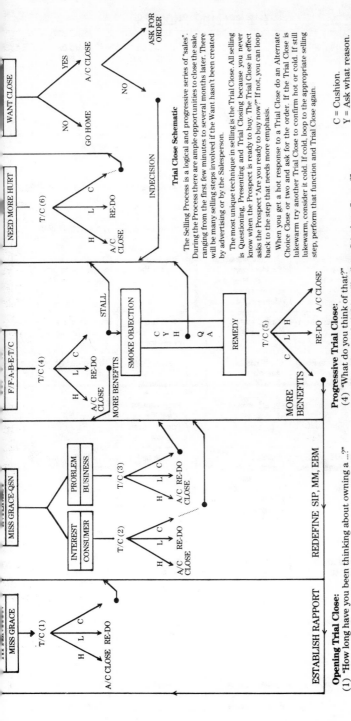

**Trial Close Schematic**

The Selling Process is a logical and progressive series of "sales". During the Process there are ample opportunities to close the sale, ranging from the first few minutes to several months later. There will be many selling steps involved if the Want hasn't been created by advertising or by the Salesperson.

The most unique technique in selling is the Trial Close. All selling is Questioning, Presenting and Trial Closing because you never know when the Prospect is ready to buy. The Trial Close in effect asks the Prospect "Are you ready to buy now?" If not, you can loop back to the step that needs more emphasis.

When you get a hot response to a Trial Close do an Alternate Choice Close or two and ask for the order. If the Trial Close is lukewarm try another Trial Close to confirm hot or cold. If still lukewarm, consider it cold. If cold, loop to the appropriate selling step, perform that function and Trial Close again.

C = Cushion.
Y = Ask what reason.
H = Hypothetically resolve.
Q = Convert to question.
A = Answer question.

H = Hot response.
L = Lukewarm response.
C = Cold response.

MISS GRACE

MISS GRACE-QSN

T/C (1)

H
L
C
A/C CLOSE RE-DO

INTEREST
CONSUMER

PROBLEM
BUSINESS

T/C (2)

T/C (3)

H
L
C
A/C CLOSE RE-DO

H
L
C
A/C RE-DO CLOSE

F/F-A-B-E:T/C

T/C (4)

H
L
C
A/C CLOSE RE-DO

MORE BENEFITS

STALL

SMOKE OBJECTION

C
Y
H

REMEDY

Q
A

T/C (5)

C
L
H

RE-DO A/C CLOSE

NEED MORE HURT

T/C (6)

H
L
C
A/C CLOSE RE-DO

INDECISION

MORE BENEFITS

WANT CLOSE

NO
GO HOME

YES
A/C CLOSE

NO

ASK FOR ORDER

ESTABLISH RAPPORT    REDEFINE SIP, MM, EBM

**Opening Trial Close:**
(1) "How long have you been thinking about owning a ...?"
"Are you serious about owning one today?"

**Tradeoff Trial Close: Consumer**
(2) "Would it be worth $xxx to be able to close more sales?"
"Is it worth 10 nights to be able to answer objections?"
"In order to achieve ..., would it be worth ...?"

**Tradeoff Trial Close: Business**
(3) "Would it be worth your loyalty to save $x,xxx a year?"
"Would it be worth 10% premium to have 24 hour delivery?"

**Progressive Trial Close:**
(4) "What do you think of that?"
"How do you feel this will ...(benefit)... benefit you?"
"If you were to go ahead, would you make any changes?"
"If it would enable you to ..., you'd probably want it?"

**Objection Step Trial Close:**
(5) What do you think about that?"

**Desire Step Trial Close:**
(6) "That's the kind of scene you want to be in, isn't it?"

A/C Close = Alternate Choice Close.

# THE SELLING PROCESS

| PROSPECT'S ATTITUDE | WHAT WE MUST DO | HOW TO DO IT | STEP | WHAT WE MUST SELL | LOGIC OF THE STEP | BUYER ATTITUDE |
|---|---|---|---|---|---|---|
| **REJECTION** | Get them excited about solving a big problem | Prompt their curiosity | **ATTENTION** | It's worth their time to listen | If one of you doesn't get excited there will be no sale | **ACCEPTANCE** |
| | Establish rapport | Justified compliment | | We are a nice person | They won't buy from you if they don't like you | |
| | Disturb Prospect with something better | Ask a question suggesting a need | | They do have a serious problem | There is no hope for a satisfied Prospect | |
| **INDIFFERENCE** | Promise to solve their problem | Relate similar successes | **INTEREST** | We are problem solvers | They must see us as a needs satisfier | **ANXIOUS** |
| | Gather information | Determine •Specific Interest or Problem (SIP) •Mini Motives (MM) •Emotional Buying Motive (EBM) | | They have a very special problem | What does the Prospect need, and why do they want it? | |
| | Be excited about helping them | Fan the spark of existing desire | | There is a way to satisfy their needs and wants | We really are a wants motivator | |
| **SKEPTICAL** | Develop benefits | •Fact/features •Advantage •Benefit •Evidence •Visual Image •Trial Close | **CONVICTION** | Product—will do the job Price/hassle is justified Peers—others will like it Priority—need it now | Tell them what's in it for them | **BELIEF** |
| | Remove any doubts/objections | •Cushion it •Ask what reason •Hypothetically resolve reason •Convert to question •Reverse/minimize (REMEDY) •Trial Close | | Reassurance | Little doubts create questions; big doubts create objections | |
| **DELAY** | Romance the product | Create a visual image | **DESIRE** | That they want the product | Let them see themselves enjoying your product | **ACTION** |
| **FEAR** | Get decision in our favor | Weigh the pros & cons | **CLOSE** | Logical decision based on need | Emotional wants must be rationalized into logical needs | **CONFIDENCE** |
| | Get an order | Assumed closes Coaxed closes Pressure closes | | A sense of urgency | It can be a long way from being sold to buying now | |

## Chapter Nine

# Objections

## Understanding And Preventing

# Secrets

- ☐ Hesitations = Rejections + Objections + Stalls.
- ☐ A sincere Objection means sincere interest.
- ☐ Objections often are a search for justification.
- ☐ Objections need not be a normal part of selling.
- ☐ You can't master selling until you can manage Objections.
- ☐ Objections are the challenge of selling.
- ☐ Don't suppress Objections; flush and answer them.
- ☐ An excited Prospect won't raise Objections.
- ☐ Attempted closes should bring out latent Objections.
- ☐ There are many ways for a Prospect to say "No".
- ☐ Objections are clues to the Prospect's thoughts.
- ☐ Objections appear logical, yet are emotional.
- ☐ Objections are not necessarily permanent.
- ☐ It doesn't mean that they don't want to buy it.
- ☐ Tangibles generate product and price Objections.
- ☐ Intangibles generate priority and peer Objections.
- ☐ Clients buy benefits, not answered Objections.
- ☐ Only a few objections come up with regularity.
- ☐ Objections are better prevented than answered.
- ☐ Preempt any Objection that you can't answer.

- ☐ To preempt an Objection you boast about it as a benefit.
- ☐ Rejections occur when you fail to create interest.
- ☐ Start with a Benefit to prevent rejections.
- ☐ Genuine Objections usually occur after Benefits.
- ☐ A sincere Objection is a question in disguise.
- ☐ Little doubts create questions; big ones Objections.
- ☐ A closing Stall means indecision due to lack of want.
- ☐ Fear of making a bad decision is the conflict.
- ☐ A Prospect's thinking is fuzzy at decision making time.

# Selling Format

**Cushion:** "I can understand how you feel."
"Thank you for being so sincere."
"I appreciate your sincerity."

**Ask What Reason:** "Obviously you have a reason for saying that. Do you mind if I ask what that reason is?"

**OR:** "Why is that important to you?"

**Resolve Reason:** "Just suppose we could resolve that to your satisfaction, then, in your opinion, wouldn't this ... be of interest to you?"

**Convert To Question:** "Well, that brings us to the question. The question is: "All things considered ...

**Product** ... will this give you all of the benefits that you need and expect of it?"

**Price** ... is the price of (or hassle-of-change) this product justified by all of the benefits you will receive?"

**Peers** ... will your peers support your choice?"

**Priority** ... can you justify the need right now?"

That is the question,isn't it?"

(**P** - "No it isn't.")
(**SP** - "Well, what is the question?")
**P** - "Yes it is."

| **Answer Question:** | **R** Reverse/Capitalize |
|---|---|
| | **E** Explain |
| | **M** Minimize/Outweigh |
| | **E** Evade |
| | **D** Deny |
| | **Y** Why (Ask "Why?") |

## OBJECTIONS ARE CAUSED BY THE SALESPERSON, NOT THE PROSPECT!

Objections are caused by the Salesperson, not the Prospect. Usually the Prospect is just sitting there minding their own business; the Salesperson is "cold calling", rather, "intruding".

With the exception of Price, *all* Objections fall into 3 categories:

(Price is not an objection since *every* price is too high until the Prospect becomes emotionally involved in what it can do for them.)

■ "I'm perfectly happy now." A Rejection.

It occurs up front while trying to get the Prospect's attention. Typically the Salesperson begins:

**SP** - "Mr. Prospect? This is D. Forbes Ley with Sales Success Institute. How are you?"

This standard opening is so trite that it is a signal to the preconditioned Prospect to shut the Salesperson off as soon as possible. Whatever you say next matters little; you have been rejected.

You then mark your prospecting card, "Not interested", and refile it. Rather, you should mark the card, "I *failed* to get them interested." Instead, seize their attention with something to excite them.

■ "it just won't work for us." A Sincere Objection.

This occurs during the presentation of benefits and is caused by the Salesperson doing all the talking. Buying is definitely not a spectator sport; they must be involved. If they are not talking, they are probably not listening either. If they are not involved, the tend to prejudge in their silence, usually a "no".

■ "I'd like to think it over." The Stall.

The classic sales killer! It simply means, "I don't want it!" At least, they don't want it enough to do something about it now, but by tomorrow they'll be cooled off even further. It is caused by the Salesperson not getting them excited enough, not hurting enough, not getting their emotions high enough to want the *product* rather than the money.

| Type | When | Serious? | Handle | Indicates | How? |
|---|---|---|---|---|---|
| Rejection | early | frivolous | hard | no interest | concede |
| Objection | middle | factual | easy | product doubt | explain |
| Stall | end | emotional | easy | indecision | HURT!!! |

| PROSPECT'S ATTITUDE | WHAT WE MUST DO | HOW TO DO IT | STEP | WHAT WE MUST SELL | LOGIC OF THE STEP | BUYER'S ATTITUDE |
|---|---|---|---|---|---|---|
| S K E P T I C A L | Develop benefits | •Fact/features<br>•Advantage<br>•Benefit<br>•Evidence<br>•Visual Image<br>•Trial Close | C O N V I C T I O N | Product—will do the job<br>Price/hassle is justified<br>Peers—others will like it<br>Priority—need it now | Tell them what's in it for them | B E L I E F |
| | Remove any doubts/objections | •Cushion it<br>•Ask what reason<br>•Hypothetically resolve reason<br>•Convert to question<br>•Reverse/minimize (REMEDY)<br>•Trial Close | | Reassurance | Little doubts create questions;<br>big doubts create objections | |

# What Is An Objection

The ability to identify, analyze and correctly answer the Prospect's Objections may be the key to your success in selling.

An Objection has different meanings under different circumstances. Therein lies most of the confusion about them. Unfortunately, there is no generally accepted definition of what an Objection is. Sincere Objections are confused with Buying Signals, smoke screens and questions.

There is further confusion in that there are at least three distinct kinds of Objections because they differ in cause. When you understand what they are and why they occur, you can get a clearer idea of what is going on in the Prospect's mind.

Rejection - If it occurs at the beginning of the interview then it is probably a "No Interest" situation.

Objection - If it occurs during the discussion of Benefits then they are seeking more information.
  Product: "Will it do the job?"
  Price: "Do the Benefits justify the price?"

Stall - If it occurs in the decision-making stage then it is a value-judgement conflict or indecision.
  Peers: "What will others think of it?"
  Priority "Do I need it now?"

Here are a few examples of each:

# Rejections

"We are perfectly happy now."
"Call me back in about three months."
"My brother is in the business."
"We will keep your brochure on file."
"We are not interested in changing now."

These all tell you that there is No Time, No Need, No Interest.

# Objections

| What They Say | What They Mean |
| --- | --- |
| "You are too big for us." | "Can you give us personal service?" |
| "It breaks down easily." | "Is there much maintenance to this?" |
| "Delivery is too slow." | "How fast is delivery?" |
| "Parts are hard to get." | "What is the parts availability?" |

# Stalls

"I want to think about it."
"I have to talk it over with my ..."
"We are interviewing your competitors."

# Buying Signals as Objections

| What They Say | What They Mean |
| --- | --- |
| "Price is too high." | Buying signal? "Help me justify it." |
| "I can't afford it." | Buying Signal? "How can I finance it?" |

In general, any kind of Objection means that the Salesperson has earned a poor grade on their report-card. Somewhere along the Selling Process an essential step was not completed, either by ommission or commission. If the Salesperson does a thorough job of covering the steps in the Selling Process there should be no Rejections, Objections, or Stalls - questions yes, but no Objections. The analogy to golf is appropriate: When it takes 10 strokes to get to the green, being a great putter still won't make you a good golfer.

# Recognizing Objections

Definition: An Objection is a *negative attitude* which may be expressed as a verbal statement or question, or as a non-verbal action that threatens the close of the sale now.

In the beginning, when you first meet a Prospect, the Objection (Rejection) is loud and clear: "No time, No need, No interest." Toward the end of the presentation the Objection (Stall) is also easy to recognize: "I'd like to think it over."

But during the presentation of Benefits the Objection may be difficult to recognize and it is here that they are most important. It can appear as:

|  |  |  |
|---|---|---|
| VERBAL: | "You are too far away from us." | Statement |
| OR: | "How can you serve us from so far?" | Question |
| NON-VERBAL: | Turns cold towards us. | |
| | Drops product with disrespect. | |
| | Starts to handle own papers. | |
| | Not talking much anymore. | |

How do you detect this sale threatening attitude? By asking questions, ie, Trial Closing. How do you answer them? By converting their feelings into questions that you can answer.

## Feelings to Questions

When the Prospect asks a sale threatening QUESTION you happily answer it. When the Prospect makes a sale threatening STATEMENT you have to convert it to an answerable question. When the Prospect shows a *negative attitude*, you must have them verbalize it as a statement or a question. The flow is:

FEELINGS→VERBALIZE→ STATEMENT→ QUESTION →SP ANSWERS

FEELINGS→VERBALIZE————————→ QUESTION→SP ANSWERS

How do you get the Prospect to verbalize a negative feeling or attitude? With a Trial Close. At any time you detect a "chill" ask them: "What do you think about that?" "How do you feel about this?" When they give you their negative statement cushion it, convert it to a question, hypothetically resolve it to smoke out any hidden Objection, and answer the real one.

# Emotions

## Salesperson's Emotions

Salespeople fear Objections, especially if they have no prepared answers. Anything that is threatening should be feared. This fear can be avoided by researching out the most probable Objections, preparing reasonable answers and memorizing them.

A positive attitude is to think of an Objection as something to be answered or discussed rather than "handled". It should be used to develop more information about what the Prospect is thinking and why.

Salespeople lose their effectiveness when they are over confident about their use of words. It is difficult to think creatively while talking, especially when just shocked by an Objection. The result is idle chatter rather than carefully planned, logical statements. You will not think productively under that kind of pressure!

You must be able to answer Objections by reflex action. Prepare answers for the ten most common Objections you receive. Keep in mind that the Prospect is also under emotional pressure and is not necessarily clear in expressing, or even knowing what their concern is.

Don't worry about having a brilliant answer to an Objection. The Prospect will buy your product for the Benefits received, not for how well you answered their Objection. A short, concise response that generally addresses the question will do.

## Prospect's Emotion

Buying is basically an emotional process. On the one hand you are making a direct appeal to the Prospect's Want emotions, "What's in it for me?" On the other hand they have to give up something to receive it, usually money; sometimes there is the risk of the product not doing the job; peer pressure may also be present. The Prospect must balance these emotions, and that is not easy.

Every decision to buy is uncomfortable for the Prospect. They are concerned about the expense, consequences, difficulties, and impulsive buying. All those may create the fear of making a bad decision that they can't easily reverse. The result is conflict for the Prospect.

If the Prospect fails to give you any feedback, they may not be interested, or at least they have a big doubt, maybe both. It is critically important to get the Objection out in the open where you can answer it. If the Prospect has some hesitation about buying your product, then it is definitely to your advantage to know that concern as soon as possible. They are doing you a favor by stating their Objection.

When the Prospect does raise an Objection it doesn't mean that they don't want your product, but rather that they have a serious concern, that you have not created a strong enough desire, or both. If desire is strong enough, a Prospect will do almost anything to have your product, even steal for it!

On a more positive note, when the Prospect raises a sincere Objection they are telling you that they have a real interest or why bother talking about it.

It is most important in answering an Objection is to understand why the Prospect raised it. Objections are the key to the Prospect's emotions. You have to know what their emotions are for their specific hesitations if you wish to close. Yet in the normal course of an interview there is too much pressure on the Salesperson and too little time to delve into their emotional reasons. Therefore, in lieu of analysis, the Salesperson must have a conceptual idea of Objections:

| Type | When | Serious? | Handle? | Indicates | How? |
|------|------|----------|---------|-----------|------|
| Rejection | early | frivolous | hard | no interest | concede |
| Objection | middle | factual | easy | product doubt | explain |
| Stall | end | emotional | easy | indecision | HURT!!! |

(Notice that the word Objection is used in a duel sense. It is the generic term for the whole subject, as well as the sincere doubt as to whether the product will do the job.)

# Preventing Objections

## Flushing Out Emotions

The single biggest reason for a Salesperson experiencing Objections is that they didn't give the Prospect an opportunity or encourage the Prospect to express their feelings about the product in the Conviction step. The professional method would be to enlist their comments by asking questions, ie, Trial Closes:

**SP** - "Mr. P, what do you think of that?"

**SP** - "Mr. P, how do you feel that would affect your ...?"

**SP** - "Mr. P, do you think that would give you the ...?"

This type of questioning will flush out their thoughts, feelings and even how much they want your product. If you have a brief discussion like this after each Benefit is presented, you will know their thinking. That eliminates surprises. You may not sell the product for reasons beyond your control, buy you will know why.

## Preempting Objections

There are some Objections that are almost impossible to deal with because they are value judgements. For example, "You are too small for us" or "You are too big for us". It is difficult to develop evidence that will disprove their claim because there is no cause-effect relationship. Such Objections are difficult for the Prospect to be specific about, even when they feel there may be potential problem. So it would be best if these Objections were prevented in the first place.

To prevent, or preempt a particular Objection, you should boast about it as though it were a Benefit. There should be no more than two or three Objections needing preempting, so developing their Benefits is easy. Just as in reversing an Objection, there are advantages and disadvantages to EVERY situation in life. You just have to do some creative thinking to see it from another viewpoint. The Benefits you develop may not be the strongest, but that too is a value judgement, yours. Since it is your product they will accept your statement as valid by virtue of you presenting it as a Benefit. They will bow to your superior knowledge. Your preemption will temper their Objection down to a minor consideration. Usually it will not be discussed or even be a serious consideration.

**Example:**

**SP** - "We deliver and our Travel Agency is sufficiently far away so that you won't lose staff time with visits to our office for travel brochures."
...when you are far away.

**SP** - "We are large. That means you will have the Benefits of our volume buying which is so important to you, yet you can the most personalized service."
... when you are a large company.

**SP** - "Because we are small we can give you the utmost in personal service, and that is really difficult to find these days, isn't it?"
...when you are a small company.

# Rejections

When first approaching a Prospect, they will have no interest in you or what you are selling. Their mind is preoccupied with other concerns. You are an intrusion until the time they can see there is something of benefit to them. Unless your opening comment offers a personal Benefit you will be rejected. Why? Simply because you haven't sparked their interest.

Typical Rejections:

"We are happy with our present vendor."
"I'm too busy now. Call me in three months."
"We are not interested in making a change now."
"We just changed and want to give the new vendor time."
"Our President's brother sells insurance."

The list goes on, but they all condense down to three basics: No time, No interest, No need. You have been rejected regardless of what they dress it up to be, and sometimes they do try to be original. Face it, you did not excite their interest. It is a simple problem with a simple solution.

If they see real benefit in talking to you, they will; they will listen with interest, regardless of what they are doing. It then follows that the most important single thing that you can do when first meeting a new Prospect is excite them as quickly as possible about your product.

Once you are rejected by the Prospect because of a weak and uninteresting opening, you force the Prospect to defend their position. Prevention of such a Rejection is infinitely easier than trying to dig yourself out of a Rejection hole. Consider this response by a Prospect from a weak opening:

**P** - "We just changed our supplier and we feel we have to give them a respectable chance."

Wow! You just got ostracized for several months. In contrast, consider this dynamic opening:

**SP** - "Mr. P, if there were a way for you to reduce your losses by $1,000 a month, you would want to talk to us about it, wouldn't you?"

**P** - "Well, yes. We couldn't afford not to."

## Recovering From Rejection

Given that you have dug the hole and you are in it, what do you do to get out?

First, you MUST cushion it to remove the sting and animosity: "I appreciate your sincerity."

After the cushion there are two choices open to you:

(1) CONVERT TO QUESTION and ANSWER IT - "Your question is 'can your expectation of superb quality justify your consideration of our service?' That is the question, isn't it?"

**P** - "Yes it is."

**SP** - "Well, we have just completed a project for the ABC company and we were complimented for our excellence in quality." (or whatever your strong suit is.) Would Wednesday afternoon or Friday morning be better for you?"

(2) REVERSE OR CAPITALIZE IT - "Your concern for quality is the very reason you should be considering our service." ... and explain the logic of that with your prepared answer.

## Intangible Rejection

The intangibles and service industries tend to chalk up more Rejections than tangible product lines supposedly because it is hard to demonstrate intangibles. It is true that the sale of intangibles is more of a "confidence and contacts" type selling. And it is also true that Salespeople tend to dramatize only Facts instead of Benefits, and that intangible Facts are difficult to dramatize. No argument, intangibles are harder to sell. But someone is out there with superior selling skills because the dollar value of INTANGIBLE services now exceeds the total of TANGIBLE products.

Services do require more selling skills. The selling skill that needs emphasis is getting the Prospect's initial attention with something that dramatically shows them, "What's in it for me."

# Objections

## (A) Trivial And Prejudiced

During the discussion of what the product can do for the Prospect (the Conviction step's Benefits) you may occasionally run into a few opinionated Objections labeled Trivial and Prejudiced.

TRIVIAL Objections show up to remind you that they are smart buyers, that they are taking reasonable precautions before buying, or just to make conversation.

PREJUDICED Objections can be mild to strong, biased, unfounded and unchanging opinions that the Salesperson dare not tangle with.

Neither of these Objections are critical:

(1) IF the Prospect has a real interest in the product, OR

(2) IF you haven't given them a reason to voice such an extraneous opinion.

Typical examples are:

**Trivial:**

**P** - "Your company makes too much money."

**SP** - "I've heard that too. I hope it's true. We are good."

**P** - "I'm not sure if I can afford it."

**SP** - "I understand."

    ... and proceed with your presentation.

**Prejudice:**

   **P** - "Only men make good Sales and Service people."

  **SP** - "I can understand your point of view. You seem like a very fair person."

     ... and go on with your presentation.

# (B) Sincere Objections

Sincere Objections can be Half-Baked or Genuine. The Prospect is serious about discussing the Benefits, but has some doubts.

HALF-BAKED: A Half-Baked Objection is one where the Prospect has only part of the truth but doesn't know it, so they have drawn a wrong conclusion:

   **P** - "I hear that it works well when it does work, but it breaks down a lot."

   **P** - "Foreign cars are hard to repair."

These objections may be true under certain circumstances, or not at all, but generally they are not true. In such a case you acknowledge what is true and then explain the facts:

   **P** - "Foreign cars are hard to repair."

  **SP** - "Yes, some are harder to repair. That's because the design required for the higher performance is more complex. Incidentally, that higher performance is something you would be excited about ..."

GENUINE: When a Prospect has a minor question about the merits of your product they will usually ask a question. These questions represent little doubts. If the question is a major concern the Prospect will often decide that their concern is overpowering and cannot be resolved. So their big question becomes an Objection. If they venture a comment on this concern it may come out as a flat statement, an Objection. Often their discussion will not indicate their concern.

**Example:**

   **P** - "You are too far away for us!"

That is now an Objection when the question really is: "I wonder if delivery will be a problem?"

**Example:**

   **P** - "You company is too big for us!"

In reality, they are concerned with your ability to give them the personalized service that large companies are reputed not to have. The comment should have been:

   **P** - "How can you give us personal service?"

     ... which you can answer readily.

**Example:**

**P** - "It breaks down too easily."

　　... when actually their concern is:

**P** - "Given the rugged terrain this vehicle has to go over, how much maintenance can we expect?"

If they ask their concerning question, you have an excellent chance to answer it. However, if they set their mind on their own conclusion and so state it, they have formed an opinion they will defend. It becomes difficult for you because you have to show respect for the Prospect's opinion - it would be devasting if you were to do otherwise; the Prospect would simply take a firmer stand, causing a confrontation.

To neutralize the sting and show respect for their opinion you must:

(a) Cushion the Objection:

**SP** - "I can appreciate your concern."

(b) Then ask them to explain why it is a concern:

**SP** - "Why is that important to you?"  OR

**SP** - "Obviously you have a reason for saying that. Do you mind if I ask what that reason is?"

(c) Then, to make certain that it is the only major Objection, you hypothetically solve the problem and ask if they want the product:

**SP** - "Just supposing we could resolve that to your satisfaction, then, in your opinion, wouldn't this be a Benefit for you?" OR ... would you want to own this today?"

A "Yes" answer frees you to convert their comment into a *question*. This is important for as long as they have an Objection in their mind they will have a negative stigma of the product.

(d) If they are convinced that it is merely a question, then an answer relieves the concern and pressure:

**SP** - "Then that brings up the question. The question is, 'Will this product provide you with years of maintenance free service you expect?' That is the question, isn't it?"

**P** - "Yes it is."

**SP** - "Let's look at these reports published in the ..."

　　... and off into the Evidence to reassure the Prospect.

If the Prospect were to say:

**P** - "No, that isn't the question." then

**SP** - "Well, what is the question?"

　　... and presumably you will hear their hidden concern.

Questions about whether or not the product will do the job are usually resolved quickly. Most vendors have enough flexibility built into their product line that one of their products will do the job. As such, a product Objection often can be solved with an alternate product. The more difficult Objections have to deal with the justification of the price; what will their peers think of it; and do they need it now. These concerns cause indecision, or STALLS.

# Stalls

Near the end of the sales interview the Prospect is under considerable pressure to decide whether the values they perceive are worth the investment; should they buy it NOW; and what will their friends and associates think about it. Certainly there is desire on their part or they wouldn't be with you to this point. Still in all, there is internal confusion ranging from simple indecision to deep conflict. Their best option is to back off from the pressure and think it over. Any reason is a good reason if it lets them bow out gracefully.

There is no agony like indecision. A Prospect's mind is a mixture of reason, emotion, dreams, and anxieties, all at the same time. The Prospect is concerned with:

- Will it do the job?                              (Product)
- Do the Benefits justify the price?               (Price)
- What will others think of it?                    (Peer)
- Do I really need it now?                          (Priority)

There is a priority to these concerns. The foremost concern is whether it will work, or do the job. Given that it will perform, the next questions are, is it reasonably priced, and is this the best deal they can probably get?

Once the concern for economic security has been established, the concern shifts to emotional security. Will their peers think well of them for owning it or will they criticize them? Given that they will be proud to own it, do they want it strongly enough to buy it now?

A Stall signals conflict; a conflict of uncertainty and anxiety VS the desire to own the product. If the desire to own is great enough they will buy, and buy NOW. No one will buy NOW unless they have a reason to buy NOW. A Stall usually means they have no reason to buy now - they don't want it badly enough! You didn't create a sense of urgency!

If you accept a Stall, hoping for them to return at a later date, you will lose 95% of the Prospects. Rarely do they think it over, and only 50% of them actually do shop around.

When the Prospect stalls go into the Desire step where you remind them of their awful problem, then assure them you can solve it, and create a Visual Image of them using and enjoying your product. You HURT AND RESCUE THEM!

For reinforcement, let us review the Hurt and Rescue:

In order to create the sense of urgency necessary to get them to buy now you must sell their problem back to them. You have to remind them of their awful problem and the undesirable consequences, and get their agreement. That's their Hurt.

The Rescue is the benefits from your solution, which is your product. You paint a Visual Image of them enjoying your product.

It doesn't hurt to exaggerate the Hurt or the Rescue, for they will accept only that portion they consider believable, they will discount it back to their level of acceptance. Here you create a vivid mental image, a memorable image they will accept in general, if not in detail.

The Hurt has the great advantage that it can be used anywhere in the selling Process where their Problem or Interest is discussed. You simply take the opportunity to agree and support the situation they are describing as a serious problem. For example, during the questioning in the Interest step:

**P** - "We do have the occasional problem in accounting mixups with our present vendor."

**SP** - "That will certainly cause great confusion when it is out of control. Besides you run the risk of paying for the same invoice twice. You are never sure whether your present vendor will notice the overpayment and return it."

That is a simple Hurt and not an exaggeration. And it predicts a serious problem.

An even simpler way of supporting them on the seriousness of their problem is:

**P** - "Well, once in a while we do get some low quality parts that have to be returned to the vendor."

**SP** - "Tse, tse, tse!"

In America this sucking sound, when the tip of the tongue is sucked away from the back of the upper teeth, means "that's terrible or ridiculous".

# ANATOMY OF
# REJECTIONS, OBJECTIONS AND STALLS

| | TIMING | TYPE | EXAMPLE | REASON | STEP | FREQ. | WHAT TO DO | HOW TO ANSWER |
|---|---|---|---|---|---|---|---|---|
| **REJECTIONS** | Phone Calling or Cold Calling | Rejection | "We are perfectly happy now." Generally, the rejection will say— "No time—" "No need—" but they all mean the same thing. | Not interested because you haven't got them interested! | Attention & Interest | Often | Prevent rejection by promising to help solve one of their biggest problems.<br><br>1. Cushion it.<br>2. a) Reverse it, or<br>   b) Convert to question and answer it. | SP— (Phoning prospect for an appointment): "Mr. P., if there were a way to reduce your losses by $2,000 you would want to know more about it, wouldn't you?"<br><br>SP—"I appreciate your sincerity."<br><br>REVERSE<br>"Your concern for quality service is the very reason you should be considering our service."<br><br>CONVERT TO QUESTION<br>"Your question is 'Can your expectations of superb quality justify your consideration of our service?' That is the question, isn't it?"<br>P—"Why is that?"<br>SP—"Yes, it is."<br>SP—"Well, we were just awarded/won/got the service ...and that means top quality. Would Wednesday afternoon or Thursday morning be better for you?" |
| **OBJECTIONS** | Early in the Presentation | Trivial | "You travel agents make too much money." | To make conversation. Not serious. | Interest | Seldom | 1. Cushion it.<br>2. Move on quickly. Don't agree with it, but don't ignore it either—rather, evade it. | SP—"Yes, I've heard that too." |
| | | Prejudice | a) "Only men make good travel agents." | Strong opinions. | Interest | Seldom | 1. Cushion it.<br>2. Stroke his self-image.<br>3. Move on. | SP—"Well, I can certainly see your point of view and the logic of it under certain conditions— if you wish, we can return to it later." |
| | | | b) "It's just too big for us." | Mild opinions. | Interest | Often | Preempt it by capitalizing on it; or by boasting about it so it will seem less important. | SP—"Being one of the largest agencies in the U.S. allows us to give you ... You bring it up as a benefit before they raise it as an objection." |
| | | Hopeless | "Our president's wife owns the travel agency we use." | Prospect cannot qualify. | Interest | Hopefully rare | 1. Cushion it.<br>2. Ask for referral.<br>3. Move on. evade it. | SP—"Well, I guess we really can't help you and I thank you for your interest. By the way, would you know of a person/company similar to you we may be able to help? Our typical client is (describe typical client)." |
| | | Halfbaked | "A good travel agency can get discounts 70% of the time." | Misunderstanding. Incomplete information. | Conviction | Sometimes | 1. Cushion it.<br>2. Explain. | SP—"I can appreciate your view, under certain conditions that is true. It really is a function of how early the traveler makes his reservations since such discount seats are limited." |
| | Middle of Presentation | Genuine Product doubt | "Your agency is too far away from us." | Need more info on the product/service. | Conviction | Often | 1. Cushion it.<br>2. Ask what reason.<br>3. Hypothetically resolve reason.<br>4. Convert to question.<br>5. Answer question—<br>   —Reverse/Capitalize<br>   —Minimize/Outweigh<br>6. Trial Close<br>7. Desire Step for Want<br>8. Weighing Close for Justification<br>   a. Decision Step<br>   b. Order Step | P—Gives an objection. (Has a doubt about something.)<br>SP—1) "I appreciate your sincerity." / "I can understand how you feel."<br>2) "Obviously you have a reason for saying that. Do you mind if I ask what that reason is?"<br>P—Gives reason. (Product, price, peer or priority.)<br>SP—3) "Just suppose we could resolve the (REASON) to your satisfaction. Then, in your opinion, don't you feel this product will definitely be of benefit to you?"<br>P—"Yes."<br>SP—4) "Well, then, that brings up a question. The question is: 'All things considered...':<br><br>QUESTION:<br>...Will this give you all of the benefits that you need and expect of it?" — Product—will it resolve my problem/need?<br>...Is the price of change to this product justified by all of the benefits you will receive?" — Price—is it worth the price/hassle of change?<br>...Will your peers/boss be happy with your choice?" — Peers—what will others think of it?<br>...Can you justify the need right now?" — Priority — do they need it now?<br>SP—"That is the question, isn't it?"<br>P—"Yes, it is."<br>SP—5) "Well, let's look at all of the benefits you will receive by going ahead with our services right now: 1)... 2)...3)..."<br>6) "What do you think about it now?" |
| **STALLS** | | Price-doubt | a) "Your price is too high, I can't afford it." | a) Needs price justified. | Conviction | Often | | |
| | | | b) "It's not worth the hassle of changing." | b) Needs change justified. | | | | |
| | | Peer-doubt | "I would like to think it over." (I wonder what they will think?") Critically important in business. You, not they, may have to sell others. | Doesn't want to look stupid to others. | Conviction | Often | | |
| | End of the Presentation | Time-doubt | "I would like to think it over." Most can't, so it's important to get the order in the first meeting. | May WANT it, but can't justify the NEED for it now. | Desire & Close | Often | | |

## Chapter Ten

# Objections

## Answering Objections

# Secrets

- ☐ Never again will the Prospect be this interested.
- ☐ An Objection has a certain degree of finality.
- ☐ Often a reflex to Caveat Emptor, "Let The Buyer Beware".
- ☐ The trick is to change the Objection into a Close.
- ☐ Some Prospects sincerely don't need your product.
- ☐ Don't sell beyond the limitations of the product.
- ☐ Don't let them see that the Objection bothers you.
- ☐ Price is not an Objection but lack of perceived value.
- ☐ Neither belittle nor magnify an Objection.
- ☐ Prepare reflex answers for all expected Objections.
- ☐ Answers to Objections need not be brilliant.
- ☐ You must keep them talking after they object.
- ☐ Answer Objections immediately, it brings conviction.
- ☐ Unanswered Objections create more Objections.
- ☐ Answer to an Objection should create desire.
- ☐ Answer must be very brief, concise - 30 seconds.
- ☐ A Stall is a decision not to make a decision.
- ☐ A Stall means the Want or Hurt is not strong enough.
- ☐ Salespeople lose 95% of the successful Stalls.

□ Cushioning shows respect for their opinion.

□ You must know why the Objection was raised.

□ Convince them it's a question that needs answering.

□ Converting it to a question makes it logical.

□ Most Objections can be reversed or capitalized.

□ A question is often a better response than an answer.

# Selling Format

**Cushion:** "I can understand how you feel."
"Thank you for being so sincere."
"I appreciate your sincerity."

**Ask What Reason:** "Obviously you have a reason for saying that. Do you mind if I ask what that reason is?"

**OR:** "Why is that important to you?"

**Resolve Reason:** "Just suppose we could solve that to your satisfaction, then, in your opinion, wouldn't this ... be of benefit to you?"

**Convert To Question:** "Well, that brings us to the question. The question is: "All things considered ...

Product ... will this give you all of the benefits that you need and expect of it?"

Price ... is the price of (or hassle-of-change to) this product justified by the benefits you will receive?"

Peers ... will your peers support your choice?"

Priority ... can you justify the need right now?"

... That is the question, isn't it?"

**Answer Question With:** R Reverse/Capitalize it.
E Explain it.
M Minimize/Outweigh it.
E Evade it.
D Deny it.
Y Why (Ask "Why").

| Trial Close: | "What do you think of that?" Then:<br><br>"If you were to go ahead with this program, would you want the Economy or Executive model?" Then:<br><br>"In your opinion, would the small or medium size be more effective?" Then: |
|---|---|

**Alternate Choice Close:** "Would you prefer the green or blue?"

| PROSPECT'S ATTITUDE | WHAT WE MUST DO | HOW TO DO IT | STEP | WHAT WE MUST SELL | LOGIC OF THE STEP | BUYER'S ATTITUDE |
|---|---|---|---|---|---|---|
| S K E P T I C A L | Develop benefits | •Fact/features<br>•Advantage<br>•Benefit<br>•Evidence<br>•Visual Image<br>•Trial Close | C O N V I C T I O N | Product—will do the job<br>Price/hassle is justified<br>Peers—others will like it<br>Priority—need it now | Tell them what's in it for them | B E L I E F |
| | Remove any doubts/objections | •Cushion it<br>•Ask what reason<br>•Hypothetically resolve reason<br>•Convert to question<br>•Reverse/minimize (REMEDY)<br>•Trial Close | | Reassurance | Little doubts create questions;<br>big doubts create objections | |

# Answering Sincere Objections

1  CUSHION
2  ASK WHAT REASON
3  HYPOTHETICALLY RESOLVE REASON
4  CONVERT TO QUESTION
5  ANSWER QUESTION
   TRIAL CLOSE
   DESIRE STEP & WEIGHING CLOSE (for STALLS)
   ALTERNATE CHOICE CLOSE

## (1) Cushion

When a Prospect raises an Objection of any type they have made a decision and taken a stand. They may have decided that:

- They are not interested.      (Rejection)
- It won't work.                (Objection)
- They won't decide now.        (Stall)

As much as you disagree, you can never prove a Prospect wrong. You cannot openly disagree with anyone and expect that person to buy. When

137

you argue they may close their minds even more. On the other hand, if you agree with their conclusion it may be insincere.

Even though you can't agree, disagree, or argue, you can show respect for their opinion:

**SP** - "I can understand how you feel."
"I can see your point of view."
"I appreciate your sincerity."

The words used in a cushion matter little, as long as you show understanding and respect for their opinion.

When a Prospect raises an Objection, they have raised a barrier. This is a critical moment in answering an Objection. A cushion removes that barrier and allows the conversation to continue.

# (2) Ask What Reason

**SP** - "Why is that important to you?" OR

**SP** - "Obviously you have a reason for saying that. Do you mind if I ask what that reason is?"

Asking the Prospect to explain their concern is the least risky position for the Salesperson. The more they talk the more they reveal. Their answer should clearly define their concern.

As the Prospect talks about their concern, they may even talk themselves out of it as their thinking clears.

A person is conditioned to answer almost any question asked, so the Prospect will usually respond to questioning. This in turn transfers pressure from the shocked Salesperson to the Prospect, thereby giving the Salesperson time to organize their thoughts.

As in all difficult sales situations the rule is "Keep Them Talking."

# (3) Hypothetically Resolve Reason

Prospect's often do not reveal their true thoughts when they raise an Objection. They may be slightly embarrassed to reveal the real reason; or afraid that if you know the real reason you might overcome it. So they may give a substitute reason and create a smoke screen. Smoke screens are as varied as the reason for not wanting to buy a product in the first place. Whatever their reason is for holding back, it doesn't matter; you must uncover their concern. Only then can it be discussed and answered.

The way to smoke it out is by gently confronting them with a hypothetical solution to their stated concern, and with that concern gone, would they now like to buy your product.

**P** - "Your line doesn't have a wide enough variety of sizes."

**SP** - "I appreciate your sincerity. If we could resolve the sizes to your satisfaction, then, in your opinion, would you want to own this today?"

When the "hypothetical resolution" is offered, the Prospect will assume that you do have the solution to their concern. If they agree that the solution removes their concern, yet do not buy, they are caught in an awkward position and must come clean. On the other hand, if they will reveal their true concern, they avoid further deception. "Hypothetically resolving" is a socially acceptable way of calling their bluff:

**SP** - "If we could resolve that concern to your satisfaction then, in your opinion, would you want to purchase it today?"

**P** - "No, not necessarily."

**SP** - "Then you must have another concern. May I ask what that concern is?"

**P**- "Well, my big concern is ..."

Then you can answer the blocking Objection.

As an option, if you want to bury the original Objection you could slip in:

**SP** - "I understand. Then your first concern, the ..., although important, is not a major concern, is that right?"

**P** - "That's correct."

Price is a smoke screen when the Prospect does not want to reveal their true concern. Price is a safe Objection because we all know intuitively that value and price are relative to the viewer, and as such it is difficult for the Salesperson to overcome.

Always check for a smoke screen on every major Objection you encounter. It is smooth, simple, and safe. When you "hypothetically" resolve their concern you promise nothing that you have to deliver.

You wouldn't want to "hypothetically resolve" every concern the Prospect has. Use it to flush out the hidden Objection that is blocking the sale. If the Prospect has more hidden Objections, something is wrong with the Prospect or with the sales interview. Use your own judgement here.

# (4) Convert To Question

Whatever your feelings are about answering an OBJECTION, answering a QUESTION is relatively easy.

When you convince the Prospect that they have a question rather than an Objection it puts them in a better frame of mind. They no longer have to defend their quickly formed negative opinion. It relieves them of that tension.

The Prospect has admitted that, except for one question, the product will benefit them. You are now out of the hole that the Prospect dug for you. The question is whether their concern can be satisfied. It may be any one of several items:

- Product — Are there enough benefits?
- Price — Justified by the benefits?
- Peers — Acceptable to others?
- Priority — Need it now?

These are the root questions. Maybe you can answer them to their satisfaction, maybe not. At least it is now a discussion and not a door closer.

The question you develop from the Objection may be general or specific, it doesn't matter. The Objection is not perfectly clear in their minds anyway. They either have to agree that it is THE question or tell you what the real question is. Either way you win:

**SP** - "Well, then, that brings us to the question. The question is: 'All things considered ...

Product    ... will this give you all of the benefits that you need and expect of it?"

Price    ...is the price of (or hassle-of-change to) this product justified by all the benefits you will receive?"

Peers    ... will your associates be happy with your choice?"

Priority    ... can you justify the need right now?"

    ... that is the question, isn't is?"

> (**P** - "No, it isn't.")
> (**SP** - "Well, what is the question?")

**P** - "Yes it is."

The Objection can be converted to a question and then the question changed slightly for ease of answering. When you ask the Prospect, "That is the question, isn't it?" you won't go too far astray. Changing it also lets them know you do understand. Once you restate it you have freed their mind.

You are now on familiar ground because you know the answers about your product and can do a great job of giving a most concise explanation to clear up the Prospect's concern.

# (5) Answer Question

The smoothest way to answer an Objection is to have a prepared answer ready. That is easy since there are fewer than a dozen Objections that occur with regularity for any product. Remember that the answer is the avenue to the sale, so invest time in developing them.

If the answer is long, you end up maximizing the problem in the Prospect's mind, so keep it brief, no more than 50 to 100 words, spoken in 30 to 60 seconds. Get to the point.

A short answer demonstrates to the Prospect that it is a minor point. If the answer is too short it will be questioned further if they are truly concerned. A long answer magnifies the concern and you buy it back by muddling up their emotional Want. You may also create more questions and doubt's in the Prospect's mind.

Neither belittle nor magnify the Objection. Remember that it is really a CONCERN and not a TOTAL Rejection. They want you to say a few words to relieve their concern. At the end they will buy the product not because of your brilliant answer to their concern but rather because they WANT it. When they raise their concern, even as an Objection, they really want and expect you to tell them it is OK.

Objections require more planning, preparation and practice than any other part of the Selling Process. Most Salespeople think they can "wing" it with Objections the way they can with product descriptions.

# The R-E-M-E-D-Y Formula

There is a formula of techniques for answering the Objection:

| | |
|---|---|
| **R** | Reverse or Capitalize it. |
| **E** | Explain it. |
| **M** | Minimize or Outweigh it. |
| **E** | Evade it. |
| **D** | Deny it. |
| **Y** | Ask why. (Try to get THEM to answer it) |

## * Reverse or Capitalize It

The best method of handling an objection is to convert it to a REASON for buying from you, that is, capitalizing it:

**P** - "Your product is in every one of my competitor's stores."

**SP** - "Why, that is the very reason you should consider carrying our product ..."

...and then Explain the reason why. Make sure you have prepared a Reverse explanation for every Objection you expect. Reverse answers are not difficult to create. Everything in life has advantages and disadvantages. Disadvantages to one are advantages to another - it is your point of view. You just have to be creative. Present the explanation as a Benefit:

**P** - "I just bought 6 month's supply of cosmetics."

**SP** - "Why, that may be the very reason that you should consider using our cosmetics right now." (Pause) OR

"The fact that you are concerned about quality is the very reason why you should be considering this."

**P** - "Oh? Why is that?"

**SP** - "Well, we have already agreed that your present cosmetics are leaving your skin a little too dry and that may cause irritation from some of the ingredients. To subject your skin to that kind of treatment for another six months is self inflicted cruelty. You deserve better than that, don't you?"

**P** - "I sure do."

## * Explain It

A simple, straight forward answer to the question. It can be used independently for a minor Objection without setting up the question first:

**P** - "It looks like it is difficult to train a secretary to operate this machine."

**SP** - "Really it is quite simple. As a matter of fact, we send in a representative to train your staff. After that, everyone is an expert." OR

**SP** - "Really it is quite simple. Here, let me show you how its done and you'll see it is easy to operate."

**P** - "It is too high for our secretaries."

**SP** - "There is an adjustment screw on the bottom to lower it with. Here let me set it in the appropriate position for a secretary."

## * Minimize or Outweigh It

No product is perfect. They all have their limitations just as well as competitive advantages. So admit it and introduce other Benefits to minimize and outweigh those limitations.

**Minimizing:**

**P** - "It only comes in Red, White, and Blue."

**SP** - "That is true. We have conducted extensive research and have found that Red, White and Blue represent 90% of the market sales. The Benefit to you is that ..."

> ... our large inventory prevents shortages on fast movers,
>
> ... you don't get caught with slow moving colors,
>
> ... your sales rep is here every week to restock,
>
> ... we have the best refund policy in the trade,

Notice how you overwhelm them with all the Benefits of your product.

### Outweighing:

**P** - "Well, $xxx is a lot of money."

**SP** - "Wouldn't it be worth a one time investment of $xxx to be able to answer Objections with ease for the rest of your career?"

OR

**SP** - "You are worth a lot more than $XXX, aren't you?"

When you admit a shortcoming avoid the combative and argumentive words "but" and "however"; they tend to build up a resistance in anyone. It is best to make a simple statement of Benefits about your product.

# * Evade It

When the Prospect gives you a Trivial or Prejudiced Objection, you have little choice except to acknowledge and evade it. The Trivial Objection is to make conversation, or an attempt to prove to oneself that they are taking reasonable care before buying. The Prejudice Objection is a mild to strong and unchanging opinion that the Salesperson dare not tangle with. You have to acknowledge both, but it is best to evade an answer:

### Trivial:

**P** - "You Salespeople all make too much money."

**SP** - "I've heard that too. I hope it's true."


**P** - "I'm not sure if I can afford it."

**SP** - "I understand."

> ... and proceed with your presentation.

**Prejudice:**

> **P** - "Only men make good sales and service people."

> **SP** - "I can understand your point of view. You seem like a very fair person."

> ... and proceed with your presentation.

## * Deny It

Whenever the Prospect make a comment that is derogatory about you, your product, or your company, deny it quickly and emphatically.

> **P** - "I've heard that this product has a terrible service reputation."

> **SP** - "I appreciate your straight forwardness. That comment crushes me and I would certainly like to know where you heard it. It is definitely not true. This product is warranted like all similar products you use. That takes the risk out of it for everyone. Since you have an initial concern I will ask my company to extend the warranty by a year just to reassure you of it's superior quality."

> **P** - "Well, that sounds like you are quite confident about your product".

## * Why? Why? Why? Why?

Question it. This technique can be used independently for any MINOR concern or Objection.

> **P** - "That color is a little too dark."

> **SP** - "WHY is that important?"

> **P** - "Because it makes me look older."

> **SP** - "Maybe, but it sure makes you look sophisticated ..."

**Summary:**

The Reverse of Capitalizing response is probably the best all-around answer. If that is not practical then Minimize or Outweigh it with Benefits.

Remember, the Objection is emotional in origin. They won't buy because of your brilliant answer to their Objection, but because they WANT it. But they often need someone to tell them it is OK, that they shouldn't worry about their concerns.

## Trial Close

A Trial Close is an OPINION asking question, while a Close is a DECISION asking question.

Since it is only an opinion that you are seeking, the answer can never hurt your progress toward the Close. It is the only way to test the Prospect's acceptance of your answer to their Objection. It will prove whether they are reassured to the point of wanting it NOW:

### Hot Response:

**SP** - "If you were to start using our product, would you want the small or medium size machine?" OR

**SP** - "In your opinion, which is the best for you, the small or the medium model?"

**P** - "Well, the medium model does have a lot of fine features."

(You have a HOT response. Close with the Alternate Choice Close.)

### Lukewarm Response:

**P** - "Well, it looks good but I'm not sure yet."

(That's LUKEWARM. Pour on more benefits.)

### Cold Response

**P** - "I am not too sure if either one would work."

(That's a COLD response. Obviously you don't know what their SIP and/or EBM are so back to the questioning in the Interest step. "Am I correct in understanding that your problem is ...?"

If the response were: "I really would like to think it over", go to the Desire step for Hurt and Rescue.)

# Desire Step & Weighing Close (Stalls only)

Desire step is to remind them of the terrible Hurt they have because of that AWFUL problem. You "bloody them up, then throw them a band-aide."

**SP-** "Mr. P, let's summarize what we have been discussing. We agree that your present car has served you well but it has seen it's day. You are now running into a lot of repairs. Worse than that, the breakdowns are interfering with your business, and you are afraid that it is going to let you down just as you are going to meet a Prospect, or some late rainy night. Isn't that right?"

"Well, this beautiful new car is tops in reliability. The manufacturer is so proud of the workmanship that they have an extended warranty. Better than that, it is one of the most luxurious cars is in it's class. You will be recognized for your fine taste in motor cars."

"Let's assume that you go ahead and purchase this car today. Six months from now you are talking to your manager about cars. All of a sudden he says 'John, come to think of it, I haven't heard of you having any problems with that new car. That's really great compared to what you had. And it sure is classy.' That's the kind of scene you want to be in, isn't it?"

**P** - "I'm still undecided." (Still indecisive, so go on to the Weighing Close where you help them sort the pros and cons in their mind.)

**SP** - "Well, I don't know if you are going to be in that picture or not. It all depends on the decision you are about to make."

# The Weighing Close

Now for the WEIGHING Close. Here you help them weigh all of the pros and cons about your product for the necessary logical justification:

**SP** - "Mr. P, you are about to make a decision and we want that decision to be a correct one. So let's weigh the reasons for hesitating against the reasons for moving ahead with us and doing so right now:

(Draw a T on a sheet of paper)

| **Reasons for hesitating:** (Let Prospect list) | **Reasons for moving ahead NOW:** (You write in your Benefits) |
|---|---|
| Loyalty | Cost savings will get you recognition. |
| Price | Nicer packaging will increase sales. |
| | 24 hr service to serve your clients. |
| | Service executive to reduce your work. |
| **SP** - "Have I missed any?" | Bonuses for your new ideas. |
| **P** - "No." | Free up capital for your expansion. |

..."Mr. P, which side weighs heavier, the reasons for hesitating, or the reasons for going ahead with our product now?"

**P** - "Well, certainly the reasons for going with you."

Let's assume they have decided that they do WANT the product. The logical question is to ask, When?

**SP** - "Would you want a delivery on Mondays or Wednesdays?"

**P** - "Wednesday would be fine."

## Close - Alternate Choice

The difference between a Trial Close and a Close is that the former is an opinion-asking question. If you have been Trial Closing along the way, there are no surprises at the Close. You know of the Prospect's problems, why they want them resolved, their thoughts about your product and their desire to buy now. Closing is now a simple choice between two minor choices:

**SP** - "Would you want this next Monday or Friday?"

To a dedicated Trial Closer the Close is assured, if their product is acceptable.

# When To Answer

There are four times you can answer an Objection:

BEFORE, NOW, LATER, and NEVER

**Before:** (PREEMPTION) In any product line there are a certain number of Objections that pop up repeatedly. Some will be specific to your product, and others general to all products, such as the "No time", "No need", "No interest", "Think it over" types.

If you have some Objections that are specific to your product that are not easily handled, then you should preempt them by boasting about them, that is, turning them into a Benefit or reason to buy.

There are advantages and disadvantages to every situation in business. You can create an advantage for every potential Objection. It may not be the best advantage, but when presented as a Benefit the Prospect is not likely to challenge the point by objecting. Your boasting about its merits then minimizes or neutralizes the Objection in the Prospect's mind.

**Example**

**SP** - "Our office is sufficiently far away so you won't lose staff time with visits to our office for travel brochures." ...when far away.

**P** - "Yes, but what about delivery?"

**SP** - "Delivery is always economic. We will deliver it at your specified time."

**NOW:** Without a doubt an unanswered Objection looks like a cover up. The Prospect may think you can't answer it, or that you are evading the issue hoping it will go away. It magnifies itself in their mind to where it may even preclude them from listening to you further. They can't get their minds off it. If at all possible answer it immediately.

**LATER:** About the only justification for delaying an answer is if the Objection raised will seriously interrupt your description of the Benefits.

This is especially true when the Benefits and the Objection are not related, such as the following:

**SP** - "... and your benefit from this new procedure is that it will reduce your down time and ..." (Interrupted)

**P** - "Your company is not big enough to service us."

**SP** - "When you see all of the Benefits in this system you'll love it. We can talk about that in a moment. Now this new procedure cuts your downtime losses by at least 25% over the lighter model. That means you can ..."

When the Salesperson told the Prospect that they would discuss that concern in a moment, the Salesperson not only promised the Prospect an answer, but also programmed the Prospect to the point to where they would be pleased with the answer. In the event that you do forget to cover it, they too may forget. Of course, if you don't have the system to handle it to their satisfaction then outweigh it with other Benefits.

**NEVER:** The only Objections/Rejections you should evade are the unimportant ones. These invariably occur early in the meeting and fall in the class of Trivial and Prejudice. The Trivial Objection is to make conversation, or sometimes it is a weak attempt to prove to themselves that they are taking reasonable care and precaution. The Prejudice Objection can be a mild to strong opinion that is unchanging. You have to acknowledge them but you do not necessarily have to answer them;

**Trivial:**

**P** - "I hear that your company makes too much money."

**SP** - "I've heard that too. I hope it's true." OR

**SP** - "I can understand your feelings."

... and go on without further comment.

**Prejudice:**

**P** -"I only want to buy from blue chip companies."

**SP** - "I can understand how you feel. You seem like a very fair person."

...and go on with your presentation.

Prejudices are biased opinions that are not pertinent to the interview. There is no apparent gain in either agreeing or disagreeing with them. Simply acknowledge the comment, stroke their self-image and move on. It is a standard rule in selling - never offer an opinion on anything other than YOUR product. If they persist, you have lost a Prospect that didn't have much want for your product anyway!

# You Sell People, Not Products

Often Objections are precipitated by the Salesperson due to lack of finesse. The strain in all people relationships is caused by lack of warm communications. Its the same in selling. So be friendly, concerned about them, and be conversational. It's hard to say "No" to a friend.

# Self-Images

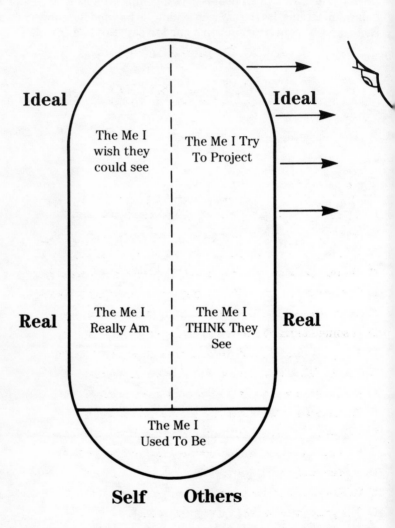

Ideal

The Me I wish they could see

The Me I Try To Project

Ideal

Real

The Me I Really Am

The Me I THINK They See

Real

The Me I Used To Be

Self        Others

## Chapter Eleven

# Motives

## Secrets

- ☐ Every Prospect must be sold logically and emotionally.
- ☐ Wants prompt the desire to buy, logic justifies it.
- ☐ People are never satisfied, they are always wanting.
- ☐ We buy because we want to and not because we need to.
- ☐ Each person has a different pattern of Needs and Wants.
- ☐ Their emotions control too much of their intelligence.
- ☐ If someone really wants something they "need" it.
- ☐ The perception of a Want is always subject to change.
- ☐ Several Wants can be motivated at the same time.
- ☐ Wants are greatly affected by outside stimuli.
- ☐ Wants are situational, therefore not predictable.
- ☐ Motivations change with time, even between sales calls.
- ☐ Feelings are only temporary, they can be changed.
- ☐ A Want may not be important until you arouse it.
- ☐ Selling is meant to arouse the Prospect's Wants.
- ☐ The pride of ownership is easy to arouse.
- ☐ You buy something to help you feel good about yourself.
- ☐ Greatest motives are Fear, Greed, Importance, and Pride.
- ☐ Fear of loss is infinitely stronger than saving money.
- ☐ Fear speeds up and confirms a decision to buy.
- ☐ Fear of loss is avoidance of dissatisfaction.

- ☐ Our projected image is the best that society will accept.
- ☐ Society must grant us the respect of that station.
- ☐ The self-image accepted by society generates our status needs.
- ☐ Status Needs are as real as product Needs.
- ☐ The symbols that support that status are all around us.
- ☐ Symbols are there with our permission to tell our story.
- ☐ Symbols can be personality factors as well as material.
- ☐ Society must see our station in life, but not see through us.
- ☐ People like to conform, to imitate the successful.
- ☐ Self-image glorifies or changes the past, discounts the future.
- ☐ The secret to everyone's surrender is their self-image.
- ☐ Self-respect may be more important than social respect.
- ☐ Everyone needs approval - the stroking of their self-image.
- ☐ We measure our success largely on the praise from others.
- ☐ Praise is the stimulant of all our achievements.
- ☐ Our self-image is our protection against despair.
- ☐ We have a greater need for stroking than for the product.
- ☐ They often need the stroking more than the product.
- ☐ The desire for approval controls our actions.
- ☐ "What will others think?" is pride defending self-image.
- ☐ We say hello to others so they will recognize us.
- ☐ All of our actions have their roots in our self-image.
- ☐ The Prospect's self-image is preoccupied until acknowledged.
- ☐ Reinforce the self-image, and do not threaten it.
- ☐ Stroking the self-image controls the Wants.
- ☐ We must be dominantly persuasive while enhancing their status.
- ☐ The tougher the Prospect the more image stroking they need.
- ☐ Always be looking for an ego-stroking reason for buying.
- ☐ Buying must be face-saving since they are succumbing to you.
- ☐ Two major factors in selling - the product and self-image.
- ☐ Buying motives must be built into the selling plan.
- ☐ Find a motivator for each level of the Wants hierarchy.
- ☐ The Alternate Choice Close protects their self-image.

# Needs and Wants

People are wanting beings; they want more of everything. They want more love, more money, more pleasure, more success, more life; just more and more. It is part of the survival instinct.

A Need is a necessity of life, a necessary evil. A Want is an inner urge which is strictly emotional in nature. It can be turned on instantly when the right emotion is prompted. When a Want is prompted, it must be justified to become a necessity or Need and, therefore, a reason to buy.

A Prospect may need something yet may not want it. If so, they probably will not buy it. Similarly, a Prospect may want something and not need it. They will buy it only if they can find the justification.

When they want it badly enough, they do indeed *need* it; they will even make up reasons for needing it. That's called rationalizing, and we can all plead guilty to that!

Each person has a different pattern of Needs and Wants. These Wants are very situational, and several can be motivated at the same time. Once justified as a Need, the Want will be satisfied with a purchase.

## Why Do People Buy?

People buy because they *want* to and not because they *need* to. People don't really *need* most of the items they do buy. Look around your home or office for the items you once thought you really needed. Ask yourself how often you have used those items in the last year. You may be embarrassed, for at least 80% of the items were probably used once or less in the last year. That hardly justifies the expense. Even now you will rationalize those ill-conceived purchases by saying, "But it's nice to have. I never know when I'll need it!" You just couldn't justify buying most of those items today! Most people do not have a sound logical reason for buying most things.

■ People buy for *emotional satisfaction!*

But you don't need to know the labels for the 150 odd motivations psychologists have identified when you ask:

**SP** - "Why is that important to you?" The answer will be their emotional reason for wanting it.

# Selling Is Motivation, Not Persuasion

Selling is MOTIVATION and not persuasion. Persuasion is coaxing, even pestering, and it is impossible to coax someone to want something. You may be able to persuade them into thinking they can afford it, or that it is better than the competitor's, or that others will like it, but you can't coax them into wanting it.

By the way, if you, the Salesperson, feel that it is morally wrong to sell someone a product that they don't need, then understand that if everyone bought only what they really needed, we would be in history's longest and deepest depression. A good part of the joy of living is satisfying Wants. So relax and learn how to motivate others into buying.

Selling, then, is a process of developing the Prospect's problems and conflicts, prompting their emotions and finding a solution with your product. Selling is the conditioning of the Prospect's emotions and the application of selling techniques to lead them to the decision to buy.

## Wants Must Be Justified

We have to deal with two facets of the Wants: the deep-seated, primitive Want that powers the Prospect into action, and the surface justification of those Wants. For example, a Prospect wants to put their child through college. The deep-seated Wants that are being prompted may be that it makes the parent look good to others, or love of family, or admiration from the child, or a complex mixture of all of these. Yet the Salesperson can only prompt the Want that is acceptable to others: "Mr. P, you have an obligation as a responsible parent to arrange a college education for your child, don't you?" The Want justified was their sense of responsibility, which is an acceptable norm of society. The deep-seated emotion of wanting to look good to others is just not acceptable.

# Pyramid Of Needs And Wants

A popular theory developed in the mid '50's is Maslow's Hierarchy of Needs and Wants. Progressing from Survival upwards, it said that the level of current concern is a Need while all above it are Wants. Once a Need is fulfilled, a person moves up to the next Want which then becomes a Need.

Yet, it doesn't explain why men risk their lives volunteering for war; nor why the poor often buy expensive items when they can't afford to take care of their kids. (They do it to improve their Self-Image, make them like themselves a little bit more).

But Maslow got hung up on the Needs, not understanding that people are driven by emotions, not logic. Better is Ley's Pyramid of Wants wherein the primary five levels are representative of our 150 odd motivations. It is not a hierarchy but rather all 150 emotions exist at the same time, some stronger and/or more excitable than others. The Salesperson only has to ask:

**SP** - "Why is that important to you?", to find the one to excite.

| Maslow's Hierarchy of Needs and Wants. | Ley's Pyramid of **WANTS**. |
|---|---|
| Self Actualization | I want to be Great. |
| Ego Enhancement | I want to be Important. |
| Social Acceptance | I want to be Loved. |
| Security | I want to be Secure. |
| Survival | I want to be Alive. |

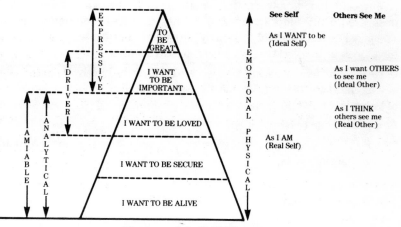

## Pyramid Of Wants

A Prospect will often pay a high price to ensure a continual want satisfaction, depending on how badly they want it:

| | |
|---|---|
| Being recognized: | Community activities. |
| Sense of importance: | Expensive belongings. |
| Feeling of belonging: | Country club. |
| Emotional security: | Getting married. |
| Physical security: | Buying a home. |

# The Powerful Motivators

Given all of the basic Wants of mankind (and over 100 have been classified), how can we crystalize these into a few selling plan actions?:

| | |
|---|---|
| **"I Want To Be Great"** | Stroke with ADMIRATION. |
| **"I Want To Be Important"** | Stroke with SINCERE COMPLIMENT. |
| **"I Want To Be Loved"** | Stroke with FRIENDSHIP. |
| **"I Want To Be Secure"** | Appeal to DESIRE FOR EASY GAIN. |
| **"I Want To Be Alive"** | Appeal to FEAR OF LOSS. |

Any Want emotion can be prompted into full bloom with a simple comment. Example: "You really deserve the best, don't you?" This may prompt them to buy the best product available, rather than one which will simply do the job. You have moved them with a few words to the top of the pyramid. It is that simple. On an unplanned basis any Want can be excited at any moment by many stimuli.

## Fear Of Loss

Mankind has a natural fear-instinct of losing something already possessed. These emotions stem from the primitive development of man. The possible loss of a tool that early man used to capture an animal must have been a dreaded tragedy, even life threatening.

Today the fear emotion of losing $1,000 is infinitely stronger than saving that same $1,000. People are very possessive, so loss of something of value is a most powerful emotion.

Compare these two statements:

"Mr. P - "With your present insulation you are LOSING at least $1,000 a year in heating costs."

versus

"Mr. P - "We can show you how to SAVE $1,000 on your heating bill."

Obviously the loss-reducing motive is stronger than the saving motive. Losing is something tangible and real - saving is intangible and therefore elusive.

## Desire For Easy Gain

Man has an overwhelming desire for Easy Gain. There is a greater desire for money that comes easily than money that has to be earned. The difference in desire is called greed. It is so powerful that it is often blinding.

Although people are well aware of the problems with the "get rich-quick" schemes, many still fall victim to them. The reason is simple; people are so blinded by desire that they will not investigate the method of gaining that wealth.

The desire for Easy Gain is prompted in the familiar "SAVE 20%" or "20% OFF" promotions of the retail trade. It is powerful when believed. A sale offering "70% OFF" is not believable so it will have to be justified. Similarly with any other "too good to be true" offering. Justify it and it will be a most powerful motivator to get them to buy.

## To Be Important/ Loved/ Great

The pyramid of needs-wants can be divided into:
Emotional well-being.
Physical well-being.

| | | |
|---|---|---|
| Actualization | To Be Great | Emotional well-being. |
| Self-image | To Be Important | Emotional well-being. |
| Acceptance | To Be Loved | Emotional well-being. |
| Security | To Be Secure | Physical well-being. |
| Safety | To Be Alive | Physical well-being. |

The greatest desire is not merely being accepted by others but to be held in awe and respect by them. That strokes the self-image. This sense of feeling important is the real security of being accepted. It transcends the 3 upper levels of the pyramid:

| | |
|---|---|
| To Be Great, The Best | I like me. |
| To Enhance self-image | WE like me. |
| Social Acceptance | YOU like me. |

The feeling of importance is intangible and difficult to gain. It takes great effort, and trial and error to earn recognition from others. Consequently, people rarely have enough and they always crave more. The desire to feel important is the *most* powerful of the motivators. Anything that strokes their self-image by making people like themselves a little more is a positive motivator.

Part of our survival instinct is personal growth. To grow, our mind continually needs evidence of who, what, and where we are, the development of our self-images.

# Self-Image

## The "ME" Image

While scaling the pyramid to self-esteem we have concern not only about how we perceive ourselves but, more important, how we think others perceive us.

From all of this we create images in our mind, our own image, the image we want to become and the image we think others have of us.

THE ME I WISH THEY WOULD SEE (The Ideal Self):

"This is what I really want to be and I wish they could see me this way. This is the way I want to be treated. I could be respected like this if others weren't so blind."

This is our personal goal in life, usually known only to ourselves. It is us at our highest level of achievement. We want to be great, to excel; And we love ourselves.

THE ME I TRY TO PROJECT (The Ideal Other):

This is a compromise between what we think they see and what we want to be. It is the image we project to others. We push this self-image as high as we can get away with, all that society will permit us, and all that the traffic will bear. If others will not accept it we may have to adjust. We will also adjust it for each reference group we join.

To project that image we surround ourselves with symbols and behaviour appropriate to that image. These are the signals to others that show them our status and station in life.

THE ME I THINK THEY SEE (The Real Other):

"I don't know what others really think of me. It scares me because I am not sure. That makes life miserable since I must always adjust this image up and down as I get signals from others. I'm always asking myself 'Is that the way they see me?'"

Our mind continually needs evidence of who and what it is. This continuous readjusting is most unsettling and it keeps us insecure.

THE ME I REALLY AM (The Real Self):

This is the image we have of ourselves. It's an assumed image because we don't know ourselves that well. We probably don't want to know the real truth. Leave well enough alone!

THE ME I USED TO BE:

"I no longer want to be reminded of what I used to be. That is gone, both the good and the bad. I'm improved now."

Our Ideal Self is the way we would like others to see us, but they won't accept that level. We compromise and project the image others expect of us, the Ideal Other image. We support this Ideal Other image with all the necessary status symbols. These manifest themselves in our car, home, friends, life style, clothing, office decor, trinkets, politics, associations and even the position in our company. As we acquire symbols, we redefine our self-image more accurately.

The various groups, associations or companies we join also help to define self-images. In the defining we may make adjustments to our Ideal Other self-image as it relates to that particular group. We may be a strong, dynamic member of a trade organization, but a regular member in a yachting group. That's OK. It depends on what we want from the association.

The status symbols of your Ideal Other self will always be changing as you climb higher and/or move sideways. They may also be redefined downward as ones' self-image is shortened by the loss of job; spouse; being "told off" by someone you respect, or any one of many other events.

While the self-image is always subject to change, it must be positive or it is shattering. If we stroke someone's self-image to a higher level they will love us. In a sales interview if we don't acknowledge their self-image or station, they will be preoccupied about that until we do. If we stroke them below their level they will literally despise us. Out we go, without a sale. We reject those that threaten our self-image and embrace those that enhance it. We also reject those that ignore our self-image or station in life. Our self-image must be recognized and respected with all honors due.

We must recognize what the self-image is and respect it. Most of the unexplained losses of sales, (when you had the better product), was probably due to a self-image problem. Loss of a competitive bid, where everything was more or less equal, may have been due to your competitor's better job of stroking the Prospect's self-image.

As we look for the Ideal Self - Ideal Other self-images of the Prospect, we must keep in mind that they are not proud of their Real Self. Don't try to find out what it is. Avoid any reference to their real self.

Even in the closing, self-image is apparent. Most people want to buy something to enhance their self-image. Yet they don't always know how to say "yes" without a loss of face or self-image by succumbing to a Salesperson! So we allow a Prospect to say "yes" by using a Close which will give the Prospect a choice, the Alternate Choice Close:

**SP** - "Would you prefer the blue or green?"

In the closing stage of the sale this same quest for approval appears as Buyer's Remorse. If the Prospect doesn't get the assurance that their purchase is a wise decision and socially acceptable from someone, even the Salesperson, they will wish they hadn't bought it. They may very well return it.

## Status Symbols

Our self-image generates status needs and symbols that in turn tell others what our status is. They need to see our status symbols so they will be able to show us the respect for our station in life. That is why we surround ourselves with the appropriate symbols. The symbols also make us feel good, a sort of self stroking that reinforces our self-image.

These symbols are all around. Everything that surrounds a Prospect is there with their permission. It is intended to tell a story. These symbols are the window to their self-image.

The Prospect will project personality status symbols as well as material symbols to define their various self-images. These too can be supported and stroked positively. Certainly a personality symbol is the easiest to create, maintain and change. It may even be more gratifying than material symbols. The Salesperson can stroke the Prospect's self-image by admiring them for a personality characteristic that even the Prospect is not aware of, providing that it is sincere and can be justified. Remember we all measure our success largely on the praise we receive from others. Some of those characteristics that a Prospect could be projecting are:

| | |
|---|---|
| Aggressive | Alert |
| Assertive | Capable |
| Cautious | Conformist |
| Contemplative | Dominant |
| Energetic | Experienced |
| Imaginative | Important |
| Impressive | Independent |
| Ingenious | Masculine |
| Powerful | Sophisticated |
| Submissive | Successful |

POOR CLASS: The poor have the same psychic needs as others. The difference is that they can't afford all the symbols necessary to define the status that they aspire to. That explains why they occassionally go out and purchase a very expensive TV, clothes, or other high priced item which they obviously cannot afford or need. They, like everyone else, are trying to generate a higher self-image and need the status symbols to define it.

The poor are like the rich, though, in that their emotions can *want* at the highest level even when basic *needs* have not yet been satisfied. The desire to be great is with us all, always. It just needs prompting to action.

MIDDLE CLASS: The middle class conforms to the station that they are trying to project. They don't dare not conform. They are great conformers because they cannot afford NOT to conform: only the rich can do that.

Although everyone wants to be an individual and be different, the degree of difference they will accept in themselves is very narrow. Few people really subscribe to being a non-conformist.

Conformity tends to make life easy. We work and play together in groups, shout together in mobs and huddle together in fear. We want to fit.

There are problems with being different. The spectre of being laughed at, sneered at, left out and unwanted is just too much. Being different invites criticism and that is upsetting.

RICH CLASS: The rich conform to a lesser degree since they are partially defining their own status symbols. Their status symbols are simpler, and more "sophisticated": Wearing a turtle neck sweater with a tuxedo to a black tie affair, while the lady wears basic black and a string of pearls.

The Salesperson must quickly read the Prospect's self-image and show the respect for that level. Preferably we should try to see the highest image that they prefer us to see: The ME I WISH THEY WOULD SEE. Stroke that self-image and you have made a friend and probably a client.

# Wants And Self-Image

These self-images correspond to the upper levels of the pyramid of Wants.

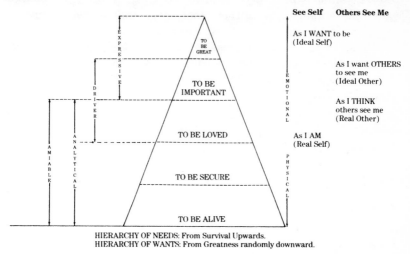

HIERARCHY OF NEEDS: From Survival Upwards.
HIERARCHY OF WANTS: From Greatness randomly downward.

# Selling

## Selling Is a Psychological Science

All during the Selling Process the Salesperson is vitally concerned with the emotional state of the Prospect. From the rather low level of acceptance received when first approaching the Prospect, it is up to the Salesperson to raise the Prospect to the emotional state of wanting to buy the product and do so now. So every step in the Selling Process must be one that conditions the emotions:

| | |
|---|---|
| **ATTENTION** | Develop rapport with a justified compliment. (Strokes the self-image). |
| **INTEREST** | Determine problem (*need*) and reason why they *want* it solved. You have to sell them the problem by showing them the Hurt of it. |
| **CONVICTION** | Discuss the benefits of your product with the Prospect to show them "what is in it for me." Activate the five basic motivators. |
| **DESIRE** | Create a vivid, emotional Visual Image of the Prospect using and enjoying the benefits. |
| **CLOSE** | Weighing the Pros (benefits) against the Cons (tradeoffs) so decisions will be rational. |

## Developing Rapport (Attention)

When you first meet the Prospect and encounter their mental attitude toward you, it is probably one of rejection. The most effective way of gaining acceptance is to pay them a sincere compliment with your reason for saying it. The compliment also serves the double purpose of getting the Prospect to think of themselves in a favorable light. Getting *their* attention by focusing on *them*, is called the ATTENTION step.

## Problem Awareness (Interest)

During the interview you must determine:
The problem the Prospect wants solved.
Their emotional reasons for wanting it solved.

Selected questions from the INTEREST chapter to develop those problems and motives are:

| Purpose | Question To Prospect |
|---------|----------------------|
| Personal | "What is your title?" |
| Personal | "How long have you been here in this position?" |
| Personal | "What is the range of your responsibilities?" |
| Personal | "What part of your position do you like best?" |
| Problem | "What problems does your industry create for you?" |
| Problem | "What help would you normally expect from us?" |
| Problem | "What is keeping you from solving that problem?" |
| Problem | "What are you doing about it??" |
| Payoff | "How would the solution make it easier for you?" |
| Payoff | "What effect would it have on you and your business?" |
| Payoff | *"Why is that important to you?"* |
| Prospect | "Who besides you will be making the decision?" |
| Prospect | "Will you introduce me if you are impressed?" |
| Prospect | "What is your step-by-step decision process?" |
| Peers | "What people problems would you perceive?" |
| Peers | "What will you need to win the support of others?" |
| Priority | "When do you plan on making the decision/change?" |
| Priority | "What is the problem costing you now?" |
| Priority | "What sense of urgency do you feel about solving it?" |

# What's In It For Them (Conviction)

During the CONVICTION step, while you are showing them how the benefits of your product will solve their problem, there is ample opportunity for you to prompt their Want emotions even more:

| I Want to Be: | Typical Comment To Prompt The Emotions |
|---------------|----------------------------------------|
| GREAT | "You deserve the very best, don't you?" |
| IMPORTANT | "That will make you important, won't it?" |
| ACCEPTED | "This will make you popular, won't it?" |
| SECURE | "You want to minimize your ..., don't you?" |
| ALIVE | "You don't want to lose your ..., do you?" |

Building a self-image phrase into the Conviction step benefit may go like this;

**SP** - "This desk is our most functional of the Executive desks. It denotes leadership, effeciency, and authority. It is symbolic of the successful business executive."

What EBM do you think your product will excite? As a matter of procedure we should prompt all five basic Want emotions. Let the Prospect fill in their specific desire, for they will recognize it immediately. If you prompt with:

**SP** - "You want to be the very best, don't you?" They will know what they want to be the best in.

**SP** - "You don't want to suffer any losses, do you?" They will know what their greatest risks are.

To emphasise your product's main benefits you should prompt those emotions that are obvious: Fear sells insurance, medicines and health care, safety devices, maintenance, education; Security sells pension plans, insurance, houses, cars, etc.

As an oversimplification, you can summarize the basic buying motives into this easy to remember grouping (5P's):

| Needs, Wants | Appeal To: | Emotional Buying Motive |
|---|---|---|
| Achievement | Perfection | Excel, be the best, love self. |
| Ego Enhancement | Pride | Self-esteem, importance. |
| Social Acceptance | Pleasure | Being liked, imitation. |
| Security | Price | Easy Gain, Greed. |
| Survival | Protection | Fear of Loss. |

# Status Needs

When the Prospect's problem is based on a status need, they may not tell you about it. Let's find out what makes the Prospect proud. Ask about their accomplishments, early background and modest beginning, ambitions, possessions, reputations, anything that strokes their self-image.

People want things to be right in life. They will glorify the past, for it is safe. They have a tendency to not want to recognize today for what it is. They will often distort, consciously or unconsciously, the real situation to make it look good. Then they will dwell on the future to excuse them from today.

They want someone to tell them that it is alright for them to be the way they are, that what they want is OK. They want someone to agree and fuss over them.

Once you have uncovered the things that make them feel good, compliment them on it. They deserve it.

If you are in the situation where they are happy with their present vendor and there is no real advantage for them to change, all is *not* lost. Remember that you are now in the unique position of being able to satisfy their psychic need, for you found out how to stroke their self-image, and that they do need. We all do.

Having stroked their self-image, go back to the product, ignoring the product satisfaction from their current vendor:

**SP** - "Mr. P, you are now in the fortunate position of being able to choose between two good products to see which has the most benefits for you. The benefits of our product are ..."

Top that off with the most dynamic words in closing a sale;

**SP** - "You deserve it, you've earned it."

... and the sale is yours.

# How To Stroke The Self-Image

We all have a deep seated need for a sense of personal worth and acceptance by others. As such, we have a constant need for stroking.

Of the three levels of emotional well being,

I want to be great.
I want to be important (self-image).
I want to be loved.

... the level that is most productive is in the stroking of the self-image. Once you have prompted the Desire to be Great in the Self Actualization level, and the Desire to be Loved in the Social Acceptance level, you can do little more than remind the Prospect about them, but you can actively stroke their self-image to a feeling of importance.

### The Strongest Motivation: Sincerely Stroking The Self-Image

Stroking the self-image is the key to the door of the Prospect's emotions. The door is open and you are welcome because they want you to see, honor and enhance their self-image. Once inside you can satisfy their wants by justifying them with needs.

In many cases the need for recognition and self-image stroking is a far greater need than the product itself. How many Prospects have bought on that basis? Have you?

The Purchasing Agent is a special case in that the only appeal you can make is an emotional appeal. This is quite contrary to popular opinion wherein the Prospect was considered to be only after the best deal. True, the Purchasing Agent should get a good deal because the lowest price is expected of a Purchasing Agent. But what are their real Wants? They want:

- The admiration of their superiors.
- Recognition for selecting quality products.
- Increased security because of their wise decisions.
- The automatic pride pumping from the expected low price.
- Keeping yourself equal or better than your competition so they won't be embarrassed for not buying the best.

We crave recognition for our qualities and achievements. It is most satisfying when someone comes along and SINCERELY comments favorably about us or our actions. We all want to be appreciated, to feel important, to be recognized, to have the approval and attention of others.

Long ago, man discovered how powerful compliments were in manipulating people. Because of its immense power, it quickly came into wide use, abuse, and finally disuse. It was even honored with its own name flattery. All of our lives we have been afraid to say something nice to others although deserved. That's why we are starved for affection and recognition.

Wouldn't it be wonderful if there were an easy way to pay a compliment and never have it slip into insincere flattery? Well there is; simply justify the compliment.

Most people deserve some recognition. You just have to be smart in spotting their positive qualities and accomplishments. Identify them, show your admiration and you win a friend. When the compliment is above their projected self-image, something they are unsure of, or never before admired, they'll love you.

Self-image is the most sensitive feeling a Prospect has that is accessible to the Salesperson. Show it the respect that it deserves and you'll be well received. Stroke it positively and they will like you. Ignore it or show it disrespect and you will be rejected. It is as simple as that.

# Pride

The most important quest a Prospect has is the maintenance, expansion, and especially the defense of their self-image. Most personal conflicts in life stem from the bruising of someone's self-image. Rejection by Prospects is largely because you didn't acknowledge and stroke their self-image soon enough, or at all.

The defender of their self-image is PRIDE, probably the greatest of buying motivators if you can use your product to nourish it. People will do almost anything, even risk their lives, to defend and enhance their self-image or pride. Handle it carefully, and don't take advantage of them.

Such is the success of the Selling Process once the Salesperson strokes the self-image, finds out the Wants, creates a vivid mind picture of the Prospect enjoying the product, and shows them admiration for their wise decision.

## Amiable (Relater)

**Intent:** To be Supportive
**Key:** Possessive
**Motto:** What do you want?
**Wants:** Peer Attention
**Time:** Now is never

### Personality Factors:

- Needs people
- Listener
- Status Quo
- No risks
- No pressure
- Counselor
- Questioning
- Insecure
- Supportive
- No goals
- No conflict
- Soft hearted

## Expressive (Socializer)

**Intent:** To persuade
**Key:** Their ego
**Motto:** Let's do it!
**Wants:** Applause for greatness
**Time:** Now is next week

### Personality Factors:

- Dreamer
- Unrealistic goals
- Creative
- Flighty
- Need approval
- Generalizes
- Persuasive
- Loves people
- Opinionated
- Fast decisions
- Excitable
- Enthusiastic

## Low Assertiveness
Avoids Risks
Needs To Follow

## High Assertiveness
(Job Oriented)
Fast Tempo, Must Dominate

## Analytical (Thinker)

**Intent:** To avoid trouble
**Key:** Preciseness
**Motto:** Get the facts
**Wants:** Activity
**Time:** Now is next month

### Personality Factors:

- Planners
- Details
- Slow decisions
- Technical
- Must be right
- Conservative
- Organizers
- Low pressure
- Logical
- Precise
- Problem solver
- Persistent

## Driver (Director)

**Intent:** To overcome
**Key:** Impulsive and impatient
**Motto:** Get it done, yesterday
**Wants:** Results
**Time:** Now is now

### Personality Factors:

- Goal oriented
- Impatient
- Task oriented
- Workaholic
- Demanding
- Decisive
- Time effective
- Blunt
- Administrative
- Opinionated
- Innovative
- Tough

## Low Responsiveness
Cold. Disciplined
No Interest In People

168

# Personalities

## Prospect Personalities

It is essential that you understand the kind of decision making process your Prospect goes through. That process is specific for each type of personality. If the Prospect is the Analytical type, a controller for example, the decision process is long and slow, very carefully studied, and must be completely free of risk. Hardly a desirable or viable business opportunity for a Salesperson. So the controller, although vitally interested in cost controls and easy to meet, may not be a closable Prospect for your kind of product.

It is estimated that 2/3 of all sales interviews are made to the wrong person for whatever reason. Herein lies a powerful reason for careful prospecting. Ask yourself/them if they have a real problem now or are they merely keeping in touch with the market; if they have budget responsibility for your product; if they are interviewing for someone else; if it is at their manager's request, or is it on their own speculation. You are now going to meet some of these "wrong" people and how to work with them if you must. Many will interview but few have the need or the authority to buy.

## Basic Personalities

Your personality is the net effect you have on others. How you behave towards others depends on your attitude. Although attitude and personality are two different entities, the manifestation of attitudes is seen by others as your "personality". Therefore, it is crucial that your attitude be acceptable to others if relationships are to be positive.

There are two key factors that reveal a person's attitude towards others:

RESPONSIVENESS: the desire to make a friend.

ASSERTIVENESS: the desire to control other people.

## Net Personalities

Everyone has degrees of both responsiveness and assertiveness. Without administering a psychological test, it is difficult to accurately measure the extent of either. It is possible, though, to observe the personality traits and estimate the degree of responsiveness and assertiveness in each person.

The summary chart depicts the resultant personalities of varying degrees of responsiveness and assertiveness. The mixture results in four distinct personalities; the Expressive, Driver, Analytical, and Amiable. Because they vary in degree it is possible and probable for a personality to be blends of each, eg, an Expressive and a Driver, an Expressive and an Amiable, etc, but not its opposite the Analytical. An oversimplification that is quite meaningful is that a responsive person is people oriented, while an assertive is job or task oriented.

The identifiable traits of each characteristic are:

| **RESPONSIVENESS:** | | **ASSERTIVENESS:** | |
|---|---|---|---|
| HIGH | LOW | HIGH | LOW |
| Relaxed | Formal | No time. | Excess of time. |
| Warm | Proper | Uses people. | Serves others. |
| Informal | Guarded | Works for goals. | Hides behind work. |

# Expressive (Socializer)

■ INTENT: TO PERSUADE (SELL)
■ KEY: THEIR EGO
■ MOTTO: LET'S DO IT!
■ WANTS: APPLAUSE FOR GREATNESS
■ TIME: NOW IS NEXT WEEK

■ A dreamer often with unrealistic goals.
■ Needs much approval and compliments.
■ Loves an audience and groups.
■ Creative ideas and dreams come easily.
■ Outgoing, persuasive and gregarious.
■ Friendly, enthusiastic and spontaneous.
■ Generates and projects confidence.
■ Has the image of the "natural Salesperson".

- Poised and meets people easily.
- Flighty, and moves from one project to another.
- Thinks quickly, makes decisions quickly.
- Acts on opinions, hunches, and intuition.
- Misjudges people because of trust.
- Often makes wrong decisions.
- Often generalizes, exaggerates, or disregards facts.
- Strives to make opinions and beliefs prevail.
- Joins groups for prestige and personal recognition.
- Ego is all over office - you know who lives there.

## Selling An Expressive (Easy To Sell)

- Easy to sell because in the emotional state of mind.
- Get them talking about themselves and their goals.
- Enjoys talking about themselves so listen and probe.
- Focus on how to make their dreams come true.
- Simply jump on their dreams with them.
- Discuss their opinions, ideas, and dreams, but not facts.
- "Nut and bolt" details bore them quickly.
- Expressives forget detail, you cover it later.
- Be entertaining, they have no patience for the bore.
- Do not hurry the discussion, they enjoy conversation.
- They want special attention from Salespeople.
- The new, different and novel excites this person.
- Don't be conservative, develop new ideas boldly.
- Try to explore alternative solutions together.
- Involve other happy clients in your stories.
- Will buy quick even without a formal proposal.
- Get them to initial a penciled agreement *now*.

# Driver (Director)

- INTENT: TO OVERCOME (CONQUER)
- KEY: IMPULSIVE AND IMPATIENT
- MOTTO: GET IT DONE - YESTERDAY
- WANTS: RESULTS
- TIME: NOW IS NOW

- Likes to control other people and situations.
- Likes to be the center of the stage.
- High achiever with good administrative skills.
- Thrives on challenges and competition.
- An individualist, self-starter and self-sufficient.
- Discontented and dissatisfied with status quo.

171

- Prefers variety, the unusual, and adventurous.
- Oriented toward productivity and bottom line results.
- Likes to move at a fast pace, impatient with delays.
- Expresses opinion quickly and vocally.
- Exhibits firmness in relations with others.
- Direct, positive, blunt and straight forward.
- Works well under pressure, makes things happen.
- Decisive in actions and decisions.
- Controls many things at the same time.
- Has a tendency to become a workaholic.
- Demanding of themselves and others.
- Susceptible to stress.
- On phone a lot, papers all about, a crisis climate.
- Closed minded: "What can you do for me that others can't?"
- Very goal oriented, fights hard for own way.
- At times stubborn, impatient, and tough.
- Accepts momentary defeat, holds no grudge.

## Selling a Driver (Normal To Sell)

- Be prepared to get to your points quickly.
- Assure Driver that time will not be wasted.
- You must be precise, effective and organized.
- Hit quick and hard because they are impulsive.
- Be firm and sure of yourself.
- Stress "What's in it for them and company".
- Focus your conversation around the Driver's goals.
- Prepare solution with clearly defined pros and cons.
- Back up your facts with solid proof.
- Provide the Driver with options for a sound decision.
- After sale, confirm that the benefits are as planned.

# Analytical (Thinker)

- INTENT: TO AVOID TROUBLE (CAUTIOUS)
- KEY: PRECISENESS AND ORGANIZATION
- MOTTO: GET THE FACTS
- WANTS: ACTIVITY
- TIME: NOW IS NEXT MONTH

- Has a strong desire to be right.
- Will adapt to situation to avoid conflict.
- Polite but indifferent.
- Cautious, conservative diplomat.

- Sometimes aloof, picky, and critical.
- Planner and organizer, proceeds in orderly manner.
- Precise and attentive to detail.
- Tends to follow established procedures.
- Environment neatly organized and structured.
- An over-reliance on data collection.
- Persistent, systematic problem solvers.
- "Show me" attitude, must see things in writing.
- Will stall decisions until facts are all in.
- Will go to your competitors for bids.
- Decisions mostly logical, little emotion.
- Once mind is made up can be very rigid.
- Surrounded by heavy objects as a protection.
- Precise, needs facts, and logic.
- Love charts and graphs.

## Selling The Analytical (Difficult To Sell)

- They ask many questions, desire information.
- Study their needs in a logical, practical manner.
- Chart the benefits for them.
- Be systematic, exact, organized and prepared.
- Support their organized, thoughtful approach.
- Will ask you for lots of factual evidence.
- Document how your product has helped others.
- List the advantages and disadvantages.
- Don't overstate their benefits.
- Suspicious of anything that looks too perfect.
- Be prepared to answer all of their questions.
- Show them how to track the results.
- The more numbers you present the better.
- Don't use a gimmick for a fast close.
- Give them a step by step timetable.
- Do not rush their decision making.
- Send followup letter on benefits and commitment.
- Assure them service will be thorough and excellent.

# Amiable (Relater)

- INTENT: TO BE SUPPORTIVE (PREDICTABLE)
- KEY: POSSESSIVENESS
- MOTTO: WHAT DO YOU THINK?
- WANTS: PEER ATTENTION
- TIME: NOW IS NEVER

- They love to be loved.
- Seek security and belongings.
- Warm, supportive and reliable.
- Sometimes seen as soft-hearted.
- Dislikes the pressure of deadlines.
- Dislike conflicts, may say what others want to hear.
- Seldom argues or openly criticizes.
- Will ask questions and is a great listener.
- Conceals feelings from others, will hold grudge.
- Very security conscious and lacks goals.
- Enjoys the known and controllable, dislikes change.
- Like to help others - excellent counseling skills.
- Slow in decisions because they fear what others will think.
- Traditionally a buck passer instead of a decision maker.
- Once under way works steadily and patiently.
- Need a lot of reassurance.

## Selling The Amiable (Very Difficult To Sell)

- Spend lot of time in the rapport buildings step.
- Take them out to lunch, get into their personal life.
- Project that you are interested in them as a person.
- Try to find out their personal goals, if any.
- Try to support their feelings.
- Study their personal needs as well as business.
- Offer personal assurance of support.
- Show them that there is minimal risk.
- Don't rush them - do offer your guidance.

## Classifying Prospect Personality

When you first approach a Prospect, quickly evaluate their people: job ratio to determine the type of personality you will be working with. All during the Rapport building step be very observant of the warmth of their personality, for this will be the key to working with them. Remember, too, that you must adjust to and blend into their personality.

You can improve your odds by doing a little pre-meeting homework. Call the Prospect's secretary and ask what type of person you are dealing with in terms of time pressure, need for detail, decision making, apparent needs; also whether anyone else will be attending your meeting with the Prospect, what they are like, and who the decision influencers are. From that you will be able to estimate the personality in advance and prepare accordingly.

You will be making your initial evaluation on the basis of the reception they give you:

**Responsiveness Behavior:**

The easy way to classify a personality is to measure their "people warmth" on the verticle axis *first*. On a scale of 1 to 10, 10 being high, how warm are they?

When warm, they enjoy people for the sake of the people; when they are cool, they see a person only as a means to their own end.

**Assertiveness Behavior:**

After you have evaluated their people-warmth (and most Americans are on the cool side), now measure their assertiveness, their desire to control others.

When they are cool toward people, deciding between a Driver and an Analytical is easy; the difference is in their *time* pressure: the Driver has no time while the Analytical has an excess of time.

When they are warm to people, deciding between Expressives and Amiables takes longer because their key difference, goals, can take longer to evaluate. Their surroundings are the early clues. An Expressive's ego shows everywhere; in the clothes they wear, their appearance, their car, their office, their business title, their awards and their self-confidence.

The Amiables are known for their lack of goals so their surroundings tend to be people oriented, rather than *success* oriented.

This evaluation should be made during the first few minutes. Although subject to refinement, your first impression is probably the correct one.

# Identifying Factors:

|          | Expressive   | Driver     | Analytical | Amiable       |
|----------|--------------|------------|------------|---------------|
| **Thinks:**  | Who?         | What?      | How?       | Why?          |
| **Wants:**   | Applause     | Results    | Details    | Approval      |
| **To Sell:** | Personal     | Benefits   | Systems    | Support       |
| **Decor:**   | Many Styles  | Organized  | Work Area  | Informal      |
| **Walls:**   | Ego Photos   | Awards     | Charts     | People Photos |
| **Desk:**    | (Varies)     | Neat Piles | Organized  | People Items  |
| **Seating:** | Close        | Power      | Functional | Cozy          |

**WARNING:** Be careful in evaluating office decor. It is a great indicator of the work side of a personality IF it is not modified by company policy (cleanup every night, etc.), controlled by their neat secretary, or maybe it's not even their office.

# Emphasis In
# The Selling Process

|             | Expressive | Driver | Analytical | Amiable |
|-------------|------------|--------|------------|---------|
| **Rapport** | *          |        |            | ****    |
| **Questions** |          | *      | ***        |         |
| **Proof**   |            |        | *          | ****    |
| **Desire**  | *          | **     | ***        | ****    |
| **Want**    |            |        | ***        | ****    |

# Potentials Of Salespeople

|            | **Strengths** | **Weaknesses** |
|------------|---------------|----------------|
| **Expressive** | Very persuasive | Too optimistic |
|            | Very self-confident | Promises too much |
|            | Enthusiastic | Talks too much |
|            | Natural Salesperson | Poor listener |
|            | Motivates others | Hurt by rejection |
| **Driver** | Good prospector | Dominates interview |
|            | Pressures to close | Talks too fast |
|            | Loves incentives | May intimidate |
|            | Must be a winner | Promise too much |
|            | Aggressive | Service inadequate |
|            | Persistent | Implusive |
|            | Closes often | Impatient |
|            | Hard Worker |  |
| **Analytical** | Well prepared | Long presentation |
|            | Technically competent | Confuses Prospect |
|            | Good followup | Rejection hurts |
|            | Good service | Not competitive |
|            | Diplomatic | Too cautious |
| **Amiable** | Likeable | Won't prospect |
|            | Good listener | Inflexible |
|            | Good teacher | Dull and boring |
|            | Well prepared | Weak on objections |
|            | Excellent service | Resists change |
|            |  | Very possessive |

# Personality Conflicts

## Salesperson vs Prospect

**EXPRESSIVE SP:** Love people, success. Innovative. Details bore.

**DRIVER P:**
Time & job
oriented.
Be businesslike. Don't waste time with small talk.

**ANALYTICAL P:**
Love detail
and proof.
Earn trust before becoming too friendly or
you will turn them off. They want product
knowledge. Minimize the socializing.

**AMIABLE P:**
Love people
and proof.
Difficult for you. They won't like your excessive
socializing. Give them personal assurances. They
are very insecure.


**DRIVER SP:** Driving, job oriented. Low on people and details.

**EXPRESSIVE P:**
Love people
and success.
Build a lot of rapport. Less emphasis in business.
You'll like the Expressive.

**ANALYTICAL P:**
Love detail
and proof.
Slow down. They want details, order and control.
Give them assurance. Give time to digest. Don't
like the new.

**AMIABLE P:**
Love people
and proof.
Give lots of facts and proof. Take it real easy.
Slow to make decisions. Be a friend. Don't
pressure.


**ANALYTICAL SP:** Steady and dependable. Easily discouraged.

**EXPRESSIVE P:**
Love people
and success.
You won't like their friendliness. Keep the facts
to a minimum. Don't bore. Be warm. Be innovative.

**DRIVER P:**
Time & Job
oriented.
Show confidence. Don't be intimidated. Be time
efficient. Stick to the high points.

**AMIABLE P:**
Love people
and proof.
Stress the proof and assurances. They are
skeptical.

| | | | | |
|---|---|---|---|---|
| **AMIABLE SP:** | Like facts, established products. Friendly, Well organized. Insecure. | | | |
| **EXPRESSIVE P:** Love people and success. | Hit the high points. Go easy on facts. Be friendly. Be innovative. | | | |
| **DRIVER P:** Time & job oriented. | Don't overwhelm with facts, just the high points. | | | |
| **ANALYTICAL P:** Love detail and proof. | Slow down so they can digest. Don't be pushy. Socialize a little. | | | |

# Salespeople Personalities

## Sales Performance By Personality

| | Expressive | Driver | Analytical | Amiable |
|---|---|---|---|---|
| **Aggressive** | Verbally | Overly | Defensively | Passively |
| **Prospecting** | Good | Will try | Wants Leads | Too shy |
| **Preparation** | Broad-brush | Too brief | Too detailed | No priority |
| **Approach** | Wordy | Blunt | Detailed | Systematic |
| **Excitement** | High | Average | Low | Low |
| **Confidence** | High | Average | Low | Low |
| **Presentation** | Broad-brush (Colorful) | Strong (Brief) | Accurate (Overwhelming) | Factual (Dull) |
| **Objections** | Snow job | Argue | Logics | Wanders |
| **Close** | Wordy | Fast | Hesitant | None |
| **Service** | None | None | Good | Excellent |
| **Paperwork** | Errors | Late | Wordy | Timely |

To clearly define your Prospect's personality, check off their observable characteristics as listed below and take it to a Psychologist or contact this publisher for interpretation:

| | | | |
|---|---|---|---|
| Achieving | Distant | Industrious | Quiet |
| Aggressive | Domineering | Influential | Rebellious |
| Ambitious | Dramatic | Inquisitive | Reserved |
| Analytical | Easy-going | Insensitive | Resourceful |
| Apologizing | Emotional | Intellectual | Responsive |
| Apprehensive | Encouraging | Jovial | Revengeful |
| Argumentative | Enterprising | Logical | Rigid |
| Assertive | Entertaining | Methodical | Sarcastic |
| Autonomous | Enthusiastic | Neat | Secretive |
| Capable | Excitable | Obliging | Self-critical |
| Carefree | Fearful | Orderly | Self-reliant |
| Cautious | Flashy | Organized | Sensitive |
| Charitable | Flexible | Out-going | Serious |
| Comforting | Forceful | Perceptive | Sociable |
| Competitive | Friendly | Perfectionist | Spontaneous |
| Consistent | Frivolous | Persevering | Suspicious |
| Controlling | Fun-loving | Persistent | Sympathetic |
| Cooperative | Hasty | Persuasive | Systematic |
| Courteous | Helpful | Plans | Takes risks |
| Curious | Helpless | Practical | Teasing |
| Defensive | Hostile | Precise | Trusting |
| Definite | Humble | Prompt | Unconventional |
| Dependent | Impatient | Proper | Unpredictable |
| Detail-minded | Impulsive | Pushy | Wary |
| Determined | Inconsistent | Quarrelsome | Worries |
| Disciplined | Independent | Quick-thinking | |

# Epilogue

Being able to blend into their personality will always be a great aid in effective selling for you are selling people and people relationships, rather than products.

## Chapter Thirteen

# Appointments
## Finding Wanting Prospects

# Secrets

- ☐ Selling is predicated on finding WANTING Prospects.
- ☐ Prospecting is the greatest challenge a Salesperson faces.
- ☐ It must be systematic and penetrating to be effective.
- ☐ Often ignored in a boom, no one is trained for a recession.
- ☐ Referrals are excellent because of the endorsement.
- ☐ Direct mail makes them aware of needs not realized.
- ☐ Advance letter prompts interest and credibility.
- ☐ Stir up curiosity, not too little nor too much.
- ☐ Keen interest will create time for the Prospect to listen.
- ☐ They lack sufficient information to refuse discussing it.
- ☐ In Business, many can say No but few can say Yes.
- ☐ The Buffer is part of your selling and their buying process.
- ☐ Recruit the Buffer for their help in your selling effort.
- ☐ You must cold call if you want new Prospects.
- ☐ The odds are great against selling to a non-decision maker.
- ☐ Always start at the top to find the decision maker.
- ☐ You seldom go wrong when you start at the top.
- ☐ Starting at the top saves time for everyone.
- ☐ If the Buffer shows interest, so may the Prospect.

- ☐ Recruit the Buffer for their help in selling.
- ☐ Buffers can assist in the pre-approach and follow-up.
- ☐ Ask Prospect for 3 pros and cons of present product.

# Wanted: Wanting Prospects

The entire Selling Process is predicated on finding WANTING Prospects. New Prospects come from two sources:

(1) Referrals, and
(2) Cold Calling:
    (a) Personal visits.
    (b) "Warm" phone calls.
    (c) Direct Mail campaign.

Who to call depends on the use of your product. If you have a general use product, contact everyone by one means or another. If you have a special use product, you will have to dig out Prospects from directories, business journals, wherever. A special use product may cause some frustration in finding new Prospects but it will be most gratifying to the Salesperson, both emotionally and financially, to discover or develop a new user. That's Creative selling.

Selling that involves eyeball to eyeball contact requires meetings. Since most Prospects offer resistence to buying, selling skills are required to establish the sales meeting. (If Prospects didn't resist buying, Salespeople would not be required).

There is no best method for ferreting out wanting buyers for any product for it depends as much on the kind of product as it does on the kind of Prospect. All methods should be used, with the emphasis on those producing the best results. Continuously upgrade each method with your creativity.

# Referrals

An excellent method of prospecting is a referral from a happy Client, or even a happy Prospect who is favorably impressed but can't buy from you presently. A Referral is the best because you also have a personal endorsement on the most important aspect of selling, YOU:

**SP** - "Frank, it is very nice being associated with you in business. I would like to have more clients like you. To that end, would you refer me to

182

someone you know who may have a need for my product? I'm going to describe an associate of yours and as soon as a name and face come to mind, stop me and tell me who you are thinking of." (Then you describe your typical Prospect. They give you a name.) "Fine. If they were to come along right now, would you introduce them to me knowing I would probably want to talk to them about my product? You would? I appreciate that very much. Frank, I wonder if you would mind doing something else that is a little different. Would you write a brief introduction of me on the back of your business card and give me their address?"

Make the description of your typical Prospect long enough to give your friend at least 30 seconds to think while you are talking. That allows their subconscious mind to come into play.

Another approach is to ask for an area referral:

**SP** - "Frank, I will be visiting other people in this area. Let me ask you a question: If you were me, who would you call on?"

**P** - "Carl McLeod over at the ABC Company."

**SP** - "Why did you select him?" (This gives you pre-approach information of their Needs, personality, etc).

When you phone the Prospect, don't waste time introducing yourself. Rather, present the referral in such a way that you create curiosity:

**SP** - "Mr. McLeod?"

**P** - "Yes."

**SP** - "Mr. Carl McLeod?"

**P** - "Yes."

**SP** - "Carl, you don't know me but we have a mutual friend in Frank Smith. Frank suggested that I give you a call when I am in this area. He feels that we may have an idea and benefit for you that worked well for him. Would this afternoon or tomorrow be better for you?"

Later on when you personally visit the Prospect:

**SP** - "Carl, I was visiting with Frank Smith over at the XYZ Company. When I asked Frank who he would suggest might have a need for our product he said you would. Let me ask you this, why do you think he suggested you?"

# Cold Calls

Cold calling means arranging a meeting with a new Prospect. Whether you contact the Propsect in person, by letter, or phone depends on several factors. Each method has its advantages. Under what circumstances is it better to cold call in person or by phone?

**IN PERSON:**

Less likely to be brushed off.

Can read the Prospect's body language.

Qualify Prospect with visual appraisal.

Personal appeal of Salesperson is utilized.

Maybe a spot presentation can be made.

Can make an appointment for a later date.

Can use visuals and demonstrate.

When the Salesperson doesn't like phones.

**BY PHONE:**

You can reach more Prospects faster.

Can separate Suspects from Prospects.

Determine Prospect's need in advance.

Save on transportation dollars.

Saves time in travel and waiting.

Saves time from cancelled meetings.

Can market your product everywhere.

East-West time zones expand selling day.

Weather is rarely a problem.

Can use scripts and take notes.

Your information is at your finger tips.

Phone calls often gets instant attention.

Can get to the point without offense.

Appearance can be at one's own comfort.

Physical handicaps won't interfere.

# Personal Visits

The typical cold call in person is to an office building or Industrial Park where there is a high concentration of likely users. The advantage is that you can contact a great number of potential Prospects with virtually no travel time. In large cities that time saving can be substantial.

When the building complex is large enough it may justify a full time Salesperson working solely that building. Not only is travel time reduced, so is all future service time. The Salesperson can also give the potential Prospect additional service attention over a long period of time. In time, almost every viable Prospect can be yours.

The efficiency of this type of prospecting depends almost entirely on the kind of product you sell. For example, photocopy paper will probably be a successful program since most offices use the product, and since the product is relatively low in value no senior decision will be required. When you are offering a "door-to-door" special discount, your sales should be especially rewarding.

The ingredients in successfull door-to-door selling are:
- Standard product - little risk for the Prospect.
- Low level, low risk decision - easy to buy.
- No hassle of change - no impact on personnel.
- Staple product - almost everyone uses it.

When selling a service the same rules apply, and the more they apply the easier it is to sell the service.

Canvassing in person can be used for searching out Prospects, qualifying them and arranging meetings as well as on-the-spot selling.

Generally, the greater your product impacts on the organization, the more selling required and at higher decision levels.

Let's take photocopy machines as an example. Virtually every business requires some sort of photocopy machine. The sales potential is:
- First machine sale.
- Replacement.
- Upgrade.

On first approaching a Prospect, or Suspect, you should do a mini survey of their present situation. Talk to a person who uses the product often:
- "Do you have a photocopy machine now?" (If not, you have a real opportunity in CREATIVE selling.)
- "How long have they had it?" (If it is old, you have an opportunity for REPLACEMENT selling.)
- "Have you outgrown it?" (A compliment that suggests the need to UPGRADE because of their growth. That gives you information on whether it is working well and if it does the job intended.)

If you are not happy with one Prospect's response try another; remember, they all have different needs and wants.

## Identify The Decision Maker

Given a positive response to the survey questions, go to the next step: Identify the decision maker.

Identifying the decision maker is critically important. If you get the wrong person you will not only waste time, but more important that wrong person may block you from meeting with the real decision maker, since they may be a decision influencer. Many have the authority to say No, few can say Yes.

The correct way to identify the decision maker is to start at the top with the President or their Buffer. The advantages of starting at the top are:

It saves time for everyone.

You need the Buffer's help in selling.

They always know the position responsibilities.

Top will know clients who reciprocate sales.

New ideas get to the decision makers quickly.

Company can select the kind of vendors they want.

Only you can present your product accurately.

You can get abused by unnecessary rejection.

Top can answer your questions freely.

Only decision makers can manipulate budgets.

Non decision makers will stall indefinitely.

Reluctant decision makers are near the bottom.

A "No" from a low level may block you from the top.

Ask them to "take me to your leader" or at least their Executive Secretary. When you meet the secretary you have to excite that person with a Probable Problem statement so they will see the value in arranging a meeting with the decision maker.

**SP** - "Ms. Secretary, we have just learned that you really need a new copier and we believe we can save you $x,xxx on the finest machine available. Would you introduce me to the decision maker please?"

Whether the Secretary introduces you personally or refers you, you have an endorsement from the President's office to the person who will make the decision.

Here is how to introduce yourself to the referred decision maker by phone:

**SP** - "Mr. Decision maker?"

**P** - "Yes."

**SP** - "I have been referred to you by your President's office to begin a study on the possible replacement of your present copier. Would Wednesday afternoon or Friday morning be better for a brief meeting?"

# The "Buffer"

Every business person receives many calls from Salespeople trying to sell their products. If the business person accepted all such calls, they would materially cut into their time and probably to no avail.

In a well managed business, screening should be expected. Only the most professional Salespeople should be allowed to use the Prospect's staff on a proposal. Hence a Buffer.

You should consider the Buffer as a part of their decision-making process. If you are not able to impress the Buffer with their wider range of idea acceptance, you are probably not going to be able to interest the decision maker either. Enlist the Buffer's interest with a Question Suggesting a Need (QSN), then ask for their help.

The Buffer's job is not to sort skilled Salespeople from amateurs, but rather to sort out those who seem to have items of current interest for their company. The Buffer will usually know of the urgently needed products as well as the company's general interests. They will probably respond to any creative offer or benefit.

When your product is not urgently needed, you must make them aware of a general problem that you can solve for them. Successful appointment making depends on your ability to create initial interest in the Buffer as well as the Prospect.

Salespeople often have a tendency to look down on, and even despise, the Buffer as a necessary evil. In reality, the Buffer is not only a necessary part of *their* decision-making process, but *your* Selling Process as well. The Buffer can be of great help in setting up the meeting, giving you pre-approach information on the decision maker, advice on how to conduct your sales interview, follow up, and even be instrumental in affecting the decision in your favor.

When you are confronted by the Buffer's inquiry as to the nature of the call, take the Buffer into your selling sphere:

**SP** - "Ms. Buffer, if there were a way... for your company to reduce your losses in..., Mr. President would probably want to know more about it, wouldn't he?"

**SP** - "Ms. Buffer, we have an exciting new solution to a problem that has been troubling your industry for a long time. We are quite sure Mr. Prospect would want to hear about it. When would be the best time to call him to arrange an interview?"

The Buffer will either:
- Put you through now.
- Tell you the best time to call.
- Suggest you send a letter.
- Suggest a different decision maker.
- Declare that the Prospect is not interested.

It is true that some Buffers may be caustic to you. That can happen in any company. The best approach is to warm them up with a few kind remarks:

**SP** - "Ms. Buffer, I can see that you, like your President, are extremely busy. We believe this is really important to your company. When would be the best time for me to call to explain it to YOU?"

Remember you are selling people and people relationships, not products alone. You are only using the product to solve the problem.

If the Buffer asks you to send a letter, then do so. The letter should be brief and full of suspense:

"Dear Mr. (President),

Your secretary, Ms. Buffer, asked that we send you this letter outlining our proposal. Your industry has been troubled lately with a serious problem in ... We have an exciting solution to this problem that you will certainly appreciate.

Please ask Ms. Buffer to expect a call from me next week to arrange a 15 minute general interest interview.

Sincerely, (Salesperson)"

The letter is short, concise and cordial. Also, it is suspenseful. If the letter were to carry all the details, either in text or with an enclosed brochure, they wouldn't need you; they have enough information to pre-judge without you; thus no interview.

When you talk to the Prospect don't try to sell them unless they are the only person that can be involved. If others can be involved, the President will probably delegate it to someone on their staff to do a preliminary investigation:

**P** - "Why do you want to see me?"

**SP** - "To get your blessing for an idea that we have in mind."

**P**- "What do you have in mind?"

**SP** - "We have a new idea in ... that may just work for you. In order to conserve your time we would want someone on your staff to look over the feasibility of it before we present it to you. They may very well be able to make the decision but it is better if it fits with your thinking. Who should we contact about it?"

**P** - "John Doe over in Operations."

**SP** - "Great. May we keep an open line so you can follow the progress?"

**P** - "Sure."

**SP** - "Fine. I'll call you in about 2 weeks."

... and off you go to John Doe with top management involvement.

If you continue to have trouble getting through to the busy Prospect, ask their Buffer for help in setting up the meeting:

**SP** - "Ms. Buffer, we are having trouble finding a time to talk to Mr. Prospect. Can you help us find a convenient time? What does their schedule look like over the next week?"

Once you have the interview arranged, send a very brief letter confirming it. Stress that you want to keep the meeting short; this keeps the Prospect from rescheduling you into oblivion; it is also very professional and you gain respect.

You can be accomplishing other goals during these discussions with Ms. Buffer:

1. Building rapport with Ms. Buffer.
2. Qualifying the Prospect by questioning the Buffer.
3. Ms. Buffer's advice on how Mr. Prospect would like the meeting conducted, their style of management, needs, wants, etc.

# "Warm" Calls

Whenever possible have a reason to call other than, "I just happened to get your name off a list". That reason could be a referral, a follow up on direct mail or a personalized letter. Having some prior event to reference makes the phone call "warm" and personal.

Advance direct mail has the distinct advantage that it can make them aware of a Need not realized. The letter can perform many functions:

- Prompt their need for it.
- Arouse their interest.
- Convince them of the benefit.
- Create a desire to own it.
- Stimulate them to action, or
- Await your phone call.

Finding Wanting Prospects will always be the most difficult job in selling. Wanting SUSPECTS proliferate in great numbers; witness the high proportion of sales presentations (2/3) being made to the wrong person. Better to spend that time searching for those Prospects that count. Having superior selling skills is of no avail when they fall on non-buying ears, yet most Salespeople have an aversion to a continuous, systematic system of prospecting.

# Wanting Prospects

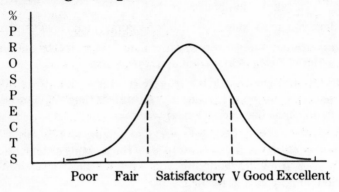

**Prospect Satisfaction**

At any given time, Prospects will be experiencing service from their vendors that ranges Poor to Excellent. No one knows how many would fall in each category, but a reliable approximation can be found in the classical normal bell-shaped distribution curve.

You can expect the following distribution of Prospects:

| | |
|---|---|
| Excellent | 5% |
| Very Good | 15% |
| Satisfactory | 60% |
| Fair | 15% |
| Poor | 5% |

The exactness of these numbers will never be known, nor will they be constant for any given area, time of year, or whatever. What is constant is that 10-20% of all Prospects are so happy with their present vendor that your chance of closing is near zero regardless of how receptive they are to your presentations. The sales attitude, "I'm going to sell them if it is the last thing I do", might very well be a self-fulfilling prophecy.

Also constant is that about two thirds of all Prospects are reasonably satisfied (Satisfactory 60%) with their present vendor. They are open to change, but it is a low priority unless you make it exciting.

Of vital interest is the 10 - 20% of those who are unhappy and ripe for a sale. These are the Prospects that need you, want your product, will be open to an interview, will not offer much resistence and probably won't do much competitive shopping. They are a WANTING PROSPECT, the only kind you should see. The big trick is in finding them. This should be your greatest effort, for your success in selling is more dependent on your ability to find Wanting Prospects than on your selling skills.

FINDING WANTING PROSPECTS: Given that the biggest secret to sales success is finding Wanting Prospects, how do you actually do it? In it's simplest form you phone survey your Prospects. Start at the top because the senior staff tend to be the most courteous, helpful and knowledgeable of their needs, know the decision makers and their degree of satisfaction. If you can do it as a blind Market Research program the data will be less biased and the Prospect more cooperative:

**SP** - "President's office please?"

**Buffer** - "Mr. Smith's office."

**SP** - "May I speak to the Executive Secretary, please?"

**Buffer** - "This is she."

**SP** - "This is D. Forbes Ley of Forbes and Associates, a Market Research firm conducting a study on the use of ... We will be sending to your personal attention a gift of ... for your cooperation. Do you have a moment to answer 10 brief questions?"

**Buffer** - "Yes I do."

**SP** -:

(1) "Do you presently use a ... (Product) ... ?"
(Will Replacement or Creative selling be required?)

(2) "How much/many do you use per month/year?"
(Qualifies the Prospect as to size or volume.)

(3) "Who is the decision maker for that product?"

(4) "What are the 3 things you like most about your vendor?"
(These points are the *competition* you must overcome.)

(5) "What are the 3 things you would like to see improved?"
(Your Opportunities, or Specific Interest or Problem, SIP.)

(6) "On a scale of 1 to 10 how would you rate them?"
(Gives you an overall rating of your expected success.)

(7) "Who/what vendor/product are you presently using?"
(The chance to develop your competitive advantages.)

They should be few and easy, certainly no more than ten.

With those questions you have found most of the vital information you need to know about a Prospect. The one important question you couldn't ask is about the people relationships, ie, the politics, but you will get that in the interview.

The greatness of the survey is that is can be done by non-Salespeople, even the handicapped, since product knowledge is not required. The method generates low cost, Wanting Prospects, and works as well on Consumers as it does on Business Prospects.

## "Happy Prospect" Strategy:

Those Prospects who are "perfectly happy" with their present vendor will all become dissatisfied in the future. The odds are that the service can't improve much and can only deteriorate. All vendors have their ups and downs, and decision makers do change.

The probability of change is substantial. The key national statistics of interest to Salespeople are:

- Any vendor will lose about 15% of their clients each year, mostly (68%) because of indifference of their staff to their clients.
- 50% of an organization's staff will turn over every 18 months.

These present golden opportunities but like gold "prospecting" is difficult.

PROSPECTING HAPPY PROSPECTS: How do you develop the Happy Prospects? Not by cold calling in person or by phone. That's a waste of time. The best method is to contact them by mail on a continuous basis. An excellent example would be to send the President a Newsletter each month, then continue month after month. Make the Newsletter valuable, with only a casual reference to your product. Repetition of high quality contact will get you an invitation when they become dissatisfied, or sooner if they accept you as an expert. The Newsletter should be an automatic mailing that can also be generated by non-Salespeople.

## Chapter Fourteen

# Appointments

## Phone Technique

# Secrets

☐ Phone selling is for *closing*, not convincing.

☐ People only learn 7% by ear, so can't convince much by phone.

☐ Can't answer an objection so use it as a reason to meet.

☐ Can't compare prices on phone, so make a price concession.

☐ Your attitude on the phone is a supreme success factor.

☐ Be bold, and talk with a feeling of command.

☐ Standing gives you the psychological advantage.

☐ Smile when on the phone or you will sound unfriendly.

☐ Smiling brings out the naturalness and removes inhibitions.

☐ The phone call should yield a commitment from them.

☐ Never ask a Prospect to return your call.

☐ Always leave an exciting/interesting message.

☐ Selling an appointment is like selling a product.

☐ Promise them an early benefit for granting an interview.

☐ Promise the Prospect an easy exit from the meeting.

☐ A pre-written script is a great advantage on the phone.

☐ Writing the script gives you a sense of authority.

☐ Scripts allow you to create and project every motion.

☐ When they call you they are motivated to buy now!

☐ Stroke phone shoppers and invite in to discuss *product*.

# Closing
# Instead Of Convincing

## Phone Selling Is Closing, And Not Convincing!

Of all the knowledge we gain, 87% comes to our brain through our sight, and only 7% through our hearing. That tells us that the hearing method of learning, for whatever reasons, is not very effective. This being true, phone selling, or Telemarketing, will be limited to the simple sales:

- SET AN INTERVIEW WITH A NEW PROSPECT.
- Sell a standard, low risk, low cost product.
- Sell more product to an established client.
- Computer calls a Prospect and sets up a call-back.

## Advantages

- Saves travel and meeting time by qualifying Prospect.
- Prospect is easier to talk to since they can hang up.
- Can use a script for opening lines and objections.
- Can use visual images to create any kind of emotion.

## Disadvantages

- You can only develop limited rapport with a Prospect.
- Lack of direct eye contact makes it impersonal.
- There may be unknown distractions or interruptions.
- You can't demonstrate the product or service.
- Meeting is too short to bring out their SIP and EBM.
- Only selling to the one sense, the hearing.

It is difficult to know when the Prospect is logically or emotionally involved. Their comments are the only way to find out if the conversation is making an impact on them. Consequently, a Salesperson has limited impact on a stranger in cold calling unless efforts are made to create responses by:

- QUESTIONING A GREAT DEAL.
- Making it a two way conversation.
- Probe for areas of discomfort.
- Being concise, Keep It Simple and Specific.
- Using simple selling techniques.
- Talking in technicolor.
- Be closing, not convincing.
- Listening for Buying Signals.
- SUMMARIZING OFTEN.

# Selling By Phone

When you are selling an interview put the emphasis on getting the Prospect to agree to a meeting, not on the merits of your product.

During a phone conversation, prove with the obvious. General proofs don't work, specific proofs do because the information is reaching the Prospect through their hearing, a most ineffective method of learning. Everything must be kept simple, clear and emphatic. Use the KISS formula: Keep It Simple and Specific. Tell them only enough to create curiosity and prevent pre-judgement.

When an objection comes up, avoid answering it. It may lead to an argument because you haven't laid the ground work in the Selling Process. Rather, use the objection as a reason for the interview:

**SP** - "Mr. P, that is the very reason why we should meet to explore the ..."

Don't accept a Stall either. They lack sufficient information to refuse further discussion. Restate their needs, then promise to resolve their problem. Selling is a Hurt and Rescue business. Sell them relief from their awful Hurt.

If the price objection comes up, you won't be successful trying to justify higher price with extra benefits. Keep in mind that a price comparison of your benefits to your competitors won't be effective on the phone. Instead, make a price or non-price *concession* that is easy to understand.

## Devices

Any kind of technique, however gimmicky, that aids in Telemarketing sales is acceptable if it is honest to the Prospect. Example:

Long Distance Phone Calls: People attach importance to a long distance phone call. Presumably, if someone goes to the expense of a long distance call it must be important. The device then would be to actually travel to a distant city and make the phone calls from there; by simulating the long distance call by using a secretary as a "long distance operator"; or using a local 800 number for a return call.

A Retail device would be to call Prospects and open with:

**SP** - "Have you bought your new ... yet?"

... and if they are in the market you will get:

**P** - "How did you know?" You have just found a Wanting Prospect.

Telemarketing success oftens depends directly on the devices used.

# Attitude

Your attitude on the phone is a supreme success factor in tele-marketing, whether promoting an interview or a product. Your attitude will give you the power to COMMAND. Everything should be directed to creating a feeling of superiority. Since the Prospect has the freedom to hang up at any time, they have less fear of the you. Without fear they can be bold, and so can you.

They must sense your strength in order for you to be influential. There are several things you can do to be more commanding and convincing on the phone:

- Give yourself a Pep Talk - "I'm strong. I am going to get the Prospect interested. I will get the appointment." etc.

- Speak louder to show strength.

- Stand up while talking with the Prospect. In your mind they are seated so you have the psychological advantage.

- Close your eyes and visualize them sitting alongside you.

- Talk with a feeling of command. You must adopt that attitude because:

  - With only a LIMITED amount of information about your exciting promise, you must convince them to meet you.

  - You have to fend off people when they push you for more details. If you give them most of the details on the phone they will have enough information to make a decision. Since no in-depth interview is involved they will rarely show interest. If their decision is NO, it may be forever. They will push for more details before committing to the meeting. To prevent that from happening do the following:

    - Avoid volunteering any more information than you mentioned in your Probable Problem statement.

    - If they ask you a question ask them to hold it until you meet (don't call it an appointment).

    - If forced to answer a question, be brief. Explain that it is an interesting question and that it opens up further discussion; then give them an Alternate Choice on a meeting time:

    SP - "Would Wednesday afternoon or Friday morning be better for you?"

# Speaking

Smile while talking on the phone. The Prospect can sense your attitude because emotion is contagious. Some people project a warm phone personality as if they were in a face-to-face situation. If you don't smile, you may sound unfriendly.

Speak at about 125 words per minute instead of your normal 225, ie, half speed. Newscasters read at 125 wpm. It is slow enough to be clear and allow the Prospect time to absorb the ideas, yet fast enough to maintain interest.

Also, check on the speed and pitch of your phone voice. If it is not pleasant, a speech therapist can help you modify it. A lower and slower voice sounds warmer, clearer and friendlier.

# Selling Goals

A Salesperson should be able to make 15 "completed" calls per day. A completed call is one where you have talked to the decision maker, regardless of that person's response. Out of those 15 completed calls, you should expect 5 new Prospects and be able to close 25% of those on the phone or in person. That is 75 new calls a week, with 25 Prospects and 6 new Clients. 15 completed calls is the daily goal in the Stockbrokering industry and it seems quite realistic for phone calling in general. You may have to adjust the figures for your product, but be careful that the adjustment applies to most of your associates and not just you.

Phone calls should yield up a commitment from the Prospect. The most positive are:

- "Let us meet" - when selling an interview.
- "Ship some" - when selling a standardized product.

If the Prospect doesn't commit to something it is a Stall. They may respond with:

**P** - "Please send me some literature/sample/proposal/letter."

That's a Stall. They are just not interested. Make them Hurt and try again for a "Rescue" meeting.

When you cannot reach the Prospect, do not ask that they return your call. Usually they won't and your constant requests creates a guilt resistance. Better to simply leave your name and state that you will call again. If it takes you many calls to reach them you can use that as a Pleasant Statement:

**SP** - "Mr. P, you sure are a busy person. Because of that you are going to appreciate my call even more ..."

# Early Benefits & Easy Exit

People are reluctant to give up their time to meet with a stranger. There should be some incentive to make it worthwhile so promise an early personal benefit, even a personal gift.

Also, give the Prospect the opportunity for an easy exit from the meeting. Remember that the Prospect sees themselves stuck for about an hour without an easy escape if they are not interested. They are willing to meet with you if it is to their advantage, but the meeting must not be a big gamble.

The way to minimize their risk is to ask for a *general interest* meeting of fifteen minutes, unless they ask it to be longer:

**SP** - "Mr. P, why don't we set up a 15 minute, *general interest* meeting to see if we have a mutual interest? Would Friday afternoon or Monday morning be better for you?" OR

**SP** - "Mr. P, we should be able to come to a reasonable conclusion in 10 or 15 minutes. If you want to pursue it we can set up another meeting. Would Wednesday... etc."

If necessary, accept an appointment even if distant in the future. Such an appointment has several advantages:

- The Prospect is less likely to be busy, *but* more subject to change.

- You have the Prospect's commitment to a meeting, even if it has to be postponed.

- It makes you appear to be very busy and therefore successful.

Follow up the phone call with a confirming memo or post card:

"Thank you, Mr. Smith, for the opportunity to present you with several new ideas to increase your sales. You will find it most interesting! See you at 11:00 a.m. on Friday, October 23."

# Withholding Information

Your objective is to obtain an interview, so you should avoid giving any sales information before the meeting. Keep in mind, though, there is no guaranteed way to avoid revealing that information over the phone.

**P** - "Could you tell me what this is about?"

**SP** - "I would be delighted to. A general interest meeting will take about 15 minutes. Would Friday morning or Monday afternoon be better for you?" (Kind of ignoring their real question.)

If it is impossible to avoid divulging information about the product, be as general as possible using the Probable Problem as a Question Suggesting a Need: "If there were a way for you to ..." statement. End it with any type of confirming question to maintain control of the conversation.

It's imperative that the Salesperson keep the purpose of the telephone call clearly in mind: it is to get the appointment, not sell the product.

## Social Attention Getter: Pleasant Statements

**SPECIFIC COMMENTS** (the best)
- "I've heard some good things about you."
- "I understand you were recently promoted."
- "(Name) said I would enjoy speaking with you." (Referral)
- "I am returning your call."
- "(Name) suggested I call you."
- "I understand that you were expecting my call."

**GENERAL COMMENTS:**
- "Your secretary seems very polite/friendly/pleasant ..."
- "We have an idea that may be of benefit to you."
- "It will take just a moment to explain why I called."
- "I have some good news for you."
- "I know your time is valuable."
- "You are probably very busy."
- "You seem to be in a very good mood."

Any kind of Pleasant Statement will be appropriate if it can lead easily into asking if it is convenient to speak now.

# Scripts

To be able to use a pre-written script is a great advantage of phone selling. Everything from a variety of attention-getting and curiosity statements, to answers for all conceivable rejections are at the Salesperson's fingertips.

The script should be laid out like a mini flip chart. You can even use a steno book standing at the upright position. Use one rejection answer per page. Tab the edge of the page with a couple of key rejection words, eg, Too Busy. You can identify the type of rejection instantly, and the answer is immediately available.

It is more difficult to convince on the phone then it is face-to-face. Yet the phone Salesperson has a golden opportunity to create and project every emotion: Happiness, sorrow, urgency, disappointment, friendliness, appreciation, excitment, sincerity, confidence and a host of others emotions that can be written into the script with visual images.

For some people "acting" on the phone may be easier than in person. With the script the Salesperson has a wonderful opportunity to speak in technicolor, to create visual images, to use powerful words, and with a conciseness that has great impact.

## Script Example

**P** - "Hello."

**SP** - "Mr. Smith?"

**P** - "Yes."

**SP** - "(Choose appropriate Pleasant Statement) ... Would it be convenient for you to talk for a few moments?"

**P** - "Yes."

**SP** - "Mr. Smith, there may be a way to reduce the capital tied up in your inventory, free up a lot of your cash and get you out of those awful problems that a cash shortage generates. If that were true, you would want to talk about it, wouldn't you?"

**P** - "Yes."

**SP** - "Would 1:30 pm today or 3:45 pm tomorrow be a better time to meet and talk about the idea?"

**P** - "I can meet with you at 1:30 pm today."

**SP** - "We'll meet at 1:30 pm then. My name is D. Forbes Ley. Thank you, Mr. Smith. See you later."

| | |
|---|---|
| **BUFFER** | "(Decision maker's name)'s office." |
| **SP** | "Is Mr. Prospect in?" |
| **BUFFER** | "May I ask who's calling?" |
| **SP** | "Yes. This is (your name). Thank you, I'll hold." |
| **BUFFER** | "Your Company?" |
| **SP** | "I'm with (company name). If you'll tell Mr. Prospect I'm on the phone I'd appreciate it." |
| **BUFFER** | "May I tell Mr. Prospect what this is about?" |
| **SP** | "Yes, indeed. If there were a way to ... (Question Suggesting a Need) ..., Mr. Prospect would probably want to know about it, don't you think?" |

| | |
|---|---|
| **BUFFER** | "I'm sorry, Mr. Prospect is in a meeting." |
| **SP** | (Cushion): "I can understand that he must be very busy. What time will Mr. Prospect be free?" |
| **BUFFER** | (She gives you the time.) |
| **SP** | "If I call you at (time indicated), would you put me right through to Mr. Prospect?" |
| **BUFFER** | "Yes." |
| **SP** | "Thank you. What is your name, please?" |
| **BUFFER** | (Gives name.) |
| **SP** | "Thank you." (Give your name and end conversation quickly.) |

# Script Format

## Selling An Interview

**P** - "Hello?"

**SP** - (State NAME as a question) _____

**P** - "Yes."

**SP** - (Pleasant Statement) _____

Is it convenient for you to talk for a few moments?"

**P** - "Yes." (If not, ask when it would be more convenient)

**SP** - Any MISS GRACE referring to a Probable Problem: _____

**MISS GRACE examples for seizing attention:**

**SP** - "Were you aware that...?  **M**ystery
**I**dea or Information
**S**tartling Statement

**SP** - "If there were a way...,
to reduce your losses in...,
with a ...,
you would probably want to know
more about it, wouldn't you?"  Ask a Disturbing Question

**IMMEDIATELY ASK WHICH TIME WOULD BE MORE CONVENIENT:**

**P** - (Chooses one of the convenient times.)

**SP** - (Confirm time, then end conversation quickly. Send a confirming note same day.)

# Selling A Product

- YOU CALL PROSPECT

**P** - "Hello?"

**SP** - (States NAME as a question:) _____

**P** - "Yes."

**SP** - Pleasant Statement (Any MISS GRACE except QSN): _____

Ask if convenient to talk now: _____

**P** - "Yes."

**SP** - Probable Problem as a Question Suggesting a Need: _____

Bridge to Interest Step: _____

Info-Getting Questions: _____

_____

Trial Close: _____

Bridge to a Specific Problem (SIP) statement: _____

Specific Problem statement: _____

Bridges to Conviction: _____

Fact/Feature: _____

Advantage: _____

Bridge: _____

Benefit: _____

Trial Close: _____

- PROSPECT CALLED YOU

**SP** - "(Your name) speaking."

**P** - (Indicates interest in a product.)

**SP** - Pleasant Statement: _____

Questions to qualify Prospect: _____

Bridge to a Specific Problem (SIP) statement: _____

Specific Problem statement: _____

Bridge to Conviction: _____

Fact/Feature: _____

Advantage: _____

Benefit: _____

Trial Close: _____

## Phone Shoppers

When a Prospect phones and asks for a price:

- ■ Never quote the price over the phone. If you do, you turn them into a price shopper.

- ■ But never say, "We don't quote prices over the phone." That antagonizes them and ruins the potential sale.

- ■ Ask what kind of needs they have for the product.

- ■ Compliment or admire them in some way:

**SP** - "I see you have taken the time to really understand the... You are the kind of client I like." OR

**SP** - "I can see you appreciate the very best. It will be a thrill to work with you." OR

**SP** - "I appreciate some one who knows the quality of a product. That makes my effort so much more enjoyable."

- ■ Ask them to come in to see all the options open to them, so they can get exactly what they want. Tell them that if you can select the time, you will commit to 30 or 60 minutes to update them on their request. The idea is to get them involved with you. Once you become their friend or consultant, they'll stop shopping.

- ■ Indicate that your competitors all have the same price, thus you can save them from running around. Tell them to ask for you, because you want to meet them.

# Rejection

Often you will be rejected on the phone; no matter how interesting your offer, there will be some who will not be excited about it — No Time, No Interest, No Need. These are the most common:

"We are happy with our present vendor."
"You'd only be wasting your time."
"I can't afford one/not in the market now."
"Can you tell me over the phone?"
"Can you send it in the mail?"
"Got a friend in the business."
"I'm too busy now; call me in a month."
"I'm really not interested."
"I don't need one; got one now."

You can easily design answers for those questions and read them from a script. Remember the wording need not be polished. It is the reasonableness of your comment that counts, not the brillance of the reply.

The Prospect's Rejection comment is a very general statement designed to close the door. Rejections are difficult to answer because of their generalities and lack of specifics. They may be true, partially true, or created for the occasion. It really doesn't matter. It is the Prospect's way of saying No; you simply didn't get enough of their interest to steal their time away from other interests.

You must "open the door" and get the conversation going again. You have to convert a rather intangible brush-off into a tangible, specific subject you can talk about.

There are 3 levels of success from this effort. The appointment may have been granted because you developed:

- Specific problem (most desired).
- General problem.
- "Moral persuasion" (least desirable).

## ■ Specific Problem:

**P** - "We are perfectly happy with our present service."

**SP** - "Well, Mr. P, if you are satisfied with your present vendor I'll respect that. That's a good position for your vendor to be in. I guess we all envy that position. While we are on that subject may I ask you two questions?"

**P** - "Sure, if they're short."

**SP** - "What are the 3 things that impress you most about your present service?"

**P** - (Gives answer. These points are your real COMPETITION.)

**SP** - "What are the 3 things that you would like to see improved?"

**P** - (Gives answer. These points are your real OPPORTUNITIES.)

**SP** - "You mentioned that you would like to see the ... improved. That's important. I can just imagine the problems that can come from that, the ..., and the ...!"

Sell the HURT. That's your opportunity. Get them disturbed by the awful problem they face. If it is not awful, make it sound awful: remember, it is all relative and to you it is awful.

# ■ General Problem:

The two best ways of handling any type of objection is by:

- ■ Reversing (capitalizing) it, or
- ■ Converting it into a question and answering the question.

Let's look at how they work on the deadly "No time, No interest, No need" Rejection:

**■ NO TIME:** "I'm too busy now."

"I'll be going on vacation soon. Call me in a month."

"This is the wrong time of the (... month, year)."

"Can you call me back in two months?"

"We are preparing our budgets now."

**SP** - "I can really appreciate your concern for time. More and more, time is of the essence in business." (Cushion)

| REVERSE | QUESTION |
|---|---|
| **SP** - " Your concern for the efficient use of time may be the very reason for considering our services." | **SP** - "The question really is 'Could you expect a substantially better service to warrant spending a little time on the project'. That is the question isn't it?" |
| **P** - "Why is that?" | **P** - "Yes it is." |
| | **SP** - "Well, we just won the award for the finest ... Would Friday afternoon or Monday morning be better for you?" |

**■ NO INTEREST:**   "We are really not interested in changing now."

"I'll have to talk it over with my boss."

"We are perfectly happy with our present vendor."

**SP** - "I can appreciate your honesty about your interest. I wouldn't expect you to be interested in another service unless you were really impressed with their quality." (Cushion)

| REVERSE | QUESTION |
|---|---|
| **SP** - "Your concern for quality is the very reason why you should be considering our service." | **SP** - "The question is: "Is our service so much better that it warrants your consideration. That is the question, isn't it?' |

**P** "Why is that?"                    **P** - "Yes."

> **SP** - "Well, we just won the
> award for the finest ...
> Would Wednesday morning or
> Friday afternoon be better
> for you?"

■ **NO NEED:** "We are getting that service now."
    "We're happy with our present agency."
    "We really don't have a need for that service."
    "We just changed and want to give them a chance."

**SP** - "I can appreciate your concern for quality service. It seems that
quality is getting more difficult to find these days."

| **REVERSE** | **QUESTION** |
|---|---|
| **SP** - "Your concern for quality is the very reason for considering our service." | **SP** - "Your question is: 'Can your expectation of superb quality justify your considering our service'. That is the question isn't it?" |
| **P** - "Why is that?" | **P** - "Yes it is." |

> **SP** - "Well, we just won the
> award for the finest ...
> Would Monday morning or
> Tuesday afternoon be better
> for you?"

Did you notice the similarity in these excellent responses? The answer in every case is almost identical. The real objective is to get the conversation going again about their problems, the only way you can be of help to them.

# ■ Moral Persuasion:

Time has created a few pet methods of begging, pleading and tricking the Prospect into agreeing to a meeting. For variety or necessity you may want to try one of them. The great defect in them is that the appointment is not based on solving their problems, except as a very indirect and intangible suggestion. They may not hold firm because of the lack of Prospect interest: "Why should I take the time to meet with them, I don't even know what they are talking about." But maybe they will work so here they are:

**P** - "I can't afford one now."

**SP** - "I can understand your position, Mr. Prospect. The purpose of my call is to request the courtesy of 15 minutes to illustrate (or demonstrate) these excellent benefits. When you are ready to acquire one, you will know all about it. Would Friday or Monday be better for you?"

---

**P** - "Can you tell me over the phone?"

**SP** - "I appreciate your early interest. Mr. Prospect, your ... business is much too complex to discuss over the phone. It will take less than 15 minutes for a general interest meeting to see if this idea will work for you. It lends itself more to illustrations. Would this afternoon or Monday morning be better for you?"

---

**P** - "I'm too busy now. Call me in a month."

**SP** - "I can appreciate that this is indeed a very busy time for you, Mr. Prospect. May I suggest a great time-saver: Breakfast on Friday at the Marriott or lunch at the golf course on Monday?"

---

**P** - "Is this an insurance agency?"

**SP** - "That is an interesting question. I don't know of any other facet of your company which can yield such a substancial cost reduction without a sizeable capital investment, do you? Would Friday morning or Thursday morning be better for you?"

---

**P** - "I can't do anything about it right now."

**SP** - "I thank you for being so honest about it. That decision is entirely up to you. It will take about 15 minutes in a general interest meeting for you to determine the time value of your savings. That's fair enough, isn't it? Would Wednesday morning or Tuesday afternoon be better for you?"

---

**P** - "I can't afford to take a chance on changing right now."

**SP** - "I'd be the last person to suggest that you take a chance on anything. You need top quality service. It will take 15 minutes for you to decide if this is what you want. Would Friday afternoon or Monday morning be better for you?"

**P** - "Can you send it in the mail?"

**SP** - "I'd be delighted to send it out tonight. I'll also need some additional information that will take less than 15 minutes. Would Friday morning or afternoon be better for you?"

---

**P** - "Can you send it in the mail?"

**SP** - "I'll be glad to. The way of establishing this cost reduction varies with a company's particular pattern, I will need certain information. That will take about 15 minutes. Would Monday morning or Tuesday afternoon be better for you?"

---

# Qualifying Prospects

It is a serious waste of your time to make a presentation to a Prospect you have no chance of closing. To that end, the Prospect must be qualified as to their:

- Need (or Want)
- Authority to buy, and
- Financial capability

This qualifying can be accomplished while you are seeking the appointment:

**SP** - "If there were a way to reduce your losses in Corporate Travel by 10 to 15% you would probably want to investigate it, wouldn't you?"

**P** - "I sure would."

**SP** - "Do you have a Cost Reduction program for your Corporate Travel now?" (The Need/Want)

**P** - "Yes, but it isn't doing much as far as I can see."

**SP** - "Well, if you can't measure it, it certainly can't be controlled." (A little Hurt) Who besides you will be making the decision to institute such a cost reduction program?" (Verifing the extent of their authority to buy)

**P** - "I would have to consult with the VP Finance but in reality their involvement is to verify the paperwork systems."

**SP** - "If you were to go ahead with this plan now would you be able to take advantage of the 1% for the 10 days payment of invoices?" (Verifying their ability to pay promptly.)

**P** - "That's an accounting decision but my impression is Yes."

**SP** - "You should be able to reduce those costs by at least 12 to 15 thousand dollars a year. That would be important to you when no capital investment required, wouldn't it? Would Wednesday afternoon or Friday morning be better for a 15 minute general interest meeting?"

## Chapter Fifteen
# Price

# Secrets

- ☐ Rarely is price the only deciding consideration.
- ☐ Price is neither high nor low; it is a relative value.
- ☐ A price objection can hide anything and everything.
- ☐ A price objection means there are not enough wants.
- ☐ Every price is too high until they see the benefits.
- ☐ The price of an unwanted product is always too high.
- ☐ Price is minor if the Prospect really wants the product
- ☐ People buy from people they like, often regardless of price.
- ☐ People seeking deals are hard to deal with after the sale.
- ☐ Don't invite price comparisons, they can't compare benefits.
- ☐ Every Prospect is a buyer at some price.
- ☐ When complex or personalized, price is less important.
- ☐ Luxury items are sold on the basis of motivated pride.
- ☐ They are thinking about buying when they ask the price.
- ☐ Features justify purchase; benefits justify price.
- ☐ The price must be justified with values and benefits.
- ☐ They often will test you to verify the best deal.
- ☐ Most will pay a fair price so long as they are not taken.
- ☐ Price = Purchase + Hassle of change + Maintenance.
- ☐ When the price is high, the extra values must be sold.

- ☐ If the extra price cannot be justified, it is mispriced.
- ☐ The rich want price justification even more than the poor.
- ☐ Quote Value-Price-Value so price is always justified.
- ☐ A mere 10% are price buyers, but many are price resisters.
- ☐ Price only ranks sixth in importance in deciding.
- ☐ When you make an attractive offer stand by it.
- ☐ You only cry once when you buy quality.

# What Is Price?

Price means different things to different people, at different times, and under different circumstances. It is a complex interrelationship between the relative values of the product, the Prospect, the Salesperson, the Company, as well as each other's competitors.

To the Salesperson, price is a stumbling block that prevents sales because it is always too high. Yet, top Salespeople choose to sell high priced products for the higher commission. Price is more of a problem in the Salesperson's mind than in the Prospect's mind.

To the Company, price is based on:

- ■ Their product's production and sales costs.
- ■ The price their competitors will "let" them charge.
- ■ Substitute products (vacation vs a new car).
- ■ Desire for certain large accounts.
- ■ What their Salespeople suggest.
- ■ A good deal of "gut" feel.

To the Prospect, the price is a sacrifice they must make in:

- ■ Dollars, both short and long term (change, service and life)
- ■ Physical effort of acquiring and implementing the product.
- ■ Hassle of change in procedures and personnel.
- ■ Peer pressure, if not a popular decision.

To all, there are emotional and logical aspects to price. If the emotional aspect is strong enough it will transcend all other considerations. A Psychologist will agree that if someone wants something badly enough, then they indeed do "need" it. Conversely, if someone really needs it, but doesn't want or feel comfortable with it, it will be an unhappy purchase.

When we think about price we only think about the purchase price, the highly visible initial out-of-pocket expenditure. Yet, the purchase price may be small compared to the long term price of maintaining the product; it may also be small compared to the hassle of change.

In the case of a service, where there is no acquisition cost, the price is in the hassle of change when there is a high personal contact between the vendor and client. Personal relationships are more difficult to change than procedures or objects.

The sale of services is also compounded by peer pressure on the decision maker. They are concerned about staff reaction to a change. In a large corporation, the attitude tends to be "don't-rock-the-boat" the pressure to maintain status quo is strong.

Similar factors are involved in a personal purchase. The constant repairs to a cheap product, plus the sneers from associates who may not like it, are all too real.

To the Prospect the price is:

**ACCEPTABLE:**

if they want it emotionally.
if the product is scarce.
if the product is being hoarded.
if it is the last one (greed).
if it is a great bargain (everyone is a buyer at some price).
if it reinforces their self-image (the pauper's Cadillac).
if they do not know what a good deal is (a consulting fee?).
if the product is unique.
if the product is a current fad.
if the product is complex.
if the product is personalized.
if pride is the motivator (luxury items).
if the product will make them look better to others.
if the Salesperson assures them that it is acceptable.

**UNACCEPTABLE:**

if it has a very low price (little value, little respect).
if the low price cannot be justified (being dumped?).
if below their station in life (have to apologize for it).
if they don't want or need it.
if they don't see the benefits in it for them.
if they feel they can get it cheaper elsewhere (being "taken").
if it is not a good deal in their mind.

Price must not be considered an objection. Like the product feature, the price must be sold, ie, justified. Price resistance is a signal that the Want is not great enough for them to exchange their dollars for the limited benefits.

## The Cost: Benefit Ratio

Price is a relative value, the ratio of the Prospect's cost to the benefits expected. In the business world it is called the cost:benefit ratio.

The Prospect's buying decision will be based on perceived value in relation to price. It is a weighing process that is going on continually in their mind. Values or benefits are not in the product but in the Prospect's mind. The Salesperson may have little direct control over the price but the Salesperson does have control of presenting the Prospect with enough reasons to buy now.

The Prospect is always asking, "What's in it for me?" The answer to this question is not *features*, but rather *reasons* and *benefits* to buy. These can be prompted into emotional wants.

When they buy, the Prospect acquires an accumulation of benefits. Rarely is any one *feature* worth the price, but it is quite possible that one *benefit* is worth the price. Another way to view it; features justify the purchase, while benefits justify the price.

# The Buying Process

## Personal vs Business Buying

Buying is an emotional process. The emotional involvements run the gamut from the Prospect wanting the item so badly that they will do almost anything to get it, to analytical Purchasing Agents wanting the recognition from their peers for low cost, high quality purchases.

Since a Prospect purchases differently for a business item than for a personal item, we should look at each separately.

### ■ Personal Buying

The price can be high as long as the Prospect feels it is justified in terms of the values and benefits offered to them. Within reason, the question "Can I afford it?" is easily resolved if the emotional Want is strong enough. So long as they can manage the monthly payments it is usually alright.

Every price is too high until the Prospect sees the benefits. When they know the price they are thinking about the cost:benefit ratio early, too early. It is all cost and no benefit, so you have to load up the benefits quickly or you will be rejected.

They will emotionally reject the product if they think the price is unrealistic. The Prospect is not unreasonable in this demand for justification. Prospects normally don't know the value of even an exceptional deal because it is so difficult to make a cost:benefits evaluation when features are different. The Prospect's emotions, not logic, will likely be the dominant deciding factor. So they need assurances that the price is justified along with the Need justification.

The Prospect will reject the product if they think it can be purchased elsewhere for less or that some one else can get it cheaper. They simply won't be "taken". They want value for their money and they can be as emotional about the unfairness of the price as they can about their desire to own.

The Prospect is always conscious of price. For the most part, a person usually knows the price range they are expected to pay before meeting you. If they don't, they are a Suspect and not a Prospect.

In the end the price has to be sold, or justified, as well as any other Benefit of the product.

If your price is higher than a competitive product you must justify the extra benefits of your product in order to justify that higher price. If they accept the justification, they must also see the need for and be willing to invest in those extra benefits.

Most people do not have a strong motivation to own or hold money, it is only a means to an end. Actually, it is burning a hole in their pocket. This is proven by the savings patterns of various nations. Statistics for the US show a 6% savings of earned income. Canada is higher at 9%. Japan tops all with 35%. In every case the pattern is constant from year to year. If they spend only for items they really need, spending habits would fluctuate wildly from year to year, which they don't. It seems that most people will always spend down to their guilt or comfort level of savings.

Since spending is a constant, it matters little what they spend it on. They will spend it for the highest priority want at that MOMENT, all the way down to their guilt level.

Within a hierarchy of Wants the priorities can change rapidly. Suppose you were passing a store window and saw an item on sale for 50% off. Normally you wouldn't buy that item. But you like it and it would be nice to have. Would you seriously consider buying it? Maybe you would. At least you would give it real consideration. If you do buy it, it is because your Easy Gain/Greed emotion has been prompted. The desire to possess is in full flame proving the old adage that "every Prospect is a buyer at some price".

Consider the purchase of shoes from a fashionable store on exclusive Rodeo Drive in Beverly Hills. Here price means little so long as others recognize the high status symbols conferred by such shoes. If the shoes are readily recognizable as an elegant product, then the Prospect's self-image is stroked as intended. When there is no recognition, then there is no benefit, and the Prospect will have to draw the attention of their Peers to the status symbol in another way.

Retail merchants know the magic of impulse items. These are items that people have not planned to buy until they see them "emotionally". At that point they want them - strickly impulse buying. The retailers take advantage of this recklessness of the emotions by strategically locating small, high priced luxury items around the necessities. The sales are most lucrative.

A Salesperson can use this recklessness of the emotions to help a Prospect justify a want. Consider these powerful influencers:

**SP** - "You really should have this - you deserve it!"

**SP** - "You only cry once when you buy quality."

Price means little, if anything, to a person who is motivated to buy. Motivation due to pride, image-stroking, greed or fear is just too powerful.

## ■ Business Buying

Corporations effectively remove the emotions from purchasing. Emotion in business purchasing is low if the purchaser is not the end-user. A Purchasing Agent will be motivated by their desire for recognition for a skillful purchase, but they will obviously not have the fiery motivation of the end-user. If a Purchasing Agent were buying a desk-top computer for their own office, then emotion would play a stronger role. If business people were allowed to purchase their own equipment, without regard to corporate peer pressure, the emotions would be just as dominant as they would be in their personal buying.

The only place where a Prospect's emotions are involved is at the leader level, but even here they feel they have to justify the purchase to their staff. They do have and are entitled to preferences, but most often this is with limited success. Peer pressure on the leader, real and imagined, has probably resulted in more no-buys then in yes-buys. Peer pressure in a corporation can be substantial.

Comparisons of price, value and quality in the business world is the name of the game. Yet, even after a rigorous comparison, price will rarely be the dominant factor. Many surveys have shown that both private business as well as government rank price only as the sixth most important consideration.

When they ask the price, that shows that they do have an interest. To keep the price from becoming dominant to the benefits the price should be given as a Value-Price-Value:

**SP** - "This state-of-the-art computer at "forty nine fifty" ($4950) will increase your order processing by at least 25%."

**SP** - "This heavy duty machine at "nine ninety five" ($995) will give your staff five years of trouble free service."

Disassociate the price from "dollars", "hundred" and "thousand" to make it seem smaller.

Every positive statement you make influences opinion. By "packaging" the price with values, ie, Value-Price-Value, benefits are maximized and the price is minimized.

# Creative Selling

There is a vast difference between Creative selling and Replacement selling:

■ **RELACEMENT SELLING:** Does the Prospect already own this type of product? If so, you are competing head-on, point-by-point with an established competitor. You have to quickly find out what the Prospect likes about their current product or vendor, the short comings and how much they are paying for it. Since the Prospect already has a need for the product, and price has been justified, all you need to do is "improve" on either the Need with more benefits or the price, either with a lower price (shame) or more non-price benefits.

■ **CREATIVE SELLING:** If the Prospect has not bought this product before, you will have to educate them as well as sell them. In creative selling, you must develop both the Need and the Want simultaneously - you "Tell and Sell". Since the degree of price acceptance varies directly with the Want satisfaction, let us consider the education of a Prospect.

## Telling vs Selling

When this is their first buying venture for your kind of product you may have to educate them. Before spending too much time, qualify them: "How long have you been thinking about buying one of these?"

You must decide if the buyer is a Prospect, or a Suspect that needs educating, and if the purpose of this sales meeting is to convince or educate, or perhaps both. If they do need educating you must determine how much time you will devote to them, and when - now, or later by appointment, or in class.

If the Prospect is just beginning a study of the product, there is little assurance that they will buy. On the other hand, if the Prospect has been seriously looking, they probably will be open to buying from the first Salesperson who finds out what they really need and want, develops the Want and then helps them justify it.

An industry profile of the consumer buying habits of a personal computer shows that the Prospect will visit a computer store seven times before buying. If the next Prospect who comes in to the computer store is making visit number six, ie, has completed most of the learning process, then the Salesperson does have an excellent chance of closing that sale. You should confirm this degree of involvement as soon as the interview begins with a Trial Close:

**P** - "How much is that little computer in the window?"

**SP** - "How long have you been considering a personal computers?"

**P** - "I've been really studying them now for three months."

**SP** - "Do you have one or two brands in mind?"

**P** - "Yes, the XYZ."

**SP** - "The reason I ask is that we have a special price on ..."

When the Prospect is just starting to study the product you may want to make this approach:

**P** - "I'm just starting. Its fascinating but complex."

**SP** - "... the reason I ask that is because we have a special $25 introductory class where you can learn all about personal computers to avoid making a big financial mistake."

What is the Prospect's profile in your market? You have to Adopt and Adapt the Selling Process to your product. If it takes considerable time to educate the Prospect, then you may want to set up classes where you are the believable consultant, rather than the Caveat Emptor Salesperson. You may be able to charge, say, $25 for a three hour class so the cost will be self-liquidating. Certainly the Prospect will be a captive buyer and you have a near certain opportunity to close them if and when they do buy.

You should teach the class since you are the expert on the product. This builds a lasting rapport with the Prospect. The classes should be conducted (a) when you are in your slow selling period, and (b) when the Prospect has the time.

As a teacher you must be unbiased about the pros and cons of the competitive products that should be considered. When the Fact/Feature and Benefit differences between your lines and competitive lines are minor, tell the Prospect that they will be just as happy with your product. All other things being equal, the Prospect will buy from you because you have become their consultant.

# Answering Price Resistance

## Price Objection

An old bromide in selling is that nothing will kill a sale like the Prospect knowing the price before they can appreciate the benefits. Like all bromides there is an element of truth. If the Prospect knows nothing about your product then the bromide is likely true, but then you have a Suspect rather than a Prospect.

The price objection is the easiest objection a Prospect can give. It can be a cover up for anything. You are never sure if that is the only reason for their hesitating or not. Regardless, it is because they do not see enough benefits to justify their sacrifices in buying the product. If they want it badly enough, they won't object. It is your primary job to get them to want it badly enough.

The Prospect balks for one or more of the following reasons:

■ They don't perceive enough Wants or Benefits.
■ They are hiding another reason for not buying.
■ They are exercising buying restraint by challenging it.
■ They are trying to bargain for a lower price.
■ They want assurance that it is the lowest price.

They may not be price objecting, but rather price *resisting*, and there is a big difference. A true price objection means they are interested, but can't see the justification. Price resisting means they want it, but are confirming that the price is the best they can do.

The Prospects that do offer price resistance are not really price shoppers. Only a few buyers are really shoppers because the success ratio of shopping is not too rewarding. The market place is really quite confusing. Where price shopping does occur is between standardized products by large volume business buyers.

The technique to sort out these differences between the "conditional objection" and the "bargaining resistance" is the Trial Close. The Trial Close will tell you how badly they want it. If the want is high, they are trying to bargain. If they are lukewarm or cold you have a price objection, i.e., not enough Wants and Benefits to offset the price.

What do you do with a price *objector?* Remember that the Prospect doesn't like the price:value relationship. So you either cut the price (shame), or start loading up more reasons why the product will soothe their Hurt from their awful situation that brought you together.

What do you do with a price *resistor*? Remind them of their Hurt, justify the price, assure them it is a good deal for them, that it is the lowest price, and offer some non-price concession to save their ego from your "no".

The shame of price cutting is that it is the easy way out. It requires no selling skill. Instead, Hurt and Rescue them, load them up with more Benefits and non-price concessions. If none of those work, then cutting the price may be the correct business alternate, but never the first; it should be your dying gasp.

## When And How To Talk Price?

The Salesperson shouldn't volunteer the price until the Prospect is ready to buy.

In most cases the Prospect knows the approximate price of the product even before meeting the Salesperson. What may not be known is *your* price range. They may be expecting a lower quality, lower priced product, and may be surprised at the high price of a product with more Feature-Benefits. That's where price justification is required.

There is only one way to justify the price and that is with more Benefits. The more Benefits, the more justification. Every Benefit is another reason to buy; it builds the emotions.

Given that the Prospect is ready to buy, but price has not been discussed, how should the Salesperson reveal the price? As a Trial Close, along the way to the Alternate Choice Close, by trading off an EBM with the price:

**SP** - "Would it be worth... (price)... to have... (their EBM)...?"
**P** - "Yes, it would."     And they are ready to close.
**P** - "I'm not sure."     And add more Benefits, i.e., reasons to buy.

The moment the price is stated, the weighing of the price against values begins. They are vividly conscious of it all during the interview. They wait and watch to see if the Benefits add up to and justify the price. Extra Benefits make it a bargain. The weighing is logical and that impedes the development of the emotional Want. It is hard to get emotionally involved with something when an "unreasonable" price looms over it.

The weighing often causes premature rejection of the product if time passes without the Wants and justifying Benefits being developed. They can even become frustrated with the questioning if the price is known before the Information Gathering is complete; they can't wait to see the Benefits.

Remember, if the Want is strong enough, there will be no objections.

Because the speculation of price can be overwhelming, the Prospect often has a premature desire to know. If some educating about the product is necessary, then you can postpone any premature price question by making a short, reassuring comment like:

**SP** - "This product is an exceptionally good value at a price I know you'll feel is more than reasonable. You'll be very pleased with it. I will tell you about that in a moment, but first let me show you how it will benefit you." (This also keeps them in a "happy" suspense.)

If the question comes up again, answer it if you know exactly what their need is, but don't dwell on it. You can take their attention off price by reinforcing it with the Benefits that triggered their Hot Button in the first; then quote it as a Value-Benefit-Value.

Another way to postpone a price revelation is:

**P** - "What is the price?"

**SP** - "At the moment, Mr. P, I really can't say. We'll have to determine exactly what you need, the quantity, the delivery and any special features. As soon as we determine your specific need I'll give you an exact price. And you'll be very happy with it."

## Preempting Price

If your price is higher than usual, you can soften it's effect by preempting it. That is, you bring up the subject as a Benefit and justify it before the Prospect complains about it. In that way you minimize any potential objection:

**SP** - "This is high priced if you are not concerned about quality. On the other hand, if you are concerned about the finer things in life, this may very well be for you."

Similarly if you have a potentially negative characteristic about your product, capitalize on it. Boast about it by comparing it favorably with something that is positive. Listerine Mouthwash has a great preemption - "The taste that you hate." They imply that Listerine, like medicine, must be good if it tastes that bad.

## Buying Signals

When the Prospect wants to know the price, it is an important Buying Signal. It means they are now considering the purchase. They have entered the decision making arena and have seen at least enough benefits to consider owning the product. Evidently the product looks desirable. They want to see if the price:value relationship is reasonable.

**SP** - "This state-of-the-art computer program for seven ninety-five will enable you to cut your processing time by 20%. (Value-Price-Value) How do you think that improvement would affect the work flow?" (Trial Close)

# Probing Budgets

Never ask the Prospect what price they have in mind. In many cases, if not most, they just don't know. If they really want it and can justify it, price is really not all that important.

In the business world, Salespeople often ask the Prospect what they have budgeted for the purchase. If it is a replacement item they can tell you. If they have not purchased the product before, they will have only limited information. They may be trying to speed up a manufacturing operation, reduce an operation's costs, etc, and no acceptable cost is known. Rather, they have to look at the justification, ie, the return on the investment. It simply has to be justified on its own merits.

# Lower Price Competition

Because price is only the sixth most important factor in selecting a product, you shouldn't lose composure when the Prospect starts pressuring. It may be a defense mechanism, a self stroking to show knowledge about your product, bargaining, exercising buying restraint, or whatever. Or they may be seeking help in justifying the purchase, that is, a Buying Signal meaning "I like it, but help me find more reasons (or excuses) for buying it."

Whether the price is higher or lower than normal, the difference between what it should be and what it really is must be justified. If a jewelry shop is running a special on jade at 50% off, the Prospect may think something is wrong with the jade so an explanation is necessary. On the other hand, some sales are self-evident, eg, 50% off the price of clothing means it is out of season. They must understand the reason for the differences.

As long as you concentrate on selling LOGICAL FEATURES you will be under heavy price pressure. When you sell EMOTIONAL BENEFITS you blur the logical part of the mind and price becomes quite unimportant. That is how expensive products are sold.

There are several other possible attacks on price pressure:
■ Point out savings that offset price:
   Method of payment/financing.
   Return policy if defective or not sold.

Service and maintenance costs.
Service response time.
Life of the product.

■ Free, non-related services reduce the price.

■ Reduce the difference to the lowest possible unit:
    **P** - "Your price is too high."
    **SP** - "How much too high?"

If they will state a figure reduce it down to a daily or unit cost and show them how little it really is:
    **SP** - "It only works out to a martini a day over the life of the product for one of the finest there is. Five years of trouble free, high quality performance is worth a martini, isn't it?"

■ Sell the Total Offer concept: Quality product by a quality vendor who will stand behind the product, and a quality Salesperson for excellence in servicing.

■ Pile on more and more values, even those that the Prospect may not need. In real estate the Salesperson knows that the Prospect can always buy cheaper else-where. They have to rely on maximizing the Benefits to minimize the price.

■ Capitalize your higher price - "Only those who appreciate fine liquor purchase this."

■ Create doubt about price cutters:

  (a) American history has not been kind to price cutters - consider the White Front chain, the Treasury stores of Penny's, the Fedmart, etc.

  (b) Anyone can cut prices if they are willing to sacrifice. "What are they sacrificing?"

  (c) Point out to the Prospect that most manufacturers have about the same costs. "Extra cost usually is due to extra values. What's missing?"

## "What's Your Lowest Price?"

Did you ever approach a rushed Prospect and get this question as their opening and closing line?

**P** - "I'm very busy. What is your lowest price?"

Sure you have. Did you ever sell such a Prospect by answering only that question? Probably not, and you never will if you answer that question to their satisfaction. Instead of quoting your lowest price, start off by questioning the Prospect as to their Needs, simply to show them there are many considerations in the "lowest price":

**SP** - "Do you mean the Deluxe or the Economy model?"

**P** - "Deluxe."

**SP** - "With or without the ...?"

**P** - "With it."

**SP** - "Current or future delivery?"

**P** - "What's the difference?"

**SP** - Well, there are many variables. If I could define exactly what you want we can prepare a proposal that you will find most interesting. Do you have a moment to answer a few questions or should we get together on Monday morning or Wednesday afternoon?

# High Price
## Theory

**THEORY:** Prospects buy products because they want its Benefits and not because they can get the 5 to 10% off. Sellers believe a lower price promotes sales, but the increase in sales is insignificant when the discount is insignificant, as 5 to 10% tends to be. In retail, 20% off is significant but usually the product was bought with the 20% discount in mind, or the goods are being dumped because of the season. Don't let the retail concept of pricing influence the business, ie, industrial pricing; that would be deadly. Discounts are the life of retail selling, and the death of business selling.

Each year 50 thousand American businesses close their doors forever. Rarely was their demise due to high prices.

Only 10% of the Fortune 500 companies make respectable profits over the long term. American management folklore is replete with crisis management, conglomerating and management upheavals. All of this is compliments of the lowest price. Someone paid the price!

Historically, the average American business has turned in about 6% after-tax profit. The necessities businesses, such as grocery stores, average 3%. Non-competitive businesses know no upper limits. It is when a company goes for high volume with a minimun of exclusive features and mediocre selling techniques that the going gets rough. A better strategy would be to invest the price discount in advanced selling skill development and reap more profitable sales.

The problem with profit is that it is RESIDUAL in nature, the left over margin between cost and the net price. When the Salesperson cuts the price, they are giving away *pure profit*. The difference to a company that sells 5% above market versus 5% below market is the difference between riches and rags:

Selling To The Wants With Benefits ⟶ Riches

vs

Selling To The Needs With Low Prices ⟶ Rags

REMEMBER: A NEED IS A NECESSARY EVIL for which the Prospect will not reward you with a high price because buying a necessity is strictly logical; there is no emotion to satisfy.

Most of your Prospects have only a vague idea on what the price of your market usually is when it is not a high volume necessity or staple item. With a lack of price knowledge they really can't be price shoppers so the Salesperson shouldn't fear it.

Neither should the Salesperson be quick to make concessions. Even when prices drop, it doesn't mean that you have to stay with the market.

When a new product comes on the market it sells well in spite of the high price. Later competition develops and the price drops rapidly as the new player takes a quick slice of the market by underselling the established price. It is easier to cut prices than it is to learn to sell well.

Once supply exceeds demand, prices drop in the scramble. As soon as a Want item becomes a Need item, the price drops. When a Prospect's Want becomes a Need, their lower need's emotions of survival and security are prompted and they will shop those lower prices the sellers promote.

The low price seller does not always get the sale. More often, the price is only secondary in nature; actually sixth in importance both for industry and government.

On the other hand, neither will a higher price materially reduce the sales volume. The further you are away from the high volume, standardized "necessary evils" products, the more pronounced this insensitivity becomes because of the inefficiency in market knowledge — no one advertises high prices.

When you sell low price, your profitability will be borderline. A small negative adjustment in the market, e.g., a recession, style change, quality demands, or material shortage and you may be dead; there is no buffer of profits or surplus capital left to survive the storm.

# How To Get a High Price

- Sell to those who appreciate and can afford quality.
- Create Benefits rather than compete with prices.
- It is the Benefits that sell, and not prices.
- Don't let Salespeople cut prices, unless they can't sell.
- Protect a price resister's ego with non-price extras.
- Don't try to sell every Prospect, it may be your last gasp.
- Offer your highest priced items first, they may go for it.
- Base prices on what traffic will bear, not costs.
- Set prices higher than what you think is reasonable.
- Raise your prices until you get some rejections.
- Build exclusive Features and Benefits into your product.
- When Prospect pressures the price, get back to Benefits.
- Don't sell the price negative "necessary evils".
- Sell to the Wants and not to the Needs.
- Sell wants, visions, ideas and not products.
- Use many visuals and visual images in your presentation.
- Create visual images of them enjoying your product.
- Make your product hard to get, easy to buy.
- Once you cut the price, it's hard to get them back on list.
- Reduce a price difference to lowest unit possible.
- Never reveal price until you must, it kills the emotion.
- Talk softly, briefly, and quickly about the price.
- Quote Value-Price-Value and then more Benefits.
- Don't cut a price, justify it with more Benefits.
- TRAIN YOUR SALES STAFF TO SELL TO THE WANTS, NOT NEEDS!

# Epilogue

Remember that if they really want it, price is not important. Building up that Want is the ultimate skill in selling. It is your greatest challenge and the most rewarding accomplishment. You are a WANTS MOTIVATOR!

## Chapter Sixteen
# Enthusiasm

# Secrets

- ☐ Enthusiasm is the priceless *quality* in every Salesperson.
- ☐ Enthusiasm is the priceless *ingredient* in every sale.
- ☐ Enthusiasm is a joyous excitement about something.
- ☐ It builds courage, and corrects bad attitudes and slumps.
- ☐ It is not the result of success, but rather the cause.
- ☐ Nothing will happen until one of you gets excited.
- ☐ Act enthusiastic and you will be enthusiastic.
- ☐ Nothing is as contagious as enthusiasm.
- ☐ Enthusiasm can be a burning desire to accomplish a goal.
- ☐ Enthusiasm is a happy self-confidence in pursuit of goals.
- ☐ Enthusiasm creates endless energy to achieve goals.
- ☐ Enthusiasm is at the bottom of all progress.
- ☐ White heat enthusiasm can melt the hardest problems.
- ☐ Enthusiasm generates its own energy.
- ☐ To get your Prospect warm you have to be red hot.
- ☐ Your enthusiasm may be your only and best evidence.
- ☐ An overdisplay of enthusiasm will defeat the purpose.
- ☐ Suppress the enthusiasm until you have a reason to show it.
- ☐ Enthusiasm is the irresistible urge of your will.
- ☐ Build it for your product by talking to happy clients.

- □ An enthusiastic Salesperson expects to win.
- □ Enthusiasm is involvement, is motivation.
- □ It may be your only advantage over competition.

# Enthusiasm Creates Miracles
## Enthusiasm Is The Priceless Ingredient In Salespeople

Henry Ford's success revolved around his belief that enthusiasm is the most valuable quality a person can have. Over his hearth he hung his now famous Fireplace Motto:

## Enthusiasm

"You can do anything if you have enthusiasm. Enthusiasm is the yeast that makes your hope rise to the stars. Enthusiasm is the sparkle in your eye, it is the swing in your gait, the grip of your hand, the irresistible surge of your will and your energy to execute your ideas. Enthusiasts are fighters. They have fortitude. They have staying qualities. Enthusiasm is at the bottom of all progress! With it there is accomplishment. Without it there are only alibis."

B.C. Forbes, editor of Forbes magazine reconfirms Ford's secret:

"What is the master key to success? Enthusiasm is the all-essential human jet propeller. Without it the highest heights are rarely reached. It is the driving force that elevates men to miracle workers. White heat enthusiasm can melt the hardest problems, can vault Himalayan hurdles. It generates immeasurable powers. It begets boldness, courage; kindles confidence, overcomes doubts. It creates endless energy, the source of all accomplishment.

Perseverance withers and dies when not perpetually fed by enthusiasm. If you dig deeply enough into the history of America's most monumental enterprises of yesteryear and today, what do you discover? Almost invariably there was one master mind, one master mind who wedded herculean work to his dreams, visions, ambitions, spurred and succored and strengthened always by his enthusiasm. "Faith without works is dead." It is enthusiasm that transmutes faith, ambition, aspiration into imperishable deeds. Without enthusiasm, nothing."

Frank Bettger in his best seller *How I Raised Myself From Failure To Success In Selling* says that "Enthusiasm is, by far, the highest paid quality on earth."

# Act Enthusiastic

Enthusiasm is defined as a "joyous excitement" about your product, yourself, your friends, you future, or whatever you are enthusiastic about.

The basis of enthusiasm is belief. In selling, it comes from belief in the miracles that your product will do for your Prospect. Only the persuaded can really persuade.

The key to showing your enthusiasm is simply to *act* enthusiastic. It is "priming the pump". William James, America's turn-of-the-century philosopher, found that "Actions and feelings go together. You can *act* as you want to and this tends to make you *feel* as you want to." Act enthusiastic and you will be enthusiastic! To "prime the pump", start off with acting animated. The animation will release your excitement which in turn will release your enthusiasm.

Acting enthusiastic, excited and animated will break you out of your shell of inhibitions and let your enthusiasm show through. This will dramatically affect your own attitudes, and the attitudes of others toward you.

## Happy Clients Create Your Enthusiasm

Sell only what you are sold on. If you don't believe in your product or your company, don't sell it. Why not see how enthusiastic you can become about your product?

Just as we can bootstrap our inner feelings with a physical action, we can get a huge dose of enthusiastic belief in our product by asking our happy clients just what they like about it. A most successful way to build product enthusiasm in new Salespeople is to have them talk to your satisfied clients. After several hours of this, the new Salespeople will be charged with enthusiasm.

## Feed Your Enthusiasm Daily

Enthusiasm must be fed on a daily basis or it will die. You must be constantly thinking about your major goals, for "you are what you are thinking about the most".

**Your motivation towards your goals is your enthusiasm.**

Your success is what you have to be enthusiastic about! Your progress toward your goals is what makes you exciting; that is your enthusiasm and it is contagious to your Prospect. This resolves the problem that if one of you is not excited, there will be no sale.

**Enthusiasm is the BREAKFAST of Sales Champions.**

The word BREAKFAST itself serves as the acronoym for the various techniques you can use in keeping your enthusiasm high:

| | |
|---|---|
| **B** | BELIEVE in the miracles of the benefits of your product. |
| **R** | RULES of selling will guide you to success. |
| **E** | EFFECTIVE public speaking will give you confidence. |
| **A** | ACT animated to shake yourself out of your inhibitions. |
| **K** | KNOW your product's benefits for your Prospect. |
| **F** | FIX your mind on the great successes of your goals. |
| **A** | ATTITUDE - forgive yourself and flush out your guilts. |
| **S** | SELF-IMAGE - rebuild it with Pep and Faith Talks. |
| **T** | TALK yourself into being excited and enthusiastic. |

# Nothing Happens Until Someone Gets Excited

It is a fact that nothing happens until someone gets excited. Give your presentation with spirit and excitement. To get your Prospect warmed up you have to be hot!

An enthusiastic Salesperson expects to win. When you are wildly excited about the benefits for the Prospect you can't help but influence the Prospect. In fact, your excitement about your product could even be the best evidence that your product is as good as you claim it to be. Remember that a lot of selling is building confidence in the Prospect. Transferring your enthusiasm to the Prospect is a powerful confidence builder. Enthusiasm is contagious!

Most sales presentations are the same old thing, presentation after presentation. The Prospects all have the same basic problems; you and your competition have more or less identical products from the Prospect's point of view; and Prospect's all have the same basic objections. So the presentations are boring. The Salesperson is not enthusiastic because they have nothing to be enthusiastic about.

When you are enthusiastic, that enthusiasm may be is the only selling benefit you have over competition, and it may be all that is necessary. Most sales are closed, not because the Prospect believes, but because the Salesperson is enthusiastic.

Enthusiasm generates its own energy. Your animation is the natural manifestation of that enthusiasm. Let that joyous excitement out. Let your voice rise or fall. Talk faster. Look happy. Let your hands be free in gesturing. Do whatever comes naturally.

Since enthusiasm is an inner spirit it's outward appearance will look different on everyone. Although your Prospect may be impressed by the calm, professional manner of the conservative Salesperson, that same conservatism will bottle up the natural enthusiasm you have for your product and hurt your sales, and the wanting Prospect.

Enthusiasm is so important to the overall success of the selling effort that the primary function of the Sales Manager is selling the Salesperson to themselves (self-image), by establishing exciting goals for them (motivation) and keeping them excited about achieving those goals (enthusiasm).

## Enthusiastic About What?

"What do you have to be enthusiastic about?" is a rather sobering question. You can't answer it because you probably don't have much to be personally enthusiastic about.

Being enthusiastic about your product is great for a selling situation. Wouldn't it be infinitely better if you were enthusiastic about yourself? A personal enthusiasm requires a different technique and produces a more lasting and satisfying outcome.

Enthusiasm is a joyous excitement, an inner spirit, a burning desire to accomplish a goal that is really important and attainable. When you want something badly enough, you will create a visualization of success that is so strong that obstacles don't matter. Much like the warm sun that draws you to it.

To make enthusiasm truly work, goals must exist that generate the excitement of success. Given that we have the goals, how do we maximize goal enthusiasm benefits? It is done with affirmations, the act of programming your subconscious mind to perform as per instructions. These affirmations can produce both short term benefits and long term dramatic changes in your personality.

Preparedly, you have to condition your mind for a new SELF-IMAGE. It requires a change to a positive mental ATTITUDE. That is accomplished by ridding yourself of your destructive guilt complex. A positive attitude allows the affirmation to generate a new self-image which in turn develops a cocky SELF-CONFIDENCE.

Self-confidence is great, but it is more of a reserve power than an activity. To really get the effort moving we have to put a driving force behind the self-confidence. That driving force is GOALS which when combined with your self-confidence generates your SELF-MOTIVATION.

The natural enthusiasm generated by goals is magnified and ensured with Pep and Faith talks. The early success dramatically changes the Salesperson's attitude about themselves which is in turn reinforces the goals and self-confidence. It is a vicious circle that feeds on and enhances itself in a most positive way.

This great confidence in your ability and drive toward desirable goals give you a natural ENTHUSIASM about YOURSELF.

THE WHOLE CONTINUUM BECOMES A SELF-FULFILLING PROPHESY.

# Vicious Circle

These qualities all feed on and enhance each other in a POSITIVE VICIOUS CIRCLE OF SUCCESS. Just as you can vicious circle yourself into failure so can you vicious circle to success. An old bromide is that "Nothing succeeds like success". That bromide is the VICIOUS CIRCLE OF SUCCESS. Little Successes begat Big Successes. It is vicious in the sense that it is generally uncontrolled.

To learn how to get into the vicious cycle of success we will proceed with the Chapters in this sequence:

ATTITUDES (To remove negative bias).
PEP and FAITH TALKS (To develop self-image).
GOALS (To direct and motivate).

```
  ┌─→ ATTITUDE → SELF-CONFIDENCE
  │                   +      ──→ MOTIVATION → ENTHUSIASM
  │                 GOALS
  └──────────────────────────────────────────────────────┘
```

The vicious circle can be negative towards failure or positive towards success.

A poor attitude and self-image rob you of your self confidence. A minimum of self confidence along with a lack of real goals will depresses you until your motivation is gone. Without the motivation toward beneficial goals you have nothing to be enthusiactic about! That feeds further on your low attitude and the cycle extends to an even lower level.

A positive cycle will propel you to success by:

- Forgiving yourself for your past reestablishes your self-image and attitude.
- Reinforcing your positive attitude with Pep and Faith talks generates a positive self confidence.
- Self confidence is a force that, when combined with realistic goals which will stretch you, creates a powerful motivation.
- Motivation towards beneficial goals creates enthusiasm.

Now you have something to be enthusastic about! That pumps up your attitude and the cycle repeats itself to a higher level of success.

## Chapter Seventeen

# Attitudes

## Secrets

- ☐ You are exactly what you think you are.
- ☐ You ACT the way you think you are, unfortunately for most.
- ☐ Nothing enhances your ability like faith in yourself.
- ☐ Most Salespeople are not sure of their own ability.
- ☐ You are what you do by habit, the good and the bad.
- ☐ First develop the habit and the habit develops you.
- ☐ Do anything daily for a month and it is a habit.
- ☐ Spectacular success is preceded by long preparation.
- ☐ Excellence is a habit and not an occasional act.
- ☐ Improve your self-image by forgiving yourself.
- ☐ Forgive yourself so you won't carry a guilt complex.
- ☐ Compete, but don't compare yourself with others.
- ☐ Winning is a learned habit.
- ☐ Babe Ruth, King of Home Runs (714) and Strike Outs (1330).
- ☐ Winners never quit achieving goals; quitters never win.
- ☐ It is always too early to quit any desired goal.
- ☐ Neither success nor failure is final unless you let it be.
- ☐ Success in selling is a race against time.
- ☐ A lack of self-confidence creates indecision in the Prospect.
- ☐ Your attitude creates an atmosphere of failure or success.

- ☐ Most Salespeople's problems stem from their attitude.
- ☐ They label themselves "disorganized"; a self-fulfilling prophesy.
- ☐ An attitude is a habit of thought that only insight can change.
- ☐ Most people don't know what a good attitude is.
- ☐ You must be positive about your product, company and client.
- ☐ You have to assume success; act, talk and think successfully.
- ☐ Worry is using an active imagination negatively.
- ☐ What a person believes, they are; what they can do, they can.
- ☐ Most are negatively programmed so success is difficult.

# You Are Exactly What You Think You Are

Most people go through life handicapped by a low self-image of themselves. This low self-image was caused by the constant criticism their parents used in raising them. It is sad that the most impressionable years of a person's life are molded by amateur parents. Your childhood environment was one of "Don't do that ...", and "Why can't you be like ...", etc. Rarely was one's self-image nourished or enhanced with a positive stroke or compliment. Only now will you believe there is no such thing as "constructive criticism".

Salespeople may be greater victims of low self-esteem because of the rejection environment they live in. Their self-image is even further pressured because selling success is a race against time.

The only good feature about a bad self-image is that it is a thought and not a permanent fixture. Any thought can be changed with the correct technique. From the self-image flows one's future thoughts, attitudes, actions, successes, or lack of same.

# How To Think Positively

Thinking positively is not simply a matter of having positive thoughts. There is some preparation of the mind that is required first.

A flushing of guilt complexes must occur before the mind can receive and operate off the new image successfully. If you were to recall all of the terrible things that you ever did, or let occur, in life it would probably be a pretty sorry mess. The one consolation is that everyone has the same problem. You are indeed fortunate that no one else can read your memory.

Throughout our lives we were responsible for terrible things because we didn't care enough; put short term pleasure before long term gain; put our own pleasure or safety before the pleasure or safety of others; made wrong decisions because of lack of care or knowledge; or couldn't achieve some goal because of lack of care, concern, training or abilities, etc. This could be an endless paragraph for it is all the things in life that didn't go your way.

The great thing about all of those failures is that you have already paid the price for failing. It was a part of growing up, of maturing, of living and of your environment.

But you only have to pay the price of failure once per happening. Even our legal system has concluded that this is the fairest system of allocating blame and penalities. When you are exposed to the penalty twice it is Double Jeopardy. That cannot legally exist, nor should you be expected to accept it in your personal life.

Yet double jeopardy does exist in your mind. You could even call it "Infinite Jeopardy" if you carry the guilt of your failures around for life. That's a huge penalty. With that penalty of guilt preoccupying your vital thinking process you will probably never succeed. The older you get the more failures your negative self-image will beget, which in turn confirms that your self-image is not so good, which in turn causes more failures, etc. It is an endless, downward spiral to failure, a negative vicious circle.

# Forgive Yourself

You have to learn to forgive yourself. You have paid for your past failures by the lack of former successes. For the most part any given failure was primarily due to your negative self-image, which you didn't know how to manage. Probably the rest of your failures were due to circumstances beyond your control. You paid the price. The world's parade has long marched by that incident. It is now another day, another life, another you. Forget the past, you cannot correct it, but you can change it a little to your advantage by glorifying the good. That is safe and healthy for your mind. You are really a pretty decent person and you know it.

Once you have decided that you won't accept an "infinite jeopardy" for your past, your self-image can be the real you. You can start to build it and your successes. Building your self-image is not a trying experience. Indeed, it is an enjoyable time. You will still have some ups and downs because you don't have control over everything out there, nor can you be a winner every time. But the new road is a pleasure to travel.

When in competition with others for an achievement, it is fine to COMPETE with them but be careful you don't COMPARE yourself to the winner. You are a unique creation and your developed talents may not match the profile sought.

Don't think of yourself as being of strenghts and weaknesses. Rather think only of the talents developed, ie, your strengths. The so-called weaknesses, which tend to label you as a failure, are simply undeveloped talents. It is your option to develop the talent now, later or never. It is a decision you make based on your current needs. So don't consider yourself a life-long failure because of your "weaknesses".

But remember, spectacular success is always proceeded by rather unspectacular preparation.

# Programming Your Mind

Now that you have forgiven yourself and have cleared out those destructive guilt complexes you are ready to rebuild your self-image.

The unique way to restructure your self-image to its proper level is with Faith Talks. In essence, you:
   (1) Establish a legimate base by counting your blessings.
   (2) Define your new personality.
   (3) Confirm your faith in achieving that personality.

The subconscious mind does not have the ability to distinguish between real life experiences and imagined (visual) experiences. It cannot think. It simply takes it's instructions from the conscious mind and performs the activities of the body as instructed. If it is told to be happy, you will be happy. If told to feel guilty, you will feel guilty.

The real trick is in making sure that the message is loud and clear, not "weak and meek".

To ensure that the meaning, signals and programming is indeed strong it must be repeated several times a day (5 to 10 times) over a period of time (a month or longer). The Faith Talks will substantially alter your personality to whatever you want it to be. Let's look at how that is done in the next chapter, "Pep and Faith Talks".

## Chapter Eighteen
# Pep And Faith Talks

## Secrets

- ☐ You are exactly what you think you are.
- ☐ A Pep talk will give you instant enthusiasm.
- ☐ Faith talks will change your basic personality.
- ☐ You program your ever-believing subconscious mind.
- ☐ Your affirmation becomes a self-fulfilling prophesy.
- ☐ Proverbs and sayings are affirmations once internalized.
- ☐ Today's thinking is where and what you'll be tomorrow.
- ☐ You must Tell and See yourself as being successful.
- ☐ All winners are self-motivated with an inner drive for success.
- ☐ 75% of patients are ill because of poor mental attitudes.
- ☐ Motivation is a matter of attitude, a habit of your thought.
- ☐ You have to act, talk, feel and think your way to success.
- ☐ In Positive Thinking you only THINK yourself to success.
- ☐ Affirmation changes expectation to a self-fulfilling prophesy.
- ☐ Our lives are limited by what we see as possible.
- ☐ Your subconscious can't distinguish between fact and fantasy.
- ☐ Pep and Faith talks are self-motivating.
- ☐ Napoleon: Tell cowards they are brave and they will be brave.

# Create Miracles With Your Mind

William James, America's foremost philosopher, declared: "The greatest discovery of my generation is that human beings alter their lives by altering their attitude of mind. As you think so shall you be."

Napoleon Hill, author of the classic *Think and Grow Rich*, agrees with James: "Faith is a state of mind which may be induced, or created, by affirmation or repeated instruction to the subconscious mind through the principle of autosuggestion. It is a well known fact that one comes, finally, to believe whatever one repeats to one's self, whether the statement is true or false."

Plato: "Take charge of your life. You can do what you will with it."

Buddha: "All that we are is the result of what we have thought."

Ghandi: "Man often becomes what he believes himself to be."

King Solomon: "As a man thinkest in his heart so is he."

From these great discoveries came the mind control technique called Affirmation. By definition, affirmation is an assertion, or a statement made positively; also, a protestation or a suggestion to the subconscious mind. The key to affirmation is that you tell your subconscious what you want to be and your subconscious merely carries out these commands involuntarily.

Perhaps the greatest liability a Salesperson has is in their low, bruised self-image. Self-image consists of 3 parts:

(1) Image they see themselves to be. At times the Salesperson is depressed by their own self-image. (Real Self)

(2) Image they wish others would accept them as. (Ideal Self)

(3) Image that society will let them project. This is a compromise between what they are and what they want to be. It is all that traffic will bear. (Ideal Other)

We are constantly programming our self-image on a moment-by-moment basis. As growing children we were programmed as we were "constructively criticized" by our amateur parents. We are programmed to some degree by everything that happens to us in life, even now as you are reading this information. Good news programs us positively, bad news programs us negatively.

The big problem in life is that we don't control enough of the programming. Until now your environment, friends, job, luck or misfortune have influenced you, positively or negatively, or both.

Wouldn't it be wonderful if you could program yourself to be whatever you want to be? The technique has a host of titles: Autosuggestion, Possibility Thinking, Attitude Control, Affirmation, or Pep and Faith talks. It all comes out the same. You are exactly what you think you are. It is a powerful weapon, and probably your only weapon against sliding morale.

# Program Your Own Mind Positively

There are two kinds of affirmation talks (1) Pep talks, and (2) Faith talks. Pep talks are for short-term pick-me-up results, while the Faith talks are for long-term major changes in personality.

## (1) Pep Talks

A Pep talk a Salesperson could give themselves just before entering a sales interview:

**SP** - "I will be enthusiastic! I will ask lots of questions and I will Trial Close at every chance I get."

That is all it takes!

## (2) Faith Talks

Since the Faith talk is for a major change in personality or character you should take some care in designing the talk. The basic formula is:

(1) Count your blessings (to boost your self-image).
(2) State your objective (your desired change).
(3) Affirm your faith in achieving the objective.

**EXAMPLES:**

**SP** - "I am very personable. I am a fine Salesperson. I have a wonderful wife and child. I am very intelligent."
**SP** - "I am an enthusiastic person. I am very involved in my product and the miracles it will give my Prospects.
**SP** - "I know I will be successful in reaching my goals because anything I really want I have always achieved."

**PLANNING:**

**SP** - "I Consider a problem as an opportunity for my creativity."
**SP** - "I have complete confidence in all that I do and plan.
**SP** - "I can reach creative decisions and solutions."

**SP** - "I face problems with courage and can solve them easily."
**SP** - "I persevere and finish all tasks that I commit to."
**SP** - "I bring great concentration to bear on all my efforts."
**SP** - "I will be a success in whatever I set my goals on."
**SP** - "I organize my work for today and the future."

## MENTAL:

**SP** - "I can master anything that I have an interest in."
**SP** - "I love new ideas and can adopt and adapt them to my needs."
**SP** - "Above all, I have superior intelligence."

## SOCIAL:

**SP** - "I feel good in expressing my like for everyone I know."
**SP** - "I show my interest by being an interested listener."

## FAITH TALK PROGRAMMING:

- Select a specific area of your life you want to change.
- State your blessings positively; visualize it.
- State your new quality as if you now possess it.
- Put it in writing:
    > Writing the affirmation will clarify your thinking.
    > You can visualize the new you.
    > Your subconscious records the written instructions better.
    > The written goal keeps you from wandering.
    > Put a timetable on your affirmations to pressure yourself.

- Repeat the affirmation to yourself several times each day.
- Ask those who are important to you to help you with your commitment.

- Act, think, feel and talk like the new you to get in the habit.

- Above all, be patient. In 30 days it will become a habit.

| Pep Talks | Versus | Faith Talks |
|---|---|---|
| Fast acting: seconds | Speed? | Slow acting: months |
| Short duration: hours | Lasts? | Long lasting: lifetime |
| Whenever needed | How often? | 10 times a day |
| 10 to 20 words | How long? | 50 to 100 words |
| Energy, enthusiasm | Benefit? | Character, attitude change |
| "Shot in the arm" | Purpose? | Rebuild self-image |
| Light in tone | Serious? | Serious in tone |
| Battle | Analogy? | War |

# Visualize For Magnification

Visualize yourself actually being the way you want to be. It is like a dress rehearsal for your subconscious mind, for the mind sees better in images. (There are those psychologists who believe the mind must translate everything into an image before the idea can be stored in memory).

Both the Pep and Faith talks must be positive, sincere and enthusiastic. You are literally programming yourself to be better than what you THINK you now are. This is not the time to be modest; your self-image is at stake.

# Category: Professional

**Goal**    Primary   — Increase annual commission to $YY,000
          Secondary — Become Sales Manager in present company

REASON FOR GOAL: I want a luxury standard of living for my family. By managing my career we can have it. I need and want more money. Becoming Sales Manager will be a major advancement.

SUPPORTING GOAL: Maintain a list of 25 Wanting Prospects.
Necessary Activities:
- Ask each Client for 3 leads.
- Ask each Prospect for 3 leads.
- Spend 4 hours each week on prospecting.
- Speak in public once per month on selling.
- Secretarial service produce 25 letters per week.
- Secretary/"home bound" make 100 calls per week.
- Create Centers of Influence, and Advisors.

SUPPORTING GOAL: Improve my presentation toward 100% closing.
Necessary Activities:
- Develop new Attention-getters (MISS GRACE).
- Improve questions for my Interest step.
- Get one new Testimonial per week.
- Develop one new emotional benefit per week.
- Develop one new act of showmanship per week.
- Absorb one selling skills program per month.
- Analyze each Presentation for pros and cons.

SUPPORTING GOAL: Streamline my paperwork.
Necessary Activities:
- Write Thank You notes in car after meeting.
- Update Prospect card in car while still fresh.
- Do sales reports on weekends: 2 hrs. maximum.

SUPPORTING GOAL: Improve Time Management so I can make more calls.
Necessary Activities:
- Record every 15 minute activity on Time Log.
- Have an alternate list of Prospects to meet.
- Carry reading materials for waiting time.
- Qualify Need/Authority/Financial *early!*
- Cold call when stranded in an area.
- Plan major and minor activities the night before.
- Be jealous of time: What is really in it for me?
- Only get involved in goal-related activities.

SUPPORTING GOAL: Maintain an Enthusiastic Attitude.
Necessary Activities:
- Visualize Goals: prompted by every cup of coffee.
- Give yourself a Pep Talk when required.
- Give yourself a Faith Talk five times each day.
- Act enthusiastic and you will be enthusiastic!

240

## Chapter Nineteen

# Goals

## (Self-Motivation)

# Secrets

- ☐ "Any port in a storm" leads to career failure.
- ☐ Goals must be activities and not results.
- ☐ Visualization the results reinforces the Want.
- ☐ Visualize the activities to program the subconscious.
- ☐ You must measure the cost:benefit of the goal.
- ☐ Goal setting is a life long activity.
- ☐ Ability is not always important to success.
- ☐ First we make the habit, then the habit makes us.
- ☐ Leadership is goal setting and goal getting.
- ☐ Planning will always save more time than it costs.
- ☐ All great achievers are great planners.
- ☐ Time management means nothing without career goals.
- ☐ Visualizing is seeing, is believing.
- ☐ Visualization gives us experience.
- ☐ The subconscious cannot sort real from imagined.
- ☐ A goal without a timetable is a dream.
- ☐ You are what you think about the most.
- ☐ Destiny is not a matter of chance, but of choice.
- ☐ Goals stop one from drifting; no purpose, no progress.
- ☐ Be goal oriented, not task oriented.

# Goals - Your Path To The Future

## Benefits Of Goals

If you don't know where you are going any road will take you there - but don't be upset if you don't like the destination.

The benefits of goal setting are quite dramatic:

**M**  MOTIVATES you to greater success.
**D**  DESTINATION is clearly defined.

**C**  CONCENTRATION of energy ensures success.
**P**  PURPOSE - gives you a sense of purpose.
**A**  ACHIEVEMENT and success are yours.

It is appropriate that the acronym of the MD-CPA degrees represents the benefits of goal setting as well as two of the highest successes one can have in education. Either degree requires goal setting for success.


# How To Select Your Goals

## (1) Crystalize Your Thinking:

YOUR GOALS MUST BE YOURS. Most of what you think now is based on habit, which in turn is based on your environment and the conditioning by that environment. It is very difficult to know yourself because of that conditioning. When you do finally understand what you want, challenge that want to see if it is really for you.

YOUR GOALS MUST BE REALISTIC AND ATTAINABLE. The higher the better. Low goals are usually ignored. Low goals have no real rewards and very little challenge. The goals must be within your reach but you must "stretch" yourself to reach them.

YOUR GOALS MUST BE POSITIVE. Our minds literally visualize a picture of each thought. Therefore, a negative image may program the mind negatively. For example, if you want to lose weight, do not tell yourself "I am overweight" or your mind will see an overweight body, the way it truly is. The image matches, negative programming results and the wrong goal is reinforced. If your desired weight is to be 170 pounds then see yourself at a 170 pounds and your mind will see the slimmer body image and respond accordingly. Its incredible, but that is the way it works.

# (2) Planning:

A small amount of planning can save an enormous amount of time in future activity, maybe even great effort and certainly great dollars. You will always save more time in your activity than the time you spend in planning the time-saving effort.

## Planning Is Always Successful
## All Great Achievers Are Great Planners

Time management means nothing without career goals to save the time for. You can save time for two purposes: (1) to have more leisure time, and (2) to reach goals faster. Since most people neither plan their leisure time nor have goals, they have no need to be proficient at saving or managing their time. So most don't. But watch a career planner or high achiever utilize their time. There is even an age old bromide about them: "Always ask the busy person, they always have time." They don't need a book or course on time managing, they could write one.

# (3) Visualize The Benefits:

## Visualizing is Seeing, is Believing

When you are watching a football game you experience the same psychological stress as the player running with the ball. The same adrenalin, hormones and body changes take place when you become emotionally involved in the play. Your mind cannot distinguish between the real emotion and the sympathetic experience you get emotionally involved in.

All thought processes must be reduced to visual images to be "seen" by the mind. Our mind operates in such a way that we will believe what we see with the *naked* eye, or even with the *mind's* eye.

## Visualizing Gives Us Experience.

The subconscious mind understands only the here and now, and not the past or future. Neither can it distinguish between the real experiences and the mental image of that same activity. So visualize your rewards as though you are enjoying them now:

> Wrong: "I want to buy a big sailboat."
> Right: "I love the ocean breeze, the keel cutting the water, the ocean spray in my face, the freshness of the air."

Even the visual images of the Desire Step are meant to prompt this same mental process. By creating a visual image of the Prospect using, enjoying, and benefiting from the product, they will have a successful mental trial. They will feel comfortable with the product after having "tried" it mentally. To the mind, experience is an image. It doesn't seem to know where that experience comes from, either a visualized experience or a physical experience. Have you ever heard of athletes visualizing their swing or their throw to make sure it is perfect? They even substitute mental practice for a physical practice. At times the mental practice can be more beneficial, because it can be more controlled.

Thoughts lead to action (subconscious activity), which lead to methods (goal setting) for the realization of goals and success.

Visualizing can be maximized by preparing your mind: Sit back, get very comfortable and close your eyes. Let your body go limp and relax all over. Your mind is now relatively clear of confusing thoughts so start to see yourself in these new goal positions. Make the image as vivid as you can. Put yourself in the scene. Smell it, hear it, taste it, as well as see it.

See the physical activities that go with the goal. Visualize yourself managing your sales force if you want to be a Sales Manager; see yourself helping one of your Salespeople close a sale; hear yourself asking the closing question and the Prospect responding favorably.

## (4) Visualize Activities

The goals we set must be ACTIVITIES and not results. The subconscious can't operate until it knows specifically what to do. For example, it may be your goal to own an expensive home on the beach. You can visualize living in the home, enjoying summer evening cocktail parties, sailing along the coast, etc. But your subconscious doesn't know what to do with that enjoyment image. In your planning on how you are going to buy the home, if you decide that you will sell $1 million dollars in the next year, your subconscious can understand and operate on the fact that you will have to sell $4,000 dollar a day average sales. You can see it mentally as well as aid in accomplishing it.

## (5) A Burning Desire

If you visualize a large, thick, juicy steak, covered with mushrooms; a fine wine, and candlelight, do you think that you may get a little hungry? If you close your eyes and visualize the scene, it's guaranteed your appetite will be activated. That's a physical thought, and an emotional appetite created by visualizing your goal. The more specific the rewards the more you kindle the desire.

When you visualize the steak, visualize it as if you were in the process of enjoying it NOW, rather than wanting it. See yourself in your chosen success.

Having a vivid image of the desire, by concentration on the activities to reach that goal, and a belief in your ability to achieve the goal you will create the emotional appetite that will have you hungering. It is yours. You have it. You merely have to go through the process of completing the required steps to realize it. It is an old bromide but always true that "where there is a will, there is a way". It just depend on how much you want your goal.

HOW DO WE DEVELOP THE BURNING DESIRE? Very simple, write down all of the worthwhile rewards you will have when you attain the goal. When you visualize and concentrate on the outcome, it stimulates your emotional appetite that creates your desire.

The big question is: "What's in it for me?" A most basic question in life. Measure your rewards against the cost to you. WARNING: write down both the costs and the rewards before starting on the goal. Develop the cost:benefit ratio of the business world. Many careers and years of life could have been more productive if the costs and benefits had been put on paper. The emotional desire of the goal must be tested against logical reality before accepting the goal. Be ruthless in that logical evaluation. If not, your easily influenced emotional mind will lead you down the garden path to a goal with a worthless reward.

# (6) Supreme Self-Confidence

Ability is not always important to success. Research indicates that most people that graduate from high school could have entered college if they had really tried and applied to a reasonable number of colleges. By the same token everyone that entered college could have earned their degree if they had had the determination and reasonable organization. Yet how many people carry a guilt complex because they never finished college? Most do. The only thing they should chastise themselves for is not having the determination to apply themselves - even now.

It is never too late to begin if you have the desire. Sir Winston Churchill was considered a failure until he was 65 years old. Peter Tchaikowsky, one of the world's greatest piano composers did not learn to play the piano until he was 39. These may be exceptions but only because they had exceptional desires to reach their goals. It all depends on how badly you want it.

YOU ARE EXACTLY WHAT YOU THINK YOU ARE. If you feel like a failure, your subconscious will effectively program you for failure and you will be successful at failing. No question about it.

By the same token, the average person can accomplish almost anything if they want it badly enough. Successful people are constantly pressing for success and are not aware of the daily sacrifices they make as a habit, but the sacrifices are there. Success for anyone is assured if they really want it. And the sacrifices may be an easy tradeoff for the other benefits of success.

## (7) Tangible vs Intangible

Tangible goals are goals of GETTING. It is there in front of you to touch, handle and smell.

Intangible goals are goals of BECOMING. Becoming means an internal change in personality traits. Also, new skills may need to be developed. For example, a Salesperson aspiring to be a Sales Manager will need to:

- Develop decision-making skills.
- Learn to overcome procrastination.
- Learn to motivate others.

## (8) Personality Changes:

Your goals must include personality changes. In your new role in life you will have a different attitude. Maybe even a different personality is required in the new role. Try to visualize this new personality and see yourself with it. You can use Faith talks to effectively create the new personality.

**First we make the habits, and then the habits make us.**

## (9) Commit Your Plans To Writing:

The mind is seldom skilled at sorting and weighing the many alternatives open to it. Writing down your goals does crystalize your thoughts.

Once the thought is committed to paper it is motivated to action; it has been programmed.

The written goals give you these benefits:

- Keep track of where you are going and how you are going to get there.
- Block out distractions. The written goal is like a checkpoint so you can stay on target.
- Written goals allow measuring and thereby gives you a feedback on your to-date performance.
- Reducing it to writing overcomes procrastination, stagnation, doubting and loss of your real goal.

# (10) Dangers In Goal Setting

(A) FEAR OF DEVELOPING PLANS FOR THE FUTURE. Most people are conditioned by society to be followers. They are not aware of it, but they fear making future plans. They are afraid to do something on their own.

(B) THE GOAL IS NOT WITHIN YOUR MEANS. At this point in your development, you may not be able to afford the price of the goal. You may not now have enough resources either in dollars, time or skills. The goal will then have to be modified or postponed.

(C) THE GOALS ARE BASED ON THE VALUES OF OTHERS. You don't realize that most of the values you operate on are not your own values, but rather those of your family and friends. Consider the goal of a young man when he boasts that he is going to uphold the family tradition by joining the Marines. After all his father was a Marine, his grandfather was a Marine, and his great-grandfather was a Marine. So he will become a Marine. Whose value system is he operating on?

You have to look at your reasons for wanting to attain each goal, and then determine if it is really something you want, rather than an unconscious desire to please others.

(D) CONFLICT WITH THE VALUES WE NOW HAVE. It is narrow minded to set one goal at the expense of the rest of our daily living. Some peole have reached outstanding goals when their one goal was pursued with an *obsession*. Putting forth *every* human effort one can muster into reaching one goal has been the usual method of all great accomplishments. But there were great tradeoffs being made that the goal seeker often isn't aware of. At times their success left sad tradeoffs. So be aware of other goals that should be considered:

FINANCIAL Goals - Being the best in a career that doesn't pay well may be a dubious goal.

COMMUNITY goals - In many careers it takes others to help you to success.

HEALTH Goals - Many have destroyed their health in the quest for success.

FAMILY Goals - Many have destroyed their families in attaining success.

SELF-IMPROVEMENT Goals - A rapidly changing world can quickly make many of your talents obsolete.

RELIGIOUS Goals - Some don't require a spiritual life until life is just about over.

PROFESSIONAL Goals - Success may not be rewarding if you have attained your professional goal but you have a tarnished and dubious reputation.

As long as you are aware that there are tradeoffs between goal attainment and a balanced life, then the choice is yours.

## Examples To Prompt Goals:

### FINANCIAL:
Be free of debt.
Buy a better home.
Obtain security for the family.
Acquire personal security.
Save more money.
Have more for investments.
Earn more money.
Have a second home.

### COMMUNITY:
Work for the community.
Start a conservation.
Perform a personal service.
Be a good team member.
Be President of civic club.
Help a favorite charity.
Help the handicapped.
Visit sick children's hospital.

### HEALTH:
Lose/gain some weight.
Get more exercise.
Cut out salt and sugar.
Take vitamins daily.
Quit smoking.
Have a good appearance.
Get active in a sport.
Get in good health.

### FAMILY:
Enhance your marriage.
Help children with education.
Buy a better home.
Increase family security.
Be closer to your children.
Retire earlier than planned.

### SELF-IMPROVEMENT:
Develop your own ideas.
Complete whatever you start.
Select goals very carefully.
Read an affirmation book.
Win more recognition.
Manage your career.
Attend some seminars.
Listen to educational tapes.

### RELIGIOUS:
See your spiritual leader.

### PROFESSIONAL:
Manage your career.
Keep business records.
Plan your advancement at work.
Win an award.
Buy, start a business.
Increase your job security.
Take advanced training.
Consider changing to new career.

(E) REDESIGN OF GOALS. At times, it is too often or too little. Situations can change rapidly. Some of these changes may warrant a change in your goals. Be especially cautious about changing long term goals, but change short term goals for the convenience of reaching the long term goals.

(F) DAILY DECISIONS. Every decision should be made in terms of its effect on your long term goals. That makes decision making on a daily basis very easy.

# (11) Deadlines Create a Sense of Urgency

If you could live forever you could accomplish any goal you desired at some point. But in life you are in a race against time when you talk about success.

A goal without a timetable is merely a dream. By putting deadlines on your goals you create several benefits:

- The deadline psychologically imprints itself on you and creates a sense of urgency.

- The deadline creates a challenge within you because of your inbread sense of responsibility.

- With the goal in sight, the deadline creates an overwhelming sense of accomplishment.

There is a problem with setting *one* deadline for a goal. You tend to leave the effort until the last minute when in reality it is almost too late and impossible to complete. With a lack of completion, you have a sense of abandonment and a loss of commitment.

To avoid risking the total success of your goals on a deadline, you should break the goal down into small "bites" to be completed at various points in time. A simple example would be a Salesperson planning to sell $1,000,000 over the next year. By reducing it to bite sizes it is more do-able:

| $87,486 per month | (21 day month). |
| $20,830 per week | (5 day week). |
| $ 4,166 per selling day | (24 days, holidays excepted). |

Look at the results daily, but don't be upset with the *daily* fluctuations. Weekly totals will also fluctuate quite a bit. Monthly totals are the combined effect of seasonality *and* selling success, or lack of same; it will then be readily apparent when more creativity is required to maintain your monthly goal.

# (12) Early Success With Goals

The sooner you experience success with a goal, the sooner you will be able to build a whole program of success. By the choice and design of goals you can control the early pattern of goal success. For your self-confidence it is desirable to have a few early successes:

| **Easy Success** | **Difficult Success** |
|---|---|
| Important Goal | Unimportant Goal |
| Near in time | Distant in time |
| Tangible | Intangible |
| Clear and Visual | Somewhat undefined |

## Watch Out For:

- DISTRACTIONS CAUSED BY OTHER ACTIVITIES.
- FRUSTRATIONS FROM FAILURES OR SETBACKS.
- OTHER RESPONSIBILITIES INTERFERING.
- PHYSICALLY TIRED OR ILL HEALTH.
- LOSING SIGHT OF YOUR GOALS.
- FAILING TO OUTLINE A SPECIFIC PLAN.

# Epilogue

Goal REACHING is the strongest motivation a human can have. Start putting it to work right now with easy successes so you can taste the sweetness of success.

## Chapter Twenty
# Strategy

# Secrets

- ☐ Adopt and Adapt your Selling to your market and Prospect.
- ☐ Consumer sales take fewer sales calls than Business sales.
- ☐ Keep business Prospects busy between calls with Key Events.
- ☐ Must get them to commit to do something before you leave.
- ☐ Business sales often require multiple approvals.
- ☐ Expense purchases are faster than capital purchases.
- ☐ When Stalled, set a future appointment or you won't be back.
- ☐ A Stall is a decision not to make a decision now.
- ☐ Must arrange next visit before Prospect gives Stall.
- ☐ The return call must be sold on its own merits.
- ☐ Once rejected, you have to start over with new curiosity.
- ☐ After a Stall, a Prospect is vulnerable to competition.
- ☐ Difficult to identify the real decision maker in a group.
- ☐ Groups: Attention, Interest, Conviction, Desire, and Close.
- ☐ Decision order: ranking, heavy user, one others defer to.
- ☐ Try to interview the key players before a group meeting.
- ☐ Must review and interview others for their SIP and EBM.
- ☐ Sell, sell, sell; don't sell, pester, pester for reentry.
- ☐ Selling involves protection from predators, in and out.
- ☐ Who controls your destiny in your Client's company?

- Who controls your destiny in your own company?
- How strong is your relationship with key contacts?
- How well have you developed your key contact's superiors?
- You must manage your client and your environment.

# Adopt And Adapt

There are times when the Selling Process is more involved than the typical one hour sales presentation to the business decision maker. It may take several visits over a period of months. When this happens you have to develop a strategy to handle that different situation. You will have to Adopt and Adapt the Selling Process.

The Selling Process is based on the fact that all Prospects go through a similar mental process: Curiosity, Interest, Conviction, Desire and Action; and that you are selling people and people relationships, rather that simply products.

The Selling Process is a universal process applying to all Salespeople and Prospects, and all kinds of markets. In addition to ADOPTING it as a new selling skill, you must ADAPT it to the specific variables you encounter. The two major variables are the type of MARKET and the type of PROSPECT. The Market refers to the Consumer or Business Prospect and is covered herein. The Prospect is covered under a separate chapter: Personalities.

## Business vs Consumer

The National Association of Manufactures conducted a survey of their member's sales success and found that 80% of the sales were made after the 5th sales call.

Yet, Frank Bettger, one of the world's leading Insurance Salespeople, and author of *How I Raised Myself From Failure To Success In Selling*, did a study on his own sales efforts and found that 93% of his sales were after the 2nd call:

|          |     |           |
|----------|-----|-----------|
| 1st call | 70% |           |
| 2nd call | 23% | Total 93% |
| 3rd+ call| 7%  |           |

Why the great difference in results? Simply different kinds of Markets - Consumer versus Business.

# Consumer Sales

Frank Bettger was selling to the lone consumer. Calling on an individual 5 times just doesn't make sense. If the Prospect isn't really interested by the first presentation, the second probably isn't going to help increase their interest. The second call may still be *"selling"* but the third definitely is *"pestering"*.

Bettger also found that he was spending 50% of his selling time to get the 7% sales from the 3rd, 4th and 5th calls. So Frank would terminate the Prospect after the 2nd call. If no sale by then, he would go back to prospecting, "Dialing for Dollars". (That is testimony to the importance of record keeping of your sales efforts!)

In a RETAIL situation the Selling Process is even shorter so you have to:

- Build rapport quickly.
- Ask them what their Interest (SIP) is.
- Find their reason for wanting the product (EBM).
- Show them how the product will solve their problem.
- Create a 25 word visual image of them enjoying it.
- Alternate Choice Close; *which* instead of *if*.

# Business Sales

In selling to a Business, the Salesperson may have to call many times to unseat a well-established vendor. Businesses usually are not reckless about switching vendors. The quick switch comes only when they are desperate and rarely is that the case.

In some situations, you may have several people to visit to have your product tested, accepted and ordered. As an example, an advanced computer system installation may take five, ten or even fifteen sales calls. Here many of the calls are survey calls for "needs evaluations", etc.

The major conquest in the business sales call is arranging to meet with the Prospect for the second, third, fourth and subsequent calls. That takes selling talent. Between each call the Prospect may lose interest or get so involved with a higher priority project that you are put on the "back-burner". Often, if the Prospect knew there were to be so many meetings involved, there may not even be a second call.

Your product line may require multiple calls as a normal pattern. If so, plan the subsequent calls even before the first is made along the Key Events that must be accomplished. Support it with data on their organizational setup, and whatever you need to develop in closing your typical sale. Don't falsely hope that you will be lucky and complete the sale on the first call. That only happens when they are desperate, or have a bad credit rating.

Not all sales are closed in a single call whether in business or consumer-retail sales. For some products the norm may even be as many as 5 to 10 calls. For example, in the sale of a PERSONAL computer, the Prospect returns to a computer store an average of 6 times before a sale is closed. A complex BUSINESS computer system the process may take a year. On the other hand, a life insurance policy may be sold in one call.

In the routine business sales presentation you can expect that the convinced Prospect will have to consult with others. This often applies even to the President, and almost always to other decision influencers. The bigger the company the more the "don't rock the boat" attitude will force the approvals of others. It is the way of business life.

# Multiple Calls

At the end of that first sales interview the Prospect's interest will be at its highest peak. Never again will it be that high. After you leave their interest starts to wane.

Now you face the problem of how to keep the interest up until the next meeting. If interest is not sustained there will be no second meeting.

There are three necessary steps that must be taken to ensure there is an open door with a welcome mat:

(1) Arrange for the day, time, and those who will be attending the next meeting. That COMMITS them. And arrange it BEFORE they tell you 'I'd like to think it over.'

(2) Get the Prospect to commit to perform a necessary step in the Selling Process that is to their advantage. These Key Events are part of their step by step decision process you identified in the questioning. That keeps their INTEREST.

(3) Arrange for a followup with the Prospect on the progress of the Key Events. That keeps them INVOLVED.

# (1) Next Meeting

Do not leave one meeting without a definite date and time for the next meeting. If you leave without it, there may not be another meeting, so stick in there.

Arrange the next meeting before the Prospect tells you, 'I'd like to think it over.' When they tell you that it means they have decided not to decide now, or maybe never. You have to execute the next step before they make that decision. That means you must know early their degree of interest and their ability to close now. How do you do that? You Trial Close all along the way.

**SP** - "Mr. P, may I suggest that there are other persons that should be consulted on this change. Why don't we arrange for a short meeting with them. The reason I suggest this is because others will probably have questions that are different than yours. Let's arrange a time for all of us. How is Monday morning for breakfast at the …?"

  **P** - "That sounds great."

**SP** - "Can you check with Mr. Decision Maker now to see if that meeting is OK?"

  **P** - "Sure, I'll have my secretary do that now."

**SP** - "Great. I'll send a confirming note to you and your associate, with a copy to your secretary so she can put it on your calendar."

# (2) Key Events

In Business there are two kinds of purchases; capital and expense. Capital purchases are the once-in-a-while machines or systems. Expense purchases are the day-to-day supplies.

**Supplies:**

In most cases a business has an established vendor for supplies. The sales effort here is to work with the Purchasing Agent or major user to show how they will benefit more from your product. The decision can be fast for a trial, and permanent if successful. Decision making is at a low level.

**Capital:**

A capital expenditure is for equipment or a system. The purchase could be a replacement, upgrading, or a new venture. Where capital expenditures are involved, several approval levels are needed because of the large dollars and/or length of time committed.

The purchase of capital items is not a spectator's activity. The buyer has several basic functions to perform:

> (1) A survey of their present position.
> (2) An evaluation of solutions possible.
> (3) Tour of vendor facilities.
> (4) Selection of a solution.
> (5) Appropriation for dollars.
> (6) Approval of others.

The way to establish an assured pattern of calls is to get the Prospect involved in a way that they are COMMITTED to perform a definite task that is important to the progress of the decision making and buying process between this meeting and the next. At the next meeting they will have to report on it. This is a Key Event. The Key Event keeps them hot between calls. Whether you are selling a product or service you must know the Key Events necessary in the buying and selling of your product. YOU must make them happen.

Examples of Key Events for a given product could be:

- Survey the staff on their present situation.
- Collect certain data pertinent to the product use.
- Approach the Prospect's manager for approval.
- Arrange to have an Appropriation drawn up.
- Presentation of your proposal at the staff meeting.
- Arrange a meeting with senior decision influencers.
- Presentation to Board of Directors.

**SP** - "Mr. P, why don't we run a small survey of your staff's evaluation of your current service. Here is a survey form that asks all the right questions. As you can see, there is no letterhead on it, so you can photocopy it to your letterhead. Have them returned to you so it will be unbiased."

Between now and the next meeting the Prospect can become very busy, too busy to accomplish their agreed-to tasks. This may result in a postponed meeting. At that point, the interest in your product may be on the "back-burner", or so low in relation to other priorities that the postponement may be indefinite.

When the Prospect has a problem performing the Key Event, your calls will tend to pressure and eventually pester them. That is devasting.

Make sure that the Prospect can perform the Key Event easily. If not, you will be stalled out until they do perform the task or you are forgotten, whichever comes sooner. You may want to suggest that the Prospect gets someone else within the organization to assist on it and you interface with that assistant. For example, suggest they enlist the aid of accounting to study the costs of the existing system. You follow up with accounting and keep the Prospect informed of the progress. Make it easy for the Prospect to perform.

# (3) Progress Followup

While interest is being sustained during a waiting period, competition may be present. Remember, the Need and Desire have been established with the Prospect so they are susceptible to competitive thrusts. The next acceptable offer to the Prospect by a likeable Salesperson may close the sale. You have to keep the Prospect interested in you and your product between calls.

Your phone calls have to be interesting. The Prospect should look forward to hearing from you because they expect you to have more benefits or other good news for them. Only incidentally can you inquire about their progress with the Key Events.

At the outset, suggest that you call the Prospect or their assistant between meetings in the event you come up with some new ideas or benefits:

**SP** - "Great. We'll see you and Mr. Prospect at breakfast. If I come up with some new ideas or benefits I'll give you a call."

**P** - "Fine."

**SP** - "I'd also like to check with your Secretary/Assistant to see if there is any way I can help with the ...(Key Event) ... Fair enough?"

**P** - "That sounds great."

# Groups

Groups pose special selling problems, and the reason for the problem is that each decision maker/influencer may have a different EBM due to their personal wants.

In reality, some Prospects may have no strong EBM when a member of a group other than peer pressure. They merely want the problem solved to reduce the work load.

This is compounded when you don't know who is dominant in the decision making process. (Rank does not necessarily denote an interest as long as their problem is solved.) Or when the decision maker could change under a new environment. Or when the current decision maker's personality could change in the presence of other levels of authority, similar to the change in assertiveness and responsiveness that often occurs between office and home. Or, as is often the case, when the decision maker is not even present.

You are open to a barrage of questions because of diversified interests. Some of them may put you on the spot, others may give you objections disguised as questions, or questions disguised as objections. Still others may object only after you leave.

In a group meeting you will not have the opportunity to identify the EBM of the dominant decision maker. So try to identify in advance the people who will be attending the meeting. Call them and offer to send along some advance material in preparation for the meeting. Better still, try to meet with them prior to the meeting if the sale warrants it. Even interview their Buffer.

There is no certain method of identifying the real or dominant decision maker or influencer during the meeting. Nevertheless, there is a procedure that you can use to target the most probable. Look to the hierarchy of power in the grouping:

> (1) The highest ranking member.
> (2) A heavy user of the product.
> (3) The one others seem to defer to.

# (1) Highest Ranking

Obviously, if no other information appears from observation, the person you should concentrate on is the highest ranking person. In most organizations when they are convinced that your product is the one for them, the sale is probably yours.

# (2) Heavy User

If there is heavy user of the product present, the highest ranked will probably want the positive input from that heavy user.

When the heavy user is positive about your product, and the highest ranked does not see any reason not to use it, you have the sale.

If the heavy user is neutral the highest ranked may want to defer judgement until later.

Obviously if the heavy user transmits a negative feeling you are in serious trouble. Once you get this negative response you have to find out quickly what interest the heavy user has in seeking a change:

**SP** - "Oh? Well, Mr. Heavy User, what challenging problems do you now see in the use of this kind of product?"

> (a) **P** - "I have trouble with the ..."
> ... and you are off and running. OR

> (b) **P** - "I really don't have much of a problem at all with it."
> ... ignore that person and go back to your original Prospect;

**SP** - "Mr. P, you mentioned that your real problem was with the ..., isn't that correct? For the sake of the group, would you elaborate on that please?"

You are now referencing back to the Prospect's problem or interest so the others will realize a problem does exists.

## (3) Defers To

When there is no highest ranking member in the group, and no heavy user, you should look to the person that others seem to defer to.

Most of time you will not receive a decision from the group in your presence unless the decision maker has a strong personality and sees that the group is in obvious agreement. You will have to wait until later to talk to your prime Prospect.

When a group is involved, its existence suggests that there is a high priority to solving the problem, else how could they justify taking the time of the other influencers. You can suspect that they are interviewing your competition as well.

When competition is active and relatively close in benefits, (which could be most of the time in the Prospect's view) the decision may turn on the smaller benefits since the major benefits should be similar. Briefly highlight those lesser benefits and leave literature describing them for comparison purposes. Detailing the lesser benefits in the meeting will be boring and will detract from the major benefits.

# Group Presentation

The presentation should follow the classic steps of the Selling Process:

## Attention:

Begin with an interesting story of another client's happy experience with the product being presented. Humanize it as much as possible. You are talking to them at their interest level. Make it a short story, and don't make yourself the hero.

## Interest:

Get them interested by telling them of the major benefits of the product. This would be the big promise, or claim. Bridge out of this step with, "You may be wondering how we can do this so let's look at the facts ..."

## Conviction:

Give them only the Fact/Features and Advantages of your product that are important to their problem. Each time stress the benefits to the company and the people involved. As you give each Benefit make it interesting. It is mandatory that you demonstrate either the Feature, Advantage or Benefit because of the limited involvement of each person. Use showmanship and excitement, because their attention is hard to hold. Use testimonials, charts, exhibits and visuals wherever possible. Since they are not personally involved, their interest is not intense. So make it exciting for them, or at least memorable.

## Desire:

This is where you do a Hurt and Rescue. Remind them of their terrible problem by using Visual Images of the awful things that can happen;

SP - "With all your capital tied up in parts inventory, your banker will be on your back, your vendors will be holding back shipments, maybe even the odd payroll check will bounce. That's quite possible, isn't it?" *(The Hurt)*

"As you have seen, our nearby warehouse and 24 hour delivery will solve that problem." *(The Solution)*

"Just imagine that you go ahead with this plan. It is six months later, and you are meeting in this very room. Your President is looking at the latest inventory report. He looks around the room at each of you and says 'Congratulations, that's great work. You have made life a lot easier for all of us.' That's the kind of scene you all want, isn't it?" *(The Rescue)*

## Close:

Summarize by doing a Weighing Close, the one wherein you weigh the pros and cons. Draw a T on a markerboard with the "Reasons to hesitate", or Concerns, on one side and "Reasons for Progressing" on the other.

SP - "As you can see, the benefits are quite substantial."

Ask for the order using a Minor Point Close:

SP - "Who will be assigned to coordinate this with us?" But don't be surprised if you get a delayed decision. Unless the decision maker is present, and the group is in obvious agreement, the decision will be delayed until they can convene on their own.

# Reentry

## Thrown Out

There is no final refusal in buying and selling. Selling is a life long process and people do change their vendors. It's just a matter of time.

While curiosity and novelty may have gotten the Prospect's interest for the first interview, it won't work for a second visit. When you do win a second interview based on the original curiosity and novelty, there will never be a third. The reason is simple, the second call was not a *sell* call where you presented new benefits to the Prospect, but rather a *pester* call where you rehashed the old.

Each sales call must be sold based on its own merits. If the Prospect wasn't interested enough to buy the first time with the benefits presented, they probably won't be interested a second time. You either have to get new benefits and/or repackage those given to a more interesting level.

So Sell! Sell! Sell! — Don't Sell, PESTER! PESTER!

# Stall

At the end of a Sales Interview when the Prospect says:

**P** - "It really looks interesting. Give me a few days to look it over and I'll give you a call."

... is a total rejection or will be in a few days. When you phone, the Prospect will be difficult to reach. When you do reach them, it will be easy for them to say "no" on the phone. YOU JUST LOST!

The problem is not with the Prospect but with the Salesperson. The Salesperson failed to get the Prospect interested enough to want to buy the product *now*. When you establish a good two way conversation you should know what the Prospect's feelings are about the value of each benefit. If the response is cold or lukewarm, then obviously you have to find new needs, wants and benefits. Once the Prospect finds a *hot* benefit there should be an automatic close.

So a Stall at the end should come as a shock to the skilled Salesperson who has a good dialog going. Since the Prospect will never be on the emotional high as they are at that time, you must do everything in your power to close *now*.

**P** - "I'd like to think it over."

**SP** - "I can understand your concern. You mentioned earlier there are too many parts tied up in inventory. It is causing a severe cash shortage and you are fearing a C.O.D. situation with your vendors and even your payroll. (The Hurt)

"With us holding your parts inventory and shipping within 2 hours around the clock, cash will increase dramatically." (The Rescue)

"Do you want to cancel your current parts orders and start using our service this week or wait until the first of the month?" (Alternate Choice close)

**SP** - "Mr. P, I'm a little surprised that you hesitate in wanting to own a ... Can you be frank and tell me what your concern is?" OR

**SP** - "Why not decide now? Knowing you will probably be busier next week, it will certainly take less time to finish now than start all over again later. What feature of the product impresses you the most in solving your problem?"

If they insist on more time to ponder about it then set up a new appointment to come back and reexamine the proposal:

**P** - "No, I still need some time to think it over."

**SP** - "Fine, Mr. P. And I'd like to thank you for taking your valuable time to consider it. Let's meet again on Wednesday afternoon or Friday morning of next week, to reexamine the proposal. Meanwhile, I'll get you some more information on the features you were impressed with."

# Reentry

Okay, you've tried everything and they won't close. So you have no alternative but to agree with their request and leave. You now have a Reentry problem.

The first step of reentry is to drop them a note the same day. Use all of these magic admirations:

- "Thank you for telling me about your ..."
  - it predisposes them to do it again.
- "Congratulations on achieving such a ...
  - makes them feel good about themselves.
- "I will be thinking of you and your ... "
  "When I find something that will fit your ... I'll call."
  - makes them feel good about you and leaves door open.

Conclude by promising a future stroking:

- "It will be a pleasure to enjoy your ...(smiling face; delightful stories; beautiful photography, etc) ... again.

A Stall is a basic problem to the Need-Desire. You are not sure now if you found their true Want, their SIP or EBM; or if you have found it, they do not have enough want for it. One thing is certain, when you next approach the Prospect you will have to reignite their interest.

You must reexamine your notes from the Information Gathering step for the SIP, MM and the EBM. Either could be wrong:

- Reconsider their SIP and EBM - this is critical since both can change in even a few days, especially the EBM.

- Review the Facts/Features, Advantages, and Benefits.
- Develop any new information you can by talking to one of their associates, Buffer, etc.

Now that you are on the outside again, you may have to be creative to get back in with a:

- Sales letter - reminding them of their awful problem and with an exciting new offer to resolve it.
- Referral help - one of your happy clients can write a letter or phone the Prospect for you.
- New phone call - with a new Probable Interest.

When you call the stalling Prospect, do NOT ask the "say-no" question:

**SP** - "Well Mr. P, what did you decide?" (P - "I don't want it.")

That invariably gets you a No in one of its many disguised forms. Rather, try something new and interesting - a new SIP:

**SP** - "Mr. P, since we last met I have been thinking about your awful problem and I have a rather interesting new approach. I know you'll be excited about it."

**P** - "What is that?"

**SP** - "Well it will take about 15 minutes for us to examine it. Will Friday or Monday be better for you?"

**P** - "Well, I'm very busy. Can you tell me about it over the phone?" (Still stalling.)

**SP** - "Sure. Wouldn't it make sense to you, as ...(Title)... of your company, to want to look at a proposal that can reduce your losses by $x,xxx a month in the ... department?"

**P** - "It sure would."

**SP** - "Great. Well, let's talk about it. Would Tuesday or Thursday be better for you?"

## Competition:

If competition is bidding for the same Client, try to convince the Prospect that Your product is the usual solution to this problem so they won't have to look elsewhere. Reemphasise the great need to have the problem solved, how much it is HURTING them. With this great emphasis on the problem you are removing them psychologically from their earlier emotional involvement with a competitor, while you are building a new emotion with new personal benefits. Selling is a HURT AND RESCUE business. Even after testimonials, similar stories, referrals and other forms of evidence, remind them of their awful hurt.

# Account Security

Wouldn't it be wonderful if all a Salesperson had to do was make presentations to Prospects? It rarely happens that way. In reality there are several major areas to selling, each emphasized by the situation:

> Prospecting - for wanting Prospects.
> Selling - to the wants.
> Servicing - to fulfill their people-needs.
> Protecting - from predators of many types.

Once you become aware of a potential problem you can use your own ingenuity to manage it. This section raises a lot of potentially disturbing possibilities that the Salesperson must face in order to manage their environment. They are not meant to scare you because most of them will never be a problem. But to manage your position effectively over time, you may have to come to grip with a lot of them. Be aware of them, and watch for them. When you see a potential problem now is the time to define it, understand the inputs that make it a problem, and try to maneuver it into oblivion.

## Product

Is it performing as intended?
Does it need enhancements?
What is competition doing in R&D?
Is it becoming obsolete?
Is it under pressure?
How does the marketplace see it?
How strong is competition?
Do your clients come to you for help?

## Peers

### OUR PEOPLE

How do I get along with my boss?
What is my boss's future?
Who controls my "selling destiny" here?
What about House Accounts?
Are there people here who can hurt me?

### THEIR PEOPLE

What is their organizational chart?
Who are the decision makers?
Who are the influencers?

How many do I know?
Who are the "up and coming"?
What is turnover like?
Who doesn't like me or us?
Who controls my "selling destiny" there?
Who will replace my Key contact?
Do they like me, and my company?

# Priorities

What are my priorities?
Do I have them planned as goals?
What are my boss's priorities? Changes?
What are my company's priorities? Changes?
What are my key contacts priorities? Changes?
What are my priorities? Changes?

# Price

What kind of pressure is my product under?
Are there price changes planned, up or down?
What effect will that change have on my Prospect?
What are competition's pricing policies?
Do my clients pressure me on price?
Can I help with services to reduce price pressure?
How profitable is this product to my client?

# Profits

Is my company really profitable?
Are high profits creating complacency?
Are low profits creating quality problems?
Is my client high profit or low profit?
Is my product profitable for them?
What happens in a recession?
What happens in a price war?
What happens when competition pressures the client?
How profitable is my product to my company?

# Problems

What are our product, delivery, billing weaknesses?
Does my client use my product as intended?
Is my client a problem account?
Are we considered a problem vendor by them?

## Predators

Who are my direct competitors?
Can my competitors introduce a replacement product?
Are competitors better in design, quality, delivery, price?
How will I know when they become aggressive?
How will I know of secret deals, price changes?

## Policies

Are their policies hard for us/others to meet?
Are our sales policies too loose, or too tight?

## Plans

What are my company's plans for me?
What is my client's plan for our mutual product?
What are my plans for my career here?
Can my company provide me with my desired career?
What do I have to be enthusiastic about?

## POWER

Who are the "seats of power" in my client's company?
Who are the major decision influencers?
Who are the power brokers in my company?
Who are our major decision influencers?

# Epilogue

Strategy in selling consists of keen insight into the workings of an organization and the best method of reaching key people who can make the decision to buy. Never expect the path to success within an organization to be a simple call; plan and concentrate on the best methods for acheiving your objective.

Thinking out your strategy is very much like the Generals planning their battles - they have to plan and manage all conceivable factors that influence the outcome. Not all factors are necessarily important but you must be at least aware of them. You Adopt and Adapt to the selling environment as you read the situation, and read it you must. A little bit of strategic thinking can go a long way toward success.

## Chapter Twenty One
# Integrated Selling Systems

## Secrets

- ☐ Salespeople are sellers, not administrators.
- ☐ Salespeople are never organized for administration work.
- ☐ A lot of selling work is truly administration.
- ☐ Automated prospecting will deliver sufficient Prospects.
- ☐ Salespeople are people oriented and not task oriented.
- ☐ Most selling campaigns are destined to failure.
- ☐ Few Salespeople have a well organized prospecting system.
- ☐ A major success factor is organized persistence.
- ☐ Computers and non Salespeople can do massive prospecting.
- ☐ An Executive computer program is the most sophisticated.
- ☐ The Executive program manages other working programs.
- ☐ An Executive program is always updated, never obsolete.
- ☐ Probability Forecasting is the wave of the future.

### The Need For Integrated Selling Systems

Salespeople are sellers and not administrators, yet a lot of the selling function is administrative in nature. Worse than that most of the administration is of little apparent benefit to the Salesperson. Without benefit there is no interest, so the Salesperson never actually organizes for administration work. No value, no respect.

■ A lot of *prospecting* is also administrative work, an effort that many consider "selling". It is a selling function but most of the initial prospecting activity can be delegated to either an automatic system or to non-sales personnel.

■ Much of the *administration* work is communicating market information from the Salesperson back to management. The company needs to know the new Prospects being contacted, the potential volumes being developed, activities of current Clients and the activities of the Salespeople. None of this has direct value to the Salesperson and in real life may not even be of much value to the company because of the manual effort required by management.

A simple, automatic system is needed to move that vital information back to management, summarize it, and display it graphically by impacting or adjusting the forecasts for Sales, Income, and Budgets. Only then will the Salesperson truly support the input system and management have "finger tip" sensitivity to the market.

Such a system is now mandatory. Without it the Salesperson cannot prosper. Too much time is being spent on prospecting, administration and travel leaving only residual time for personal selling.

## Desired Output:

In addition to automatic prospecting, the ultimate design is a graphic display that shows future sales detailed as the "for sure" activity of current clients, plus the probable sales from the Prospects being courted. The system also allows a detailed analysis of the buying activities, thus the Salesperson can overview assigned markets at leisure. It should look like this:

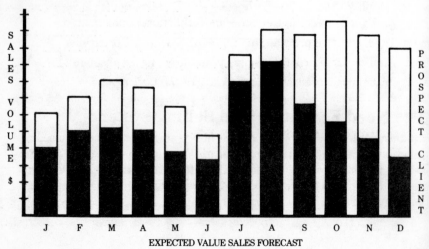

EXPECTED VALUE SALES FORECAST

| Forecast For Month Of: | Expected Value Forecasts | | |
|---|---|---|---|
| | Client + | Prospects | = Total |
| Commissions | $9,046 | $3,178 | $12,224 |
| Total Sales | $91,135 | $31,783 | $122,918 |
| Contribution to Profits | $31,135 | $9,374 | $40,509 |
| Net Profit after Tax etc. | $4,725 | $2,224 | $6,949 |

## Reports:

### FOR SALESPERSON:
- Updated CLIENT sheets, Rolodex cards, labels, 3x5 cards, etc.
- Updated PROSPECT sheets, Rolodex cards, labels, 3x5 cards, etc.
- Daily calendar of who to visit, phone or write.
- Master File Printout.

### MISCELLANEOUS:
- Analysis of success of an Ad campaign.
- Analysis of success of a Mailing List.
- Analysis of success by SIC code.
- Analysis of success by Zip Codes.
  ...as X Prospects - Y Appointments - Z Clients, eg, 40P/10A/7C.

### GRAPHICS:
- Industrial Client's buying History for specific periods.
- Total Client's buying History for specific periods.
- Forecasted Client's buying Potential for specific periods.
- Forecasted Prospect's buying Potential for specific periods.
- Commissions by Client and by Prospect by specific period, etc...

### PROSPECTING:
- A fully automated prospecting system to deliver a predetermined number of Wanting Prospects per period.

# Selling Campaign
## The Problems

## Unorganized Salespeople:

There is a fair amount of self discipline required in selling. Salespeople by their very nature are people rather than task oriented. Consequently, their ability to organize themselves is typically low.

Due to the nature of selling most Salespeople find it very difficult to maintain organized paperwork. Maintaining and updating records that result from the efforts of selling seems impossible to achieve. For similar reasons, a continuous selling campaign is almost sure to fail.

The Salesperson's problem in keeping a selling campaign organized occurs in the lack of support of the basic program tasks that must be performed. Those tasks are:

- System SOURCE of new Prospects to contact.
- System to MAIL letters to Prospects.
- System of CONTACTING Prospects.
- Recording contact RESULTS.
- Strategic plan to CLOSE Prospect.
- System to FOLLOW UP on Prospects contacted.
- Closing DOCUMENTS, surveys, demonstrations, etc.
- System for FOLLOWING UP new Client.
- System for SERVICING new Client.

The campaign is analogous to a chain: break one link and everything that has been done to date becomes lost. A major break in the chain and the Salesperson loses the system. Even with some neglect, time sets in and a hot Prospect becomes cool. Before long you literally have to start all over again.

Few Salespeople have a well organized system working. Those that do enjoy substantial success because organized persistence in selling is a major success factor. The organized persistence is that which needs to be relegated to a computer or non-sales personnel. It is the system that ferrets out Wanting Prospects.

Most often a successful sales team is "managed" by a sales secretary who keeps the paperwork system in order. Usually it is a manual procedure and is only as effective as:

- The design of the selling system, and
- The skills of the secretary operating the system.

Again, the system is delicately held together, and over time it is most ineffective.

## Total Market Selling:

Most product lines are designed to serve a wide variety of buyers. When advertised, all models are offered. Their full range product line has a series of models that can service the entire market.

Assuming that a product line is designed to be all things to all buyers, the seller must then have a system for selling to all segments of their market.

The total selling effort will consist of a full range of media, from Newspapers, TV Commercials, prospecting with Direct Mail, Salesperson presentations, to account Servicing; along with the Direct-to-Consumer sales, and Retail stores. To cover all bases the selling system must be sophisticated.

For optimum results these selling activities, ie, prospecting and selling future Clients, plus servicing current accounts, must be integrated into the daily operating systems of top management by way of impacting the forecasts they view on a daily basis.

# Selling Campaigns

## The Solution

## Computer Systems

To have an effective on-going selling program the system has to be automated and of indefinite duration. The only simple automatic system with the total flexibility necessary is a computer system programmed to fulfill all activities.

Sales and Marketing programs have been designed both for the giant computers of the large companies, as well as the general market Personal Computers. Both the large and small systems designed for sales have a major defect in that they were designed as a COMPLETE sales system package, thereby making enhancements very difficult. There is no easy way for a quick updating and as such the program has a built in obsolescence problem. In effect, these programs tend to be glorified mailing system of lists and letters.

The software manufactures of working programs boast of greater capability in their programs than warranted. On the other hand, a few software manufacturer's have started from scratch to write a total selling system only to end up with programs that have limited capability and flexibility because of the massive interdisciplinary programming required.

As a rule software manufactures become known for one specific program. The development of such a complex program, and the intensive competition that threatens it's obsolescence, forces them to perform a massive amount of reprogramming. Since software manufactures are also relatively small, there is little likelihood that they will branch out into other specialized programming. The resources demanded are massive and therefore limited. The net result is that we cannot look to the software companies to write large state-of-the-art integrated programs that will serve Salespeople, and at the same time update management with sophisticated forecasting.

# Executive Programs

Every computer program is obsolete the day it is issued because new ideas and updates are becoming available on a daily basis. Once you buy a program you are locked into it for years, along with its good and bad features. You are then unable to take advantage of advancements in other systems as they become available.

One way to overcome the problem is to design an Executive program that MANAGES a group of other independent working programs. The Executive program integrates them for a variety of interrelated activities. There is then no limit to the capability of the Executive program. As an example, an Executive Sales program could manage a:

- Database management program to be used for client files, updating, sorting, client retrievals, etc.

- Word Processing program that would be used for writing personalized letters, proposals, reports, etc.

- Spread sheet program that can handle budgets, forecasts, analysis of results against forecasts, and a variety of mathematical items.

- Directory program that can check the spelling and grammar in written material.

- A mailing program that can print labels, sort by attributes, merge letters, check for duplicates, etc.

- Networking programs that interconnects as many company terminals, and receive input from outside services and Input programs.

- Miscellaneous programs such as Expense accounts, matching the Personality profiles of the Prospect and the Salesperson into a stategy, etc.

Once you have the Executive program operational the working programs will be updated from time to time by their individual manufacturers, thereby assuring you of the latest technology. Major updates in the working programs usually are marketed for about 10% of the cost of the original program.

An Executive program needs no programming update, since its sole effort is to manage the functions of the working programs. As the author of the Executive program senses a need to add more functions or change to a more advanced working program, it is a simple effort of slipping in the specialized program. It is effortless to the user.

Above all, the Executive program will be of menu design meaning that the user requires no training other than how to turn the computer on. The program gives you the options and you simply choose the option desired. It leads you by the hand through all activities, thereby allowing both you and non-sales personnel to input.

Executives programs are the only way to combine all of the features necessary for a TOTAL selling system, a system wherein the Salesperson's daily successes are available as graphic forecasts on the computer for corporate management.

# Input Design

The data that you will need to be develop in time are:

| Information | Prospect | Client |
|---|---|---|
| History | * | * |
| Key Contacts (DM/I) | * | * |
| Organizational Chart | * | * |
| Selling Strategy | * | 0 |
| Servicing Strategy | 0 | * |
| Their Competition | * | * |
| Their Priorities | * | * |
| Their Profitability | * | * |
| Their Problems | * | * |

# Sales Forecasting

Salespeople have difficulty in getting concise, timely, and accurate information to management about the accounts that are *almost* closed. At times the impact of a new major account can be substantial; it can be devastating if that estimate is too high or too low.

**FORECASTS TOO LOW:** When a sales force is effective and about to acquire several new major accounts, the company may not be staffed in time for the increase. Instead of growth the accounts may be quickly lost because of the "stumbling" on the first few orders. We all know that the first few orders are critical when two new organizations, unfamiliar in each others ways, are about to interface.

**FORECASTS TOO HIGH:** It is assumed that a company will lose about 15-20% of its business each year for reasons beyond their immediate control. These reasons run from employee indifference (estimated as 68% of the problem), to clients going out of business. Therefore, a

# Typical
# Sales Success Strategy
# (SSS) Record

Mr/Mrs/Ms/ _____ Title _____

First name _____

Last name _____

Street _____ Suite _____

City _____ State _____ Zip _____

Company _____

Street _____ Suite _____ PO BOX _____

City _____ State _____ Zip _____

Reports to: _____ Title _____

Manager? _____ Date met? _____

Phone (___) _____-_____ Ext _____
Watts (800) _____-_____ Ext _____

Direct (___) _____-_____

SIC Code _____

Their Estimated Sales $ _____ MM   (Qualifier #1 thru 4)

Our Potential Sales    $ _____ MM   (Qualifier #5 thru 9)

Seasonality, % by qtr. 1st _____ 2nd _____ 3rd _____ 4th _____

Selling History (Permanent) _____
_____

Selling History (Auto delete) _____
_____

Service History (Permanent) _____
_____

Service History (Auto delete) _____
_____

Qualifiers 1 2 3 4 5 6 7 8 9 10 11 12 13 14 15 16 17 18 19 20
SELLING STRATEGY: _____
_____

Their Competition: _____

Their Priorities: _____

Their Profitability re us: _____

Their Problems: _____

company has to acquire 20% more new business each year just to maintain a status quo. If the sales force is ineffective over a period of time the negative impact on their company will be devastating.

Wouldn't it be great for management to have instant access to the impending new account activity? An Executive program must have this unique feature, programmed to impact your forecasts with meaningfull numbers.

In its simplest form this is how it works:

**SALES PROBABLITIES: SMITH, JOHN, PHX DIV.**

| Company | Type | Seasonality | $ Potential | Prob | Expected $ |
|---------|------|-------------|-------------|------|------------|
| ABC Inc | **P** | NORMAL | $750,000 | .8 | $600,000 |
| RST Inc | **P** | NORMAL | 80,000 | .9 | 72,000 |
| XYZ Inc | **P** | .75x4th | 450,000 | .3 | 135,000 |
| HJK Inc | **C** | NORMAL | 100,000 | (.5) | (50,000) |
| Etc. | | | | | |

**P** = Prospect. C = Client.

# Probability Forecasting

Probability is the Salesperson's best estimate of the chances of success in getting or holding the account.

Nothing is certain in the business world except probabilities. A probability is your educated guess based on all known factors. As new data enters you modify probability, and as such probability may be subject to constant changes, which is reality. That's fine, because it is your latest estimation reduced to a number.

A probability is very similar to the estimation: "On a scale of 1 to 10, 10 being tops, what do you think about the ...?" A simple number is a most effective method of reducing the many intangible variables into a number meaningful to the computer.

Incidentally, a 100% probability is defined as 1.0. A lesser probability of 0.6 would mean a 60% chance of happening.

The calculation above is a weighted Expected Value; the weighting is the total sales volume times the probability of the Salesperson's getting the account. If the account is $100,000 per year and the Salesperson estimates that they have 60% change of closing the account in the next 30 days then the expected value is:

$100,000 x .60 = $60,000 Expected Value (EV)

Each time the Salesperson receives an impression of the account's changed potential they modify the probability up or down. The same information is also available for existing accounts, some that may even be in trouble as in the case of the HJK Inc above.

The Expected Value is mathematically sound and is an accepted standard forecasting technique used by Operations Research in the business world. With a large number of accounts the accuracy is most impressive. It is easy to increase the reporting accuracy by modifying the probabilities for those Salespeople who are too optimistic or conservative in their estimates.

An expected sales increase or decrease can be impacted on the sales forecasts in an Executive program, which in turn impact on the projected Profit and Loss and even the "What if?" budget forecasts of the company.

Note that the established Budgets are not being changed; rather Sales, Income and Budget FORECASTS are constantly being updated. Forecasts that change substantially are early warnings to management that budgets may need adjustment.

It is relatively easy to create a "What if?" budget based on the updated forecast. By including the accountant's "Fixed, Semivariable, Variable Cost" formula into the spreadsheet of a working program, a most realistic budget can be displayed. It too will adjust every time the Salesperson changes their estimate about a present or future Client. Management will then have finger-tip sensitivity to their market.

There is no end to the benefits from the Probability Forecasting of change. It especially allows for substantial growth in an orderly and profitable manner. It will also warn management that the expected change, up or down, may be too great and the business should be buffered against the possibility of one or two large accounts being acquired as expected, or current ones being lost. That will reduce the crisis management.

## Selling Strategy

With modern computer systems there is no reason why the strategy of selling a particular account can't be institutionalized.

In most corporate accounts there may be only one decision maker (D/M) but many decision influencers (D/I). It is possible that the D/M may only make a decision after listening to the D/I's. Some D/M's may want to explore the sale personally, depending on their degree of delegation, interest or importance of the purchase. Be what it may, it is important in strategic planning to know who the D/I's are and their degree of conviction in the selling process:

# Stage In The Selling Process

| Prospect | D/M/I? | Attention | Interest | Conviction | Convinced |
|----------|--------|-----------|----------|------------|-----------|
| Smith, J | D/M * | YES | | | |
| Jones, R | D/I | YES | YES | YES | 0.8 |
| Brown, P | D/I | YES | YES | | 0.5 |
| Carver,T | D/I | NOT YET | | | |
| Dayton,B | D/I | YES | NO | NO | NO |

No skill is required to read the current situation of this Prospect account. What would you do? Answer: Reinforce Jones and Brown, try to find out what Dayton's problem is, meet with Carver and the D/M Smith. Now the details of the strategy can be worked out.

# Sales Campaign

## Various Ways Of Prospecting:
- Referrals (the best but limited).
- Cold Calling (in person or by phone - slow).
- Ads with coupons for Prospect response.
- Telemarketing (massive phone calls by non-sales).
- Letters: where Salesperson phones (limited campaign).
- Letters: where Prospect responds (massive campaign).

The method lending itself to the greatest response of Wanting Prospects is a massive letter campaign. It can be easily automated and operated by non-sales personnel. When highly qualified Prospects are uncovered their SSS Record can be turned over to the Salesperson for personal contact. They will be maintained until the prospect becomes a Client or the prospect is sustained on a Newsletter mailing status.

The system begins with a list of names entered into a Sales Success Strategy Record. This becomes the base for the entire activity.

**INITAL MAILING:** A mailing is the most productive way to start any sales program. Even the Telemarketing Salespeople advise making their initial contact by mail. A "warm" phone call is more respected and effective than a totally cold call.

There can be a variety of one page letters residing in the Word Processing program, any one of which can be assigned to any Prospect. The working program will record the code number of the letter used in the Selling History section of the SSS Record.

# Corporate Sales:

For the BUSINESS market there are two letter systems to choose from:

MASSIVE MAILING: THEY CALL YOU. This saves the Salesperson time but the response will be lower. How much lower depends on a variety of factors. As a minimum it should bottom out at the direct mail's historic response rate of 1-3%.

(The usual method in selling CONSUMERS is to buy a mailing list of Prospects that have a commonality of interests with your product. For example, the subscribers to Fortune magazine probably have a commonality of interest in high technology products, books on business, business seminars, and expensive gifts, etc. The reply is via mail with a coupon or via an 800 number. The response runs 2 to 3%. The mailing can go on indefinitely to the same prospects at spaced intervals with equal success.)

LIMITED MAILING: YOU CALL THEM. These are personal letters that require the Salesperson to make a follow up phone call. The number of mailings is limited to the time available for the Salesperson to phone the Prospect. Even ten letters a day can be heavy. Often the Prospect cannot be reached on the first call and soon the number of calls per day may reach 50, a mix of new calls and many follow up calls from prior days. It is not a good technique to have the Prospect return your call so you have to adjust the mailings rate up or down depending on the backlog. This method requires that you be most selective in choosing the Prospects simply because of your high personal attention.

A more effective program would be a combination of both these systems. Mail out several letters, each referencing an earlier letter or even promising a new one. Eventually mention that you will be calling them. By then they should be aware of you, your company and your product. The hot ones may call you immediately. The lukewarm will be conditioned for your future call.

The letter should be a simple one page, one hundred word message of interest. EXAMPLE:

# Sales Success Institute, Inc.
425 Vista Flora Avenue,
Newport Beach, Ca, 92660
(714) 542-7777

Mr. John Prospect,
President,
ABC Inc,
123 Main Street,
Anycity, Ca, 90009

Dear Mr. Prospect,

There is trouble in River City and there could very well be trouble in your Sales Department.

There IS trouble in your Sales group if we can train them to increase your sales by 25% and they don't accept the offer!

That's too good to pass up. We'll even guarantee results. I'll call you next week to set up a 15 minute general interest meeting.

Sincerely,

D. Forbes Ley
Executive Director

PS: River City was where Howard Hill proved that you've got to "Hurt and Rescue" them in THE MUSIC MAN.

**SAMPLE CAMPAIGN DESIGN:** Three standard Sales letters (A,B,C) are mailed to a Prospect, followed by a phone call (Step 4).

If the phone call produces an appointment, two more salutary letters are generated, one confirming the appointment and a Thank You note after the meeting.

If no appointment, then go to to three more Sales letters (D,E,F).

If the appointment produces a client then remove the file from the campaign and recode as a Client.

If the appointment does not produce a client, then back to three more Sales letters (G,H,I) followed by another phone call (Step 10), etc., and the cycle keeps repeating:

## Step Letter

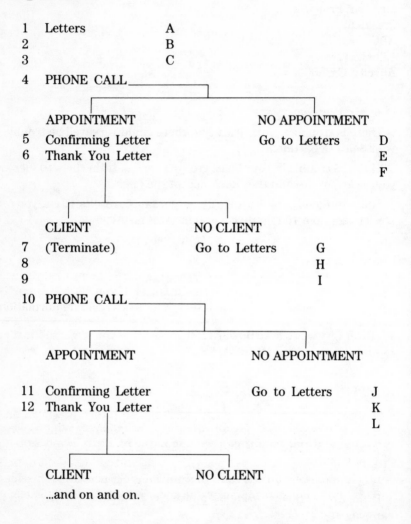

| Step | | Letter |
|---|---|---|
| 1 | Letters | A |
| 2 | | B |
| 3 | | C |
| 4 | PHONE CALL | |

| APPOINTMENT | | NO APPOINTMENT |
|---|---|---|
| 5 | Confirming Letter | Go to Letters | D |
| 6 | Thank You Letter | | E |
| | | | F |

| CLIENT | NO CLIENT |
|---|---|
| 7 | (Terminate) | Go to Letters | G |
| 8 | | H |
| 9 | | I |
| 10 | PHONE CALL | |

| APPOINTMENT | NO APPOINTMENT |
|---|---|
| 11 | Confirming Letter | Go to Letters | J |
| 12 | Thank You Letter | | K |
| | | | L |

| CLIENT | NO CLIENT |
|---|---|

...and on and on.

Keep the concept and letters simple. The program can be modified to each Prospect by selecting a different sequence of letters for each mailing.

The program must also contain two unique features:

- The ability to introduce new names into the system without designing a new system, and
- The ability to delete a name either to:
  - (a) Client file.
  - (b) Trash - not a Prospect.

INITIAL PHONE CALL: The phone call is made to the Prospect within a few days of expected receipt of your letter. The ONLY purpose of this brief call is to set an appointment.

**SP** - "Mr. P, you should have received my letter a few days ago. Would it make sense to you to want to know more about a system that will help reduce the losses on your office supplies?"

**P** - "Yes, it would."

**SP** - "Great. What we need to do now is set a general interest meeting. Would Wednesday afternoon or Friday morning be better for you?"

At the time you make the call, but before you speak to the Prospect, ask their secretary for as much basic data for your sales record as she will give you. When you finish the call make out an Edit memo sheet with the new data on it for input into the Prospect file.

**SELLING STRATEGY:** After the phone call, a strategy has to be developed for future contacts. If you did not get the appointment you will need to send additional letters to the Prospect. If you get the appointment, then begin the pre-approach search for sales related information about the Prospect's needs, wants, personality, etc., and off into the sales interview.

# Epilogue

The computer system will literally organize your total sales efforts and activities in letter campaigns, follow up, time allocation, call reports, management reports, sales and commission forecasts, plus a host of other extras. The program is for your benefit and the required data is easy to input. The outcome will dramatically impact on your selling efforts, and get management interested and involved in your daily selling.

## Publisher's Note

Sales Success Press has taken the entrepreneural step of having such an Executive Program written for its readers. The program was designed in terms of the author's requirements for a Totally Integrated Selling System.

The Executive program was written to manage the best state-of-the-art software for databases, word processing, spreadsheets, decision making, accounting programs, etc.

The Executive Program is menu driven, meaning you can do it yourself without any training. For those whose time is limited Sales Success Press will set up the entire System in both hardware and software, and train the operators for out-of-pocket expenses. In other words, there is no charge for the Executive Program. You just buy the software and/or hardware parts through Sales Success Press at the manufacturer's suggested list price, and we will set it up for you. We will train free of charge at our location in Los Angeles. The software system will be maintained and enhanced for an annual fee of 10% of the original purchase price.

Since pricing has always been highly volatile in the computer industry, the only rational way of pricing such an integrated system is to charge only the manufacturer's suggested list price for each component part.

The programs that are functionally part of the Executive Program are LICENSED to the reader for multiple machine use by the software manufacturer. The Executive Program itself will be on LOAN from the Sales Success Press for an indefinite period of time.

This program has been endowed for the life of this book.

# Chapter Twenty Two
# Scenario

A scenario is defined as (1) a working script of a motion picture, or (2) an outline of a proposed series of events. Both are intended here, though the motion picture is still in book form. Although the scenario is typical, it has been expanded to reveal the widest variety of selling techniques.

This scenario is a dialogue between a skilled Salesperson and a Prospect. The product chosen is corporate business travel, an intangible service, essentially non-price competitive and with services virtually identical to competition. The services may be somewhat new to the Prospect, yet are reasonably available from many other vendors. Sales depend almost entirely on the selling ability of the Salesperson.

**BUFFER** - "(President's name) office."

 **SP** - "May I speak to ...(President's name) ...?"

**COMMENT**: Always start at the top. You may even end up talking with the President if your ability to resolve their current needs is essential. If not, you will be directed to the assigned decision maker for your kind of product. It saves everyone time when you work with the assigned decision maker rather than spin your wheels with non-decision makers.

**BUFFER** - "May I tell him who's calling?"

 **SP** - "Yes. This is (your name). Thank you. I'll hold."

**COMMENT**: "I'll hold ..." is gentle pressure to put you through.

**BUFFER** - "Your company?"

 **SP** - "I'm with (company name). If you'll tell Mr. Prospect I'm on the phone I'd appreciate it."

**COMMENT**: This is steady, gentle pressure to put you through.

**BUFFER** - "May I tell Mr. Prospect what it is about?"

**SP** - "Yes, indeed. If there were a way to reduce your business losses by at least $20,000 a year, Mr. President would probably want to know about it, don't you think?"

**BUFFER** - "It certainly sounds like something Mr. Prospect would be interested in. One moment please, for Mr. President."

**P** - "Hello."

**COMMENT**: The Buffer was screening your call. In a well managed business this should be expected. Only the most professional Salespeople should be allowed to involve a company's staff.

The Buffer is part of their decision making process in the sense that she can encourage or abort your efforts. Because the Buffer can supply pre-approach information that can be critical to your efforts, as well as facilitate the follow up, you should enlist the Buffer by treating her with the same respect as the Prospect.

At times, the Buffer may be the one who influences the decision the most, depending on their stature in the company. If you can't get the Buffer's interest with your Probable Problem statement ("If there were a way ..."), with her wider range of acceptance, you probably won't be able to get the Prospect's interest either. Unless you favorably impress the Buffer, your road to success will be indeed rough. Here the Probable Problem was presented as a Question Suggesting a Need (QSN).

**SP** - "Hello, Mr. President. By the way, your secretary sure is a pleasant person to talk to; besides she was most professional in finding out the purpose of my call. (1) Is it convenient for you to talk for a moment?"(2)

**P** - "Yes it is."

**COMMENT**: (1) A Pleasant Statement compliments him about his secretary (The C in MISS GRACE). Since the Buffer screened you the Prospect is probably receptive. (2) Asking if they have the time to spend a moment with you is a courtesy since you are somewhat of an intrusion.

**SP** - "Mr. Prospect, as President of your company, wouldn't it make sense to you to explore a travel management system that will reduce your losses by at least $20,000 a year?"

**P** - "It would, but we are very happy with our present service."

**COMMENT**: You have only seconds to capture their attention and interest, so get to the point by promising to help them resolve one of their probable problems. The QSN, "If there were a way ...", is specific in "what's in it for me". The Probable Problem is a shot-in-the-dark about some problem they are probably having because most of their industry has it. In the business world cost reductions are always of interest but "reducing losses" sounds more rewarding because of the "devastating losses".

You use a Probable Problem because you do not have any specific information about a real problem they may be experiencing. If you have developed rapport with the Buffer, she could have given you a specific problem. In lieu of a specific problem, make the Probable Problem broad enough to grab their interest, yet not specific enough that it will cause rejection. If they are not experiencing your Probable Problem, then give them a different QSN until you do get their interest. Often they will reject you with the "No time, No need, No interest" type of comment.

**SP** - "Well, Mr. President, if you are satisfied with your present vendor, I'll respect that. That's a good position for your vendor to be in. I guess we all envy that position, and we are always concerned about what is important to our clients; it's hard to see it from your point of view. While we are on the subject may I ask you two questions?"

**P** - "Sure, if they're short."

**COMMENT**: The Salesperson moved away from the general rejection that was impossible to answer and maneuvered the Prospect into a specific subject. You want them talking about their problem in an area where you have benefits available for them.

**SP** - "What are the 3 things that impress you most about your present service?"

**P** - "Good delivery, pleasant staff, and a good reporting system.

**COMMENT**: These 3 services are your competition. By asking the Prospect about the good points first puts them in a cooperative mood, for we all like to talk about our pleasantries.

**SP** - "And what are the 3 things that you would like to see improved?"

**P** - "Well, pricing could be a little better; maybe a faster phone service; and maybe more attention to detail."

**COMMENT**: These are your opportunities! Now you have him talking candidly about the service. No company has a perfect product, because quality is always relative to your expectations and the performance of others, competitors or not.

**SP** - "You mentioned that the pricing could be improved. That's important, especially in corporate travel where prices are high and subject to wild change. I can just imagine the confusion, frustration and embarrassment when several of your people have tickets for the same flight, all with substantially different prices. There has to be serious losses there. The big problem is that you don't know why that happens, so you are helpless to control it. We could enlighten you with a few good ideas on that in a 15 minute general interest meeting. Would this afternoon or Friday morning be better for you?"

**P** - "I'm quite interested in what you have to offer but at the moment I'm super busy. Will you meet with our controller and let him sort out the details? Cost reductions are the controller's function. Tell him I'm very interested in your approach."

**COMMENT**: Hurt and Rescue. Here the Salesperson is selling their problem back to them, impressing on them that they do have a serious problem. If they are not sufficiently disturbed by the problem they will not be moved to correct it. The Salesperson can create a visual image of how much the problem could hurt the Prospect if it got out of hand. (Dentist: "Should I fill this tooth now or wait until it really hurts you?")

**SP** - "That's fine. May I ask one favor?"

**P** - "Sure."

**SP** - "May I have the commitment from you to discuss the controller's report with you, and maybe meet you personally? You are the only one with the broad-scope of concerns necessary for this decision."

**P** - "Sure."

**COMMENT**: You now have an assignment to study with a decision influencer and the President's endorsement. The controller will be very happy to meet with you. You also have an open door back to the President if you need it.

# LATER

**Buffer** - "(Controller's name) office."

**SP** - "May I speak to Mr. Prospect?"

**Buffer** - "May I tell him who's calling?"

**SP** - "Yes. This is (your name). I have been asked to meet with Mr. Prospect to work on an assignment for your President."

**Buffer** - "One moment please."

**P** - "Hello."

**SP** - "Mr. Prospect?"

**P** - "Yes."

**SP** - "This is (your name) of (your company). Your President has asked that I meet with you to detail out a corporate travel system that he is interested in. Would this afternoon or tomorrow morning be better for you?"

  **P** - "Tomorrow at 9:00am would be fine."

**SP** - "That's great. See you at your office at 9:00am tomorrow."

# LATER

**BUFFER** - "Mr. Prospect, I would like you to meet SP (your name)."

  **P** - "Hello, SP."

**SP** - "Hello, Mr. Prospect. Thank you Ms. Buffer. Well, Mr. Prospect you sure have an admirable operation here ..."

**COMMENT**: ATTENTION - A sincere compliment is the best ice breaker. This is where you build rapport, i.e., getting the Prospect to like you. You do that by centering attention on them by talking to them about something in which they are interested.

**SP** - " ...The reason I say that is that most accounting departments are usually disorganized. As we were walking through your accounting section, I couldn't help but notice how well organized every person and thing is. It is sure impressive looking. How did you get it so well organized?"

  **P** - "Well, I'm an organizer at heart. I don't feel good unless everything is well organized and running by some system."

**COMMENT**: Most Salespeople feel uncomfortable about extending a compliment because it might be considered insincere, i.e., flattery. When you can justify the reason ("The reason I mention this ..."), then it's sincere.

**SP** - "That fits in with what your President said about you. He was most complimentary about your talents. You two seem to work well together. Why is that?"

  **P** - "We have been working together for a long time and our goals are quite similar. We each have a lot of respect for the other. That's why everything is so efficient."

**COMMENT**: Ask the Prospect why they are like that, why did they ...? and so forth. These are essay-type questions that get the Propsect talking freely about their favorite subject, themselves. They will have to be doing a lot more talking later on, so the proper attitude must be established here. Stay in this step until they feel good about talking about themselves. It shouldn't take more than 3 to 5 minutes.

**SP** - "Well, Mr. Prospect, that indicates that you are really a general manager at heart. How does the wide spectrum attitude of general manager help you in your responsibilities?"

**P** - "Instead of just looking at the accounting control function, I'm very concerned about the long term direction and effects on any current decisions. Good management of today has to produce good results in the future."

**COMMENT**: This is the second essay-type question to get the Prospect to want to talk to you freely, i.e., get them to accept you as an interesting person. Also, you are looking for a word, phrase or idea on which to bridge out of their personal interests into your reason for being there.

**SP** - "Good management is the very reason why I am here ..."

**COMMENT**: This bridges their personal interests into a mutual reason for being together.

**SP** - "...If there were a way for you to reduce your travel losses by $20,000 a year, it would make sense to explore it in detail, wouldn't it?"

**P** - "Absolutely. Our travel expense is our second largest expense after salaries. We know we don't have the mechanism for managing it the way we should."

**COMMENT**: - One of the best interest-getting lines in selling. Its a Question Suggesting a Need, including a promise of a solution to a serious problem. It also confirms their interest with the leading question, "... You would probably want to know more about it, ..."; followed by a suggested agreement ... wouldn't you?" A very powerful pair of influencing statements.

**SP** - "The reason I mention this is because of what we are doing now for the ABC Corporation at their various offices across the U.S. Maybe we can help you too."

**P** - "That would be very nice, indeed."

**COMMENT**: A "similar situation" solution reinforces the Prospect's interest because you have helped others, so maybe you can help them too. You can also replace it with the more general: " We have been doing that for several other firms in the area, and maybe ..." The word "maybe" is like a mild challenge, and is more effective than "we can do the same for you". A challenge creates curiosity.

**SP** - "To conserve your time, would it be okay to get the answers to a few questions?"

**P** - "Sure."

**COMMENT**: A simple request for permission to ask questions of concern. If you don't ask for permission, you run the risk of being considered pushy.

**SP** - "Your title was listed as "controller". Is that correct?"

**P** - "Really it's VP Finance, but those titles are almost interchangeable."

**COMMENT**: Question: PERSONAL. Start off with a very simple question. Also verifying that person's position.

**SP** - "What is the range of your responsibilities?"

**P** - "Everything from arranging the finance of the company to running the cost reduction programs."

**COMMENT**: Question: PERSONAL. Verify that the Prospect's responsibilities really do cover your product. Also, it encourages them to talk more about themselves.

**SP** - "What is the most enjoyable part of your travel duties?"

**P** - "Well, it is a glamorous part of business. Some of it rubs off even though I don't travel much. I do get to inspect a few hotels and arrange for future meetings."

**COMMENTS**: Question: PERSONAL. Get the Prospect to talk more about their situation. Have them talk about the nice things first.

**SP** - "What problem does our industry create for you?"

**P** - "The very high cost of travel is hurting us, and even our best efforts don't seem to be too effective in controlling costs."

**COMMENT:** Question: PROBLEM. This rather clinical approach to their problems surprises the Prospect. They get the feeling you are looking for ways to help them, rather than the typical sales approach. You are discussing a serious problem (SIP) which just coincidentally is the same problem that gained their initial interest.

**SP** - "What help would you normally expect from us?"

**P** - "Well, we don't know much about the travel industry. It is huge. Our efforts in the past have been most ineffective. Even a 10% cost reduction would be great."

**COMMENT:** Question: PROBLEM. What kind of a solution is the Prospect expecting? Do we have the capability of keeping them happy?

**SP** - "What is preventing you from solving this problem?"

**P** - "We did outline a policy and delegated it to the secretarial staff to control. We now know that expecting them to control their boss's travel created a serious conflict."

**COMMENT**: Question: PROBLEM. This can reveal the conflicts of interest within an organization. Wherever there are people, there are political pressures. Questioning flushes them out.

**SP** - "What are you doing about that problem now?"

**P** - "Nothing really. We seem to react rather than act, which indicates that we need an outside, independent contractor to monitor it for us."

**COMMENT**: Question: PROBLEM. At this point the Prospect is leveling with the Salesperson about their problems. That is because the questioning started out general, and progressively probed deeper as the rapport between the Prospect and the Salesperson developed.

**SP** - "How would solving the problem effect you?"

**P** - "I feel that part of my responsibility is having good control over business travel expenses. Good control, even without a sizeable cost reduction would be a big plus."

**COMMENT**: Question: PAYOFF. The first question that asks ..."What's in it for me?" This line of questioning should be persued until you find an emotional benefit for the Prospect. Here the Propsect is concerned with what others think about their capabilities. This is a Mini Motive (MM), that is, the desire to take control over the situation. You can follow up with a series of similar questions to develop more MM's:

(**SP** - "When you get the control established what would that do for you?"

**P** - "Be able to design a policy that is meaningfull both from a dollar and people point of view.

**SP** - "How would others feel about that?")

**SP** - "Why is that important to you?"

**P** - "Well, it frustrates me to have it generally known that one of my responsibilities are not under control."

**COMMENT**: Question: PAYOFF. The Prospect is concerned now about the way others are judging their performance and wants to strengthen the respect for their position. The EBM is that the Prospect is suffering from loss of respect.

**SP** - "What would it be worth to you to solve the travel control problem?"

**P** - "It would make me feel good all over, and give me a great sense of accomplishment."

**COMMENT**: Question: PAYOFF. Self-satisfaction and a sense of accomplishment are important to the Prospect. Both are MM's.

**SP** - "Who, besides you, will be making the decision to change travel services?"

**P** - "Basically, me. But, since we have been using our present travel agency for many years, their owner knows our President so I'd have to check with him."

**COMMENT**: Question: PEERS. In a corporation rarely is one person the final decision maker. Anyone making a decision is concerned about how it will be accepted by others in the group. Here we make it clear we expect that others will be involved.

**SP** - "If you are favorably impressed with our service, would you accompany me when I meet with Mr. ...(decision maker) ...?"

**P** - "Oh yes, indeed. You can do a better job presenting the benefits of your service than I can."

**COMMENT**: Question: PEERS. This pre-arranges and committs the Prospect to a future meeting with the decision maker. Also, it preempts the Prospect from making the presentation on your behalf.

**SP** - "What people problems would you perceive by changing?"

**P** - "We are really a very professional organization. If our management says we are going to change the travel service, the secretaries won't let their personal feelings be involved. A dollar is a dollar."

**COMMENT**: Question: PEERS. In corporations, personal contacts can have major influences over decisions. Where intangibles are involved, as in the service industry, personal ties can create "logical justifications" for just about any action. Those things happen frequently. You have to know about them.

**SP** - "When would you plan on making the decision and the change?"

**P** - "The decision could be made within a few days and the change within 30 days."

**COMMENT**: Question: PRIORITY. This also tells you whether or not they are studying other alternatives or competitors, and also whether they feel bound by any existing agreements.

**SP** - "What is it costing you now not to have a reasonable solution to the business travel problem?"

**P** - "If 10% is a reasonable cost reduction and we are doing $20,000 per month, that is a savings of $2,000 per month."

**COMMENT**: Question: PRIORITY. Now the Prospect is aware of what the problem is costing them.

**SP** - "What sense of urgency do you feel now about solving the problem?"

**P** - "$2,000 a month savings without any capital investment is great. That's over $20,000 a year! It can make us really hussle."

**COMMENT**: Question: PRIORITY. Obviously, the Prospect now has a sense of urgency. This would preclude such Stalls as "We'd like to think it over".

(These questions should be reduced to a paper form that the Salesperson can complete during the interview. You should ask or get the answers to all standard questions. The form can also list various closes you may want to use.)

**SP** - "Based on what you have told me, there is a way we can provide you with a substantial cost reduction and at the same time reduce the pressure and frustration in controlling your business travel".

**P** - "Good."

**COMMENT**: You have determined that their Specific Interest (SIP) is to control business travel expenses. The Prospect's Emotional Buying Motive (EBM) is that he feels that others doubt he is doing his job properly (a loss of respect). He is also concerned about his self-satisfaction and sense of accomplishment, but these are lesser motives to the respect he requires.

**SP** - "You are probably wondering how we can do this, so let's look at the facts."

**P** - "Fine."

**COMMENTS**: CONVICTION STEP - You are going to present only those Facts/Features, Advantages and related Benefits of your product that will solve the Prospect's problem.

**SP** - "We will monitor and maintain your business travel across the U.S. according to your corporate policy ..."

**P** - "That sounds like a big effort."

**COMMENT**: FACT/FEATURE - This is the special feature of your product that will help solve their problem.

**SP** - " ... so you will be organized for an effective cost reduction program of about $2,000 per month."

**P** - "That's a lot of effort and money."

**COMMENT**: ADVANTAGE. The feature of your product creates an advantage. You then translate those tangible advantages into the emotional benefit that makes a Prospect want to have your product.

**SP** - "That will give you the management control you feel your level of responsibility requires. At the next management meeting you can present a comprehensive report on how successful the new control system really is. That will be well received."

**COMMENT**: BENEFIT - What benefits are there in it for the Prospect? Spell them out. Let them see themselves in the happy scene with a Visual Image of themselves enjoying the benefits of your product, the only thing they really buy.


**SP** - "Here is a sample of a corporate policy we modified for another company, along with the guidelines and action points we monitor. We will accept the financial responsibility for monitoring this policy."

**P** - "That is a simple and effective control policy. We could probably adopt it as is."

**COMMENT**: EVIDENCE - Evidence dispels doubt. They don't want a claim or promise of what you can do. They want proof. The evidence also gives them the opportunity to get involved.


**SP** - "What effect do you feel it would have, first, on your travelers and, second, on your internal controls?"

**P** - "The travelers wouldn't mind the restrictions because they are not unreasonable, and they are in the company's best interests. Our people are loyal to the company. As far as internal control is concerned it is excellent. Much better than I had expected. But how can our company monitor it?"

**COMMENT**: TRIAL CLOSE. After the benefit presentation the Salesperson tests the waters to see how well received it is. If hot, then Trial Close progressively into the Alternate Choice Close. If lukewarm present the other benefits that are pertinent to the problem's solution. Here the Prospect is hot but wants more information.


**SP** - "Here is a sample of the control report that both summarizes and yet details just where there is tight control, and where policy has been exceeded. It can be produced on a weekly basis so new procedures can be timely. On any occasion that we know in advance where it will be exceeded, we can notify you so you can make a decision. You will also receive a consolidated management control report for the travel from all of your offices across the US."

**P** - "All across the U.S., huh? That sounds really great."

**COMMENT**: FACT/FEATURE - This is the second Facts/Feature the Salesperson is presenting in order to solve the Prospect's problem.

Present only those features which contribute to solving their problem. Unnecessary discussion is the way Salespeople talk themselves out of a sale, because the Prospect's mind becomes muddled.

**SP** - " If you can't measure it, you can't control it. Here is the measuring device. Here is your control."

**P** - ."That's basic to management.

**COMMENT**: ADVANTAGE - The advantage translates the feature into problem solving language that the Prospect can understand.

**SP** - "This report will enable you to show management the results of your control, so you'll get the recognition you deserve."

**P** - "That'll be nice."

**COMMENT:** BENEFIT - You actually have to explain what their personal benefit will be. Rarely can they translate the Fact/Feature and Advantage into a Benefit without help. The salesperson promtped an emotional Want with the words "So you'll get the recognition you deserve". Other emotional prompts could be:

"You deserve the very best, don't you?"

"That will make you look important, won't it?"

"That will make you popular, won't it?"

"You want to maximize your..., don't you?"

"You don't want to lose your..., do you?"

**SP** - "Here are a few more samples of the computer reports you will be receiving. Notice that in the Loss Reduction Report it actually shows where they saved and where they overspent."

**P** - "That's comprehensive reporting, yet a clear overview."

**COMMENT**: EVIDENCE - This can come in many forms: logical evidence consists of Demonstrations, Exhibits and Statistics. Emotional evidence are Testimonials, Similar Stories and Understatements. A Prospect has to be sold both logically and emotionally so you should present evidence to both mind's.

**SP** - "How will that tie in with the control system on your side of the business?"

**P** - "It will be great. The systems we have now will blend in beautifully with yours."

**COMMENT**: TRIAL CLOSE. "How is ...?" ... is a Trial Close and this one gets you another favorable response. Notice that the Prospect's involvement is imperative if you are going to close the sale. Buying is not a spectator sport, rejecting is. There will be few objections when you are Trial Closing but maybe some questions that could have been objections if there were no dialogue. Certainly, if there are any objections they will be easy to answer because of their involvement. At this point, you can either Trial Close again and then try an Alternate Choice Close or go directly to the Alternate Choice. It doesn't matter because they differ only in degree. You will never get in trouble with either since they are only questions about how they feel or think about something.

**SP** - "If you were to go ahead with our system, do you feel that you would want to modify the reporting?"

**P** - "Probably not. It looks complete. As for going ahead with you, we do have a loyalty problem with our present supplier."

**COMMENT**: TRIAL CLOSE. Response has flushed out a concern. The Salesperson has to flush out this loyalty objection. Loyalty is a Stall due to indecision. It is also a dangerous situation since the Salesperson has developed the Need-Desire and the Prospect can always go back to their present supplier and ask them if they can duplicate your services. This isn't ethical and not much of a reward for creativity but it happens quite frequently. Few companies today have a lasting advantage over competition. It is a matter of time, effort and dollars until they catch up.

| **Response To Trial Close** | **Where To Go Now** |
|---|---|
| Hot | Go into Alternate Choice Close. |
| Lukewarm: | |
|     No Objection, ie, a Stall | Hurt and Rescue, T/C and Close |
|     With Objection | Answer, T/C and Close. |
| Cold: | |
|     To Benefit | Re-examine SIP, MM, EBM |
|     To a Trial Close | Consider an Objection |

**SP** - "I appreciate your sincerity."

**COMMENT**: CUSHION - The Salesperson has just cushioned the objection. It shows respect for the Prospect's opinion but not agreement. This takes the conflict out of the remark.

**SP** - "Obviously you have a reason for saying that. Do you mind if I ask what that reason is?"

**P** - "Well, we've been with our present agency for 10 years and we feel loyal to them. There are some real securities in that, and there are personal relationships."

**COMMENT**: ASK FOR THE REASON - The Salesperson asks for their reason. It is a challenge to the Prospect to explain just what is causing them to hesitate.

**SP** - "Suppose you felt that we also deserved that kind of loyalty. Then your opinion, don't you feel our services will definitely be of bene to you?"

**P** - "Yes, I believe so."

**COMMENT**: HYPOTHETICALLY RESOLVE REASON - Hypothetically Salesperson is resolving the reason in order to confirm that this is only hesitation or concern.

**SP** - "Now then, that raises a question. The question is: 'Does our fi have the personalization of service that warrants such long te loyalty?' That is the question, isn't it?"

**P** - "Yes, it is."

**COMMENTS**: CONVERT TO QUESTION - Even though the Prospect s. earlier they wouldn't be concerned about the secretary's reaction, they have some second thoughts about it.

**SP** - "... We select our agents on the basis of personality and desire serve their clients. That is very important to us. To allow different types of personality, we will assign from 4 to 6 agents your account so your secretaries can choose to work with the o they have a natural rapport with."

**COMMENT**: ANSWER THE QUESTION. The Salesperson answers question as quickly and as concisely as possible. Since most sell situations develop the same dozen objectives over and over, Salesperson should have the answers well developed.

**SP** - "What do you think of that?"

**P** - "It sounds like you have all the bases covered but I'm not too su

**COMMENTS**: TRIAL CLOSE - This is a simple Trial Close and response is lukewarm. It is a Stall objection. Now the Salesperson can on to the Desire Step to "Hurt and Rescue" them.

**SP** - "Mr. Prospect, let us summarize our discussion so far. At moment, you feel you are lacking in overall control of your busin travel and you feel pressured to correct it. Not only is y reputation with the President at stake here, but more importan the respect that your staff has for you. Isn't that right?"

**P** - "Yes, it is."

**COMMENT**: DESIRE STEP - The Hurt and Rescue. Remind the Prosp what they are hurting from. You can even create a visual image of th hurting here. When you have to use the Desire step it means that Prospect likes your product but the cost:benefit ratio is not good enou

Their want is not strong enough. The Desire step is an EMOTIONAL persuasion, a method of building the Want by appealing to the emotions. If the Prospect does not want to buy the product at the completion of this step, you go into the Weighing Close where you do a LOGICAL persuasion, that is, you help them justify the Want that they developed.

**SP** - "From what we have discussed, you can see that we have the mechanism to establish control, generate an excellent cost reduction and get the pressure off of you."

**P** - "Agreed."

**COMMENT**: PROMISE THE RESCUE. Your product has all the Fact/Features, Advantages and Benefits the Prospect needs.

**SP** - "Let's assume that you go ahead with our services. It is 6 months later when you are in a staff meeting. Your President asks you for a status report. You pass him the latest Travel Expense report showing a substantial reduction. He studies it, looks up and says, 'John, this really looks good. I appreciate it. Thank you.' That's what you want, isn't it?"

**P** - "Most definitely, but I would like to think it over."

**COMMENTS**: THE RESCUE. You are creating a Visual Image of a happy scene in which the Prospect can see themselves enjoying the benefits of your product. You are fanning an existing spark of desire into a flame. They call it "romancing the product". It works equally well for tangible products as well as for intangible services in the business environment for they are seeing themselves enjoying the benefits. The ending question is also a Trial Close. If it is hot, go to the Alternate Choice Close. If not, go to the Weighing Close.

**SP** - "Mr. Prospect, let's take a closer look at the ideas that may cause you to hesitate and weigh them against going ahead with our services, and doing so right now."

**P** - "Okay."

**COMMENT**: WEIGHING CLOSE - Even though the Prospect seemed satisfied with your answer to the objection, their concern probably will not be completely eliminated; rather it will only be minimized; they will still remember it. You have to logically justify it for them.

**SP** - "In the ideas that may cause you to hesitate, you mentioned loyalty and service. Were there any others?"

**P** - "No."

**COMMENT**: To make sure the Prospect has it clear in their mind that the benefits of your product far outweigh any concerns or shortcomings, both have to be brought out in the open. This buries their objections and prevents Stalls and Buyers' Remorse (changing their mind a few days later).

**SP** - "Now the benefits you would receive by going ahead with our services now are: (1) a $2000 per month cost reduction, (2) a control reporting system and (3) a sense of accomplishment and the recognition for getting a complex system under good control."

**COMMENTS**: The weighing of their concerns against the benefits is especially important in the sale of services where more often than not there is no "order blank" to sign. Here closing can be continuous over weeks or months before the service is actually in full swing. Even the slighest flaw in the start-up can reverse the Prospect's decision.

**SP** - " Mr. Prospect, which side weights the heavier?"

**P** - "Your benefits, of course."

**COMMENT**: Now into the multiple close.

**SP** - "I agree. Would you prefer 4 or 6 of our staff assigned to your account?"

**P** - "I think we should start with 6."

**COMMENT**: You may wish to use a simple Alternate Choice Close for a starter. This choice between two minor points takes the pressure off the Prospect by not creating the big fear of "Do I, or don't I?" You assume they will and you don't want to confront them with the big Yes or No decision.

**SP** - "Would you like to have your travel document case printed with your company's logo?"

**P** - "Yes, my management would like that."

**COMMENTS**: This Is a Minor Point Close, half an Alternate Choice Close. Again this takes the pressures off the big decision and places it on a tiny one.

**SP** - "Who should I see in the Art Department for the logo?"

**P** - "See Mary and tell her I said it was okay."

**COMMENT**: You may want to get someone else involved in the change, so you ask for their permission to perform a Key Event with another person, e.g., get the artwork prepared.

**SP** - "What I need to do is call our computer center to set up your file. Do you mind if I use your phone for a local call?"

**P** - "No, not at all. Be my guest."

**COMMENT**: This is a pressure close, the Physical Action close. You are never sure if one closing question is sufficient so a series of closes is necessary. At this point you may want to do something forward such as using their phone to set up the account with your office. If they are not ready to get involved with you, they will hesitate here.

**SP** - "We should arrange a "Travel Update" meeting for your secretaries. Would this Friday or next Friday be better for your staff?"

**P** - "Next Friday by all means. It will take us a few days to organize it."

**COMMENT**: Now more people are involved in the Closing. The momentum has begun.

**NOTE**: With the exception of those comments relating specifically to the travel product, all the Salesperson's lines should be memorized or reduced to writing.

# THE SELLING PROCESS

| PROSPECT'S ATTITUDE | WHAT WE MUST DO | HOW TO DO IT | STEP | WHAT WE MUST SELL | LOGIC OF THE STEP | BUYER'S ATTITUDE |
|---|---|---|---|---|---|---|
| **R E J E C T I O N** | Get them excited about solving a big problem | Prompt their curiosity | **A T T E N T I O N** | It's worth their time to listen | If one of you doesn't get excited there will be no sale | **A C C E P T A N C E** |
| | Establish rapport | Justified compliment | | We are a nice person | They won't buy from you if they don't like you | |
| | Disturb Prospect with something better | Ask a question suggesting a need | | They do have a serious problem | There is no hope for a satisfied Prospect | |
| **I N D I F F E R E N C E** | Promise to solve their problem | Relate similar successes | **I N T E R E S T** | We are problem solvers | They must see us as a needs satisfier | **A N X I O U S** |
| | Gather information | Determine <br>•Specific Interest or Problem (SIP) <br>•Mini Motives (MM) <br>•Emotional Buying Motive (EBM) | | They have a very special problem | What does the Prospect need, and why do they want it? | |
| | Be excited about helping them | Fan the spark of existing desire | | There is a way to satisfy their needs and wants | We really are a wants motivator | |
| **S K E P T I C A L** | Develop benefits | •Fact/features <br>•Advantage <br>•Benefit <br>•Evidence <br>•Visual Image <br>•Trial Close | **C O N V I C T I O N** | Product—will do the job <br>Price/hassle is justified <br>Peers—others will like it <br>Priority—need it now | Tell them what's in it for them | **B E L I E F** |
| | Remove any doubts/objections | •Cushion it <br>•Ask what reason <br>•Hypothetically resolve reason <br>•Convert to question <br>•Reverse/minimize (REMEDY) <br>•Trial Close | | Reassurance | Little doubts create questions; big doubts create objections | |
| **D E L A Y** | Romance the product | Create a visual image | **D E S I R E** | That they want the product | Let them see themselves enjoying your product | **A C T I O N** |
| **F E A R** | Get decision in our favor | Weigh the pros & cons | **C L O S E** | Logical decision based on need | Emotional wants must be rationalized into logical needs | **C O N F I D E N C E** |
| | Get an order | Assumed closes <br>Coaxed closes <br>Pressure closes | | A sense of urgency | It can be a long way from being sold to buying now | |

## Chapter Twenty Three

# Selling Summary

**Selling Technique**     **Salesperson's Comment**

## The Pre Approach

Interview associates, Buffer.
Use your eyes and ears as you
enter. Ask questions of
receptionist. It is very
important to pre-interview
before a group presentation
where you must identify and
sell the key person.

## The Attention Step

A short time, 3 to 5 minutes. To
get Prospect's mind off what
they are doing, and to get them
to like you - building Rapport.
Talk to them briefly about
some-thing in which they are
interested, themselves first.

(A) SOCIAL ATTENTION GETTER: Brief. Any social pleasantry used by Salespeople to establish adequate Rapport with Prospect. (Should also be used if a CLIENT is distant or unfriendly).

1)(a) Pay a sincere Compliment or show admiration - develops a positive awareness of you.
— Anything that will make them like themselves a little more.
— Anything they are unsure about.
— Anything we see good about them.

"Hello, Mr. Prospect. You sure have an impressive operation here ..."

(b) Tell them why you like that quality - keeps you honest, builds credibility. Justify the compliment!

"... The reason I that is that most accounting departments are usually disorganized. As we were walking through your accounting section, I couldn't help but notice how well organized every thing and person is. It sure is impressive looking...

(c) Introduction, if necessary.

(d) Opened ended question - "How was that ...(quality)... developed?" (Must listen carefully here in case you have to recompliment because of inadequate rapport so far).

"... How did you get it so well organized?"

(e) Indicator:

(1) If adequate rapport, make a brief compliment and bridge to business.

(2) If inadequate rapport, repeat the cycle with a new compliment. Ask another open ended question.

"Well, Mr. Prospect, that sort of indicates that you are really a general manager at heart. How does the wide spectrum attitude of general management help you in your responsibilities?"

(3) Do a Bridge to Business.

"Good management is the very reason why I am here ..."

There are several techniques for getting a Prospect's Social and Business Attention. They are summarized by the acronym MISS GRACE. You should develop all 81 combinations and vary their use for freshness. Keep the social use separate from business, eg, a Gift without your name is a Social Attention Getter, but with your name it a Business Attention Getter.

* M   Mystery.
* I   Information or Idea.
* S   Startling statement.
* S   Survey or Service, free.

* G   Gift.
* R   Referral from a
      happy client
      "Mr. Prospect?"
      "Mr. John Prospect?"
      "You don't know me, but
      have a mutual friend
      in Bob... Bob suggested
      I call you. I'm ..."
* A   Ask a question that will
      interest them, or suggest
      a need or problem.
* C   Compliment or admire
      them.
* E   Exhibit, displays or
      samples

(B) BUSINESS ATTENTION
GETTER: Bridge to BUSINESS
ATTENTION GETTER, the
Disturbing step. Any sales
statement or question used by
the Salesperson to develop
Problem awareness or pre-
existing Interest.

"... If there were a way for you
to reduce your travel losses by
$20,000 a year, it would make
sense to explore it in detail,
wouldn't it?"

In a general way you remind
them of a problem they
probably have, the Probable
Interest or Problem (PIP).
Then, make a big promise. A
critical 30 seconds. The PIP will
be different for different
industries, companies, and
even visits.

Bridge from BUSINESS
ATTENTION GETTER to
Interest Step. You are
promising to solve their
Probable Problem in order to
develop their Interest about
your product.

"The reason I mention this is
because of what we are doing
now for the ABC Company at
their various offices across the
U.S. Maybe we can help you
too."

# The Interest Step

Probing to Uncover the Close. A long step. Keep digging until you find their SIP, MM and EBM.

Discover their Need and Want and fill it emotionally.

Selling is a HURT and RESCUE business.

People want to save money not for the sake of saving money, but for some other reason. Money only spells progress.

PROBABLE INTEREST OR PROBLEM. PIP is the biggest of their problems in your product area. It has to be a NEED to them.

EMOTIONAL BUYING MOTIVES: Reasons why they are interested in having their problem solved.

MM = Mini Motive, an lesser buying motive that contributes toward reaching the Prospect's EBM, eg., save time, money, etc. What they want to do with your product or what they want it to do for them. Mini Motives tend to be tangible items, like saving dollars and time. If you keep probing for Mini Motives you will get to the more emotional EBM.

"To conserve your time, would it be okay to get the answers to a few questions?"

PERSONAL
"Your title was listed as Controller. Is that correct?"

"What is the range of your responsibilities?"

"What is the most enjoyable part of your travel duties?"

PROBLEMS
"What problems does our industry create for you?"

"What help would you normally expect from us?"

"What is keeping you from solving this problem?"

"What are you doing about that problem now?"

PAYOFF
"How would solving the problem effect you?"

"When you get the control established what would that do for your?"

"Why is that important to you"

"What would it be worth to you to solve that problem?"

PAYOFF: Emotional Buying Motive, EBM. The most important reason to solve the big problem. A WANT. More emotional than a Mini Motive. WHY they want to solve the problem to satisfy their real WANT. Our affluent society satisfies most NEEDS. They need to satisfy WANTS, they are more powerful.

The SIP/MM/EBM is the thread that holds the presentation together. It shows up every-where in the Selling Process.

The questions are designed to:
(1) Get the Prospect talking,
(2) Get answers to progressively more delicate questions. Can ask as few or as many as needed to get the information.

SPECIFIC INTEREST OR PROBLEM. You are giving them back what they gave you in the questions. The SIP.

PROSPECT
"Who, besides you, will be making the decision to change?"

"If you were favorably impressed with our product, would you accompany me when I meet with Mr. ...(decision maker)...?"

PEERS
"What people problems do you perceive in changing?"

"What will you need to win the support of others?"

PRIORITY
"When would you plan on making the decision and the change?"

"What is it costing you not to have a reasonable solution to the problem?"

"What sense of urgency do you feel about solving that problem?"

"Based on what you have told me, there is a way we can provide you with a substantial cost reduction and at the same time reduce the pressure and frustration in controlling your awful problem."

# The Conviction Step

Now adjust your presentation to the kind of person you are working with.

"You are probably wondering how we can do this, so let's look at some of the facts."

**FACT/FEATURE**
  Only give them Features that pertain to their problem solution.

"We will monitor and maintain your business travel across the U.S. according to your corporate policy ..."

**ADVANTAGE**
  Explain why that Feature is an Advantage for them.

"... so you will be organized for a major loss reduction program of about $2,000."

**BENEFIT**
**SAMPLES OF BRIDGE:**
"So.., thus.., and so..,
therefore.., gives you..,
which means to you..,
which means you
will have .., which
will allow you to..."

"That will give the management control you feel your level of responsibility requires."

**EVIDENCE**
Evidence support Fact/ Features, Advantages, Benefits and Claims. A Claim is a Fact that the Prospect doubts so it needs proving. Your problem is that they will rarely tell you what they don't believe so you have to prove almost everything.

"Here is a sample of a corporate policy we modified for another company."

307

EVIDENCE will convict the RASCAL:

**R** Relevant to the situation.
**A** Accuracy is a must.
**S** Specificity for belief.
**C** Clarity for understanding.
**A** Acceptable to Salesperson.
**L** Long enough to convince, short enough to interest.

Trial Close confirms their desire for Benefit. "How would that affect your ...?"

When you ask them how they FEEL, it puts them into the emotional mind; how they THINK, puts them into their logical mind. Most of the time you want them in the emotional mind.

Evidence supporting a Benefit is important in intangible services.

CONFIRMING, Logical Evidence:
Demonstrations
Analogy
Statistics

INVOLVING, Emotional Evidence:
Similar Stories
Testimonials
Understatements

"What effect do you feel it would have, first, on your travelers and, second, on your internal controls?"

"If you can't measure it, you can't control it. Here is the measuring device. Here is your control."

"Here is a sample of the control report that both summarizes and yet details just where there is tight control, and where policy has been exceeded.

"This report will enable you to show management the results of your control, so you'll get the recognition you deserve."

"How will that tie in with the control system on your side of the business?"

"If your were to go ahead with our system, do you feel that you would want to modify the reporting?"

Conviction step must satisfy
these concerns:
 SIP: Product must solve
        problem.
        It is worth the investment,
        price or hassle of change.
        Others will think well of it.
EBM: They really need it NOW.


DRAMATIZING REAPS CASH:
**R** Relevant to the product's use.
**E** Emotion should be excitement.
**A** Appropriate to the situation.
**P** Personally acceptable to you.
**S** Something different interest.

**C** Contest: Can Prospect do it?
**A** Action makes it more exciting.
**S** Striking to make it memorable.
**H** Hands on by the Prospect.

CUSHION AN OBJECTION: To
get back in step and in
conversation with Prospect.

"I appreciate your sincerity."

ASK WHAT REASON: Get them
to elaborate on it.

"Obviously you have a reason
for saying that. Do you mind if
I ask what that reason is?"

HYPOTHETICALLY RESOLVE
REASON: Will force out any
hidden objection or concern.

"Just supposing you felt that
we also deserved that kind of
loyalty. Then, in your opinion,
don't you feel our services will
definitely be of benefit to you?"

CONVERT TO A QUESTION:
and confirm that it is the real
question. They usually will.
Remember the objection is
emotional in origin.

"Now then, that raises a
question. The question is: 'Does
our firm have the
personalization of service that
warrants such long term
loyalty?' That is the question,
isn't it?"

ANSWER THE QUESTION:
quickly and concisely. Keep it
down to less than a minute
and less than 100 words or you
end up magnifying it.

"... We select our agents on the
basis of personality and desire
to serve their clients. That is
very important to us. To allow
for different types of
personality, we will assign from
4 to 6 agents to your account
so your secretaries can choose
one for natural rapport?"

TRIAL CLOSE: to see how the
Prospect accepts the answer.

"What do you think of that?"
"How do you feel that will  help
your staff to accept  their new
agents?"

# The Desire Step

When your Prospect agrees
that it will solve their Problem
or satisfy their Interest but still
wants to think it over, then go
to the Desire step for "Hurt and
Rescue", ie, building their
emotional Want.

Most important technique of
all. Less than 1% of use it. Can
be used anywhere, at any time
to increase their Want.

THE HURT: All desire is built
on a feeling of lack, want, or
hurting. Motivational selling is
satisfying some desire that
serves as a motivation to buy.
But they have to visualize their
real Hurt before they can be
really motivated to do
something about it.

"Mr. Prospect, let us summarize
our discussion so far. At the
moment you are seriously
lacking in overall control of
your business travel and are
being pressure to correct it.
Not only is your reputation
with the President at stake
here, but also the respect your
staff has for you. Isn't that
right?"

THE SOLUTION: Assure them that you can solve their awful problem.

THE RESCUE: Pick your Prospect up mentally and carry them into the future. Let them see themselves using and enjoying your product or service.

When creating Visual Images, appeal directly to the senses that make sense - seeing, hearing, touch, smell and taste. Use vivid words and ideas. "Touchdown" is vivid. You must create a mental picture. It must be visualized.

"As you can see that we have the mechanism to establish that control, generate an excellent cost reduction and get the pressure off."

"Let's assume that you have gone ahead with our services. It is 6 months later when you are in a staff meeting. Your President studies your latest travel control report showing a very substantial reduction. He looks up and says, "John, this is really good. Congratulations." That's what you want, isn't it?"

# The Weighing Close

IF the Prospect is still indecisive following the Visual Image bridge into the Weighing Close for logical justification.

Every person goes through a weighing process in making a decision. Since most items are "apples and bolts" it is difficult to compare accurately. Most people are negatively biased so they can't weigh objectively on their own. You must organize the weighing for the Prospect.

"Mr. Prospect, let's take a closer look at your concerns and weigh them against going ahead with our services now.

"In your concern, you mentioned loyalty and service. Are there any others?"

| Concerns | Reasons in Favor |
| --- | --- |
| Loyalty | All our benefits that solve their: |
| Service | |

_____SIP
_____MM
_____ MM
_____EBM

"Did I miss anything in our discussion?"

"Now the benefits you would receive by going ahead with our services now are:
- A $2,000 cost reduction
- A control reporting system
- A sense of accomplishment
- Recognition

"Mr. Prospect, which side weighs the heavier?"

Try to keep these concerns to one or two words each. These are "concerns" only, so don't glorify or magnify them.

After the Prospect answers, ask for the order with the Alternate Choice Close:

"I agree. Would you prefer 4 or 6 of our staff assigned to your account?"

Never use the word "objection" with a Prospect, use "concern".

"Would you like to have travel document case printed with your company's logo?"

It doesn't matter which side is the longer as long as each side is honestly stated.

"We should arrange a "Travel Update" meeting for your secretaries. Would this Friday or next Monday be better for your staff?"

"Who should I see in the Art Department for a logo?"

"What I need to do now is call our computer center to set up your file. May I use your phone for a local call?"

# Epilogue

Selling can be easy and enjoyable when you:
- Get them excited.
- Get them to like you.
- Find their real Interest or Problem.
- Ask: "Why is that important to you?"
- Sell them their Hurt with a Visual Image.
- Offer a solution with a Visual Image.
- Always be Trial Closing.
- Close on every hot Trial Close.
- Use the Alternate Choice Close.

COLOPHON

PRINTER: Delta Lithograph, Van Nuys, CA
EDITOR: Keith Terry, Newport Beach, CA
BINDER: National Bindery Company, Pomona, CA
TYPESETTING: Graphic Concepts, Laguna Hills, CA
TYPE STYLE: Century 10/12, 10/16

## MEET THE AUTHOR

D. Forbes Ley, MBA (York '69), is a former Dale Carnegie Sales Cours
Instructor and has been selling a variety of both tangible and intangibl
products and services for an entire career.

## ISBN LISTING OF BOOKS BY D. FORBES LEY:

ISBN 0-9613319-0-9          Hard Cover edition of The Best Seller.
ISBN 0-9613319-2-5          Soft Cover edition of The Best Seller.

## SPECIAL EDITIONS

Brief Special Editions written for specific selling situations:

ISBN 0-9613319-1-7          The Best Seller: of *Automobiles*
ISBN 0-9613319-3-3          The Best Seller: of *Insurance*
ISBN 0-9613319-4-1          The Best Seller: of *Travel Services*
ISBN 0-9613319-***          The Best Seller: of *Portraits*
ISBN 0-9613319-***          The Best Seller: of *Real Estate*

Mr. Ley and Staff are available for sales seminars, consulting and help
in closing a major account. For more information call:

(714) 542-7777 CA
(800) 772-1172 US